"Using the robust new tools of Christian and power model of God that reflects biblical teac traditional themes. Yet this model carefully updates traditional notions and so provides a compelling alternative to contemporary views of God that stray from biblical moorings. This is just the kind of contribution analytic philosophers ought to make to theology. I greatly appreciate this book."

DAVID K. CLARK, PROFESSOR OF THEOLOGY, BETHEL SEMINARY

"Jay W. Richards's The Untamed God is a commendably clear, well-researched introduction to the power of essentialist metaphysics to help us think clearly and correctly about God. It models well the ways philosophy and theology both support and balance each other. Allies and opponents of his views will join their own debates with greater precision and fruitfulness for having worked through his book."

W. JAY WOOD, ASSOCIATE PROFESSOR,
DEPARTMENT OF PHILOSOPHY, WHEATON COLLEGE

THE UNTAMED GOD

A Philosophical

Exploration of

Divine Perfection,

Immutability

and Simplicity

JAY WESLEY RICHARDS

IVP Academic

An imprint of InterVarsity Press
Downers Grove, Illinois

InterVarsity Press
P.O. Box 1400, Downers Grove, IL 60515-1426
World Wide Web: www.ivpress.com
E-mail: email@ivpress.com

InterVarsity Press® is the book-publishing division of InterVarsity Christian Fellowship/USA®, a movement of students and faculty active on campus at hundreds of universities, colleges and schools of nursing in the United States of America, and a member movement of the International Fellowship of Evangelical Students. For information about local and regional activities, write Public Relations Dept., InterVarsity Christian Fellowship/USA, 6400 Schroeder Rd., P.O. Box 7895, Madison, WI 53707-7895, or visit the IVCF website at <www.intervarsity.org>.

Cover design: Cindy Kiple

ISBN 978-0-8308-2734-3

Printed in the United States of America ∞

Library of Congress Cataloging-in-Publication Data

Richards, Jay Wesley, 1967-
    The untamed God: a philosophical exploration of divine perfection,
immutability, and simplicity / Jay W. Richards.
        p. cm.
Includes bibliographical references and index.
    ISBN 0-8308-2734-X (pbk.: alk. paper)
1. God—Attributes. 2. Essence (Philosophy) 3. Philosophical
theology. 4. Christianity—Philosophy. I. Title.
    BT130.R53 2003
    231'.4—dc21

                                                                                    2003008236

P	21	20	19	18	17	16	15	14	13	12	11	10	9	8	7	6	5	4	3	2
Y	26	25	24	23	22	21	20	19	18	17	16	15	14	13	12	11	10	09			

To Ginny and Gillian

CONTENTS

ACKNOWLEDGMENTS

There are a number of people who deserve credit for their valuable help, some for the formation of the ideas found in this book, others for insightful and sometimes detailed advice on the manuscript.

I would like to thank Diogenes Allen, Daniel Migliore and Bruce McCormack for their oversight, guidance and advice on an early version of this book. I especially appreciate their tolerance and magnanimity, since none, so far as I know, quite agrees with my argument. Serendipitously, it was during a lecture on Karl Barth by Bruce McCormack that the central argument first occurred to me. Bruce also persuaded me that Barth was worth taking the trouble to read carefully at a time when I found Barth's prose, well, indecipherable. Engaging seminars by Saul Kripke and Scott Soames in the philosophy of language helped shape my analytic approach to a number of philosophical questions.

In addition, I would like to thank Alvin Plantinga for both his influence, which will be obvious, and his encouragement in publishing this manuscript. My interaction with William Dembski, which first began at Princeton, should also be apparent. William Lane Craig provided a number of important nuances in my treatment of divine immutability and prevented me from making a few serious blunders. Greg Welty provided some crucial insights and distinctions on the doctrine of divine ideas just a few weeks before I completed the final manuscript. And Bryan Cross and Alex Pruss offered valuable arguments on the doctrine of divine simplicity, which helped me clarify certain parts of my argument.

For countless editorial suggestions I am indebted to my lifelong friend Jonathan Witt, who teaches English literature and offered the priceless perspective of an educated reader who does not specialize in philosophy or theology. Thanks also to my editor, Gary Deddo, for many more editorial suggestions and for taking on this project.

Preparing this book would have been impossible without the support of the Discovery Institute and my colleagues there: Bruce Chapman, Steve Meyer, John West and many others. Discovery is an intellectual community than which none greater can be conceived.

Finally, I would like to thank my wife, Ginny, who early on tolerated hundreds of dusty library books—which consumed probably 25 percent of the cubic space of our bedroom at Princeton—and graciously endured many arcane conversations as I worked through the constellation of theological conundrums explored in the following pages. Any mistakes remaining—and there are probably a few still lurking—are, of course, my own.

ABBREVIATIONS

1/1   Karl Barth, *Church Dogmatics,* vol. 1, part 1 (Edinburgh: T & T Clark, 1975, 2nd ed.)

1/2   Karl Barth, *Church Dogmatics,* vol. 1, part 2 (Edinburgh: T & T Clark, 1956)

2/1   Karl Barth, *Church Dogmatics,* vol. 2, part 1 (Edinburgh: T & T Clark, 1957)

3/1   Karl Barth, *Church Dogmatics,* vol. 3, part 1 (Edinburgh: T & T Clark, 1958)

4/1   Karl Barth, *Church Dogmatics,* vol. 4, part 1 (Edinburgh: T & T Clark, 1958)

AD   Charles Hartshorne, *Anselm's Discovery: A Re-examination of the Ontological Argument* (LaSalle, Ill.: Open Court, 1965)

BH   Charles Hartshorne, *Beyond Humanism: Essays in the New Philosophy of Nature* (Chicago: Willet, Clark & Co., 1937)

CSPM   Charles Hartshorne, *Creative Synthesis and Philosophical Method* (LaSalle, Ill.: Open Court, 1970)

DR   Charles Hartshorne, *The Divine Relativity: A Social Conception of God* (New Haven, Conn.: Yale University Press, 1948)

LP   Charles Hartshorne, *The Logic of Perfection and Other Essays in Neo-Classical Metaphysics* (LaSalle, Ill.: Open Court, 1962)

MVG   Charles Hartshorne, *Man's Vision of God* (LaSalle, Ill.: Open Court, 1941)

NTT   Charles Hartshorne, *A Natural Theology for Our Time* (LaSalle, Ill.: Open Court, 1967)

OOTM Charles Hartshorne, *Omnipotence and Other Theological Mistakes* (Albany: SUNY Press, 1984)

PCH Lewis Hahn, ed., *The Philosophy of Charles Hartshorne* (LaSalle, Ill.: Open Court, 1991)

PSG Charles Hartshorne and William L. Reese, eds., *Philosophers Speak of God* (Chicago: University of Chicago Press, 1953)

RSP Charles Hartshorne, *Reality as Social Process* (Boston: Beacon, 1953)

ST Thomas Aquinas, *Summa Theologica*, trans. fathers of the Dominican Province (New York: Benziger Brothers, 1947)

God is whatever it is better to be than not to be, and He, the only self-existent being, makes all other things from nothing.

Anselm, *Proslogion*

There is in God both supreme necessity and supreme contingency. This supreme contingency in the essence of God which is not limited by any necessity, the inscrutable concrete element in His essence, inscrutable because it never ceases or is exhausted—is his will.

Karl Barth, *Church Dogmatics* 2/1

INTRODUCTION

Taken separately, the core tenets of theism pose little difficulty for the believer: (1) God exists. (2) He created the world—meaning, everything other than God—in such a way that the world owes its existence and individual features to him. (3) God created the world freely—that is, nothing external or internal to God compelled him to create this or any world. The world, in other words, might not have existed or, as philosophers often put it, God's choice to create the world and the existence of the world are contingent. On this view then, God enjoys freedom and sovereignty vis-à-vis the world. Another way to put this is to say that God exists *a se* (or has the property of aseity), meaning that he exists from and of himself and does not depend on anything outside himself for his nature or existence. Everything else, in contrast, depends upon God for its existence.

Additionally, most theists believe that God is superlative or maximally perfect in whatever ways it is possible and desirable to be so. Thus God is perfect in knowledge, power, goodness, love, freedom, existence, holiness, justice and the like. As the great medieval theologian Anselm (1033-1109) famously expressed it, God is *that than which none greater can be conceived.*

Of course, a Christian theist also would profess that God exists as three persons, Father, Son and Holy Spirit, while still being one God; that the Father sent the Son to earth as the man Jesus; that Jesus in turn lived a specifically human life, during a particular segment of human history, was executed by crucifixion and was raised from the dead.

And if Christian theists profess these things, presumably they take these claims to be meaningful and consistent with each other. The conjunction of at least some of these propositions, however, quickly leads to a thorny conceptual thicket from which it is difficult to escape with the package intact. For example, if God is perfect, how can he change from a state of perfect power and knowledge to a state of relative ignorance, suffering and degradation? More generally, how can he change at all, since, if he is perfect, any change would presumably be from a perfect to a less-than-perfect state? And if he is perfect, why would he create anything at all? Does not the notion that God created the world imply that, even if there is nothing lacking in God, at least it is better that the world and God exist, than that only God exist? But if so, what has become of the assertion that God is perfect in himself?

Another conundrum involves the notion of God's sovereignty. If God depends on nothing other than himself, then it seems inappropriate to say that he has various properties, such as perfect goodness, perfect knowledge and the like, since he would then be dependent on transcendental concepts or universals. In a sense, he would be composed of them. Certain concepts, like Platonic forms, in some sense seem to precede God's essence and existence. And this would certainly violate his sovereignty.

To resolve these dilemmas, many classical theologians have adopted the doctrine of divine simplicity, which takes several forms. The advocate of divine simplicity may say that God's properties and essence are identical not only with each other but also with God himself. So there is no sense in which God depends on anything other than himself. But this seems to imply a somewhat different idea, namely, that God does not have properties or an essence. Rather, God just *is* what we would otherwise take to be his properties and essence. So God is not omnipotent, omniscient, perfectly just and loving. Rather, God is omnipotence, omniscience, perfect justice and, as the epistle of 1 John tells us, love (1 Jn 4:8).

Both of these closely related claims, however, seem to create a host of new problems. Simplicity so defined not only appears to conflict with the notion that God is perfect in various ways and so has various distinct perfect-making properties. It also seems inconsistent with such Christian beliefs as the Trinity, creation and incarnation. How can the Son's being born of the Virgin Mary be identical with, say, divine omnipotence? How can the Son being begotten by the Father be identical with the Spirit's proceeding from the Father and the

Son? How can God choosing to create the rhinoceros be identical with, say, God's necessary existence? These claims imply not only that God does have an essence and various properties but also that at least some are not identical with each other. And what does it even mean to say that God is not omnipotent and loving but rather omniscience and love? Are these simply poetic ways of speaking, or is there something more to it?

The problems get even stickier if we maintain that God need not have created the world. For then it appears that God has chosen from alternatives. But whence come the alternatives, and why would a sovereign God have to choose from among them? Surely if he is sovereign he would choose not only what is actual but also what is possible. For that matter, if God is in control of everything, what sense does it make even to speak of contingencies? Surely contingent events and objects will at best be only apparent. In reality, however, everything will be merely one part of a grand theologically determined system.

As we will see, such problems can multiply like seedy guests at an open-bar reception. Anyone interested in the viability of Christian theology will want to resolve them. In this book, I propose such a resolution. It's simple: *Christians should affirm that God has an essence, which includes his perfections and essential properties, and should attribute to God essential and contingent properties.* If we can do so properly—and that is not as easy as it seems—we can resolve many of the troubling implications in the classical concept of God. I will refer to this view as theological essentialism, or simply essentialism. At first blush, this suggestion may sound trivial. But this strategy carries with it certain ontological commitments, some of which require departing from certain traditional ideas. Once we have made a full accounting of the issues, through analysis, careful definitions and adjustments for different philosophical contexts, it should become evident that such departures are minor. In fact, I will argue that essentialism is, in the final analysis, a properly Christian answer, which, on the most important matters, preserves not only traditional motivations but also its more perplexing claims.

The journey to this answer requires a detour into territory not familiar to most Christians or theologians. Recent developments in logic, particularly modal logic, provide conceptual tools that can help resolve long-standing problems in the Christian doctrine of God. In the chapters that follow, I will develop and apply certain essentialist[1] concepts—derived from contemporary modal metaphysics and possible-worlds semantics—to the Christian doctrine of God. Essentialism as such is neither a full-fledged doctrine of God nor a doctrine of the divine perfections. Rather, it is a proposal for how we can attribute certain things to God, remain logically consistent and preserve the tradition.

Although it's a bit pedantic, let me summarize the chapters that follow. A roadmap may make a trip less adventurous, but it also makes it less confusing. In chapter one, I consider some preliminary matters necessary to frame the issue properly. The first of these is what is often called classical theism: that treatment of God's essence and attributes that spans most Western theological reflection, becoming most explicit in Thomas Aquinas, the Protestant Scholastics and Protestant confessions, and continues to the present day in many Roman Catholic and Protestant circles, especially in Anglo-American Christian philosophy. The second is a description of three central themes that have guided theological reflection and debate in the Christian tradition, including the various proposals we consider: biblical normativity, the Principle of Perfection, and the Sovereignty-Aseity Conviction. I argue that while these themes give rise to certain problems in the classical concept of God, they are nevertheless intrinsically Christian ideas. For that reason, the Christian theologian and philosopher should oblige them. Third and finally, I discuss the concept of essence as a theological category in the Christian tradition. This concept provides a point of contact between the traditional language for God and contemporary essentialism, which is bolstered by modal logic and possible-worlds semantics.

In chapter two I introduce and explain relevant aspects of modal logic, possible-worlds semantics and essentialism; and challenge the opinion current in theological circles that essentialism is philosophically indefensible and passé—a refutation necessary if essentialism is to be of any use to theology. I

---

[1] I define theological "essentialism" as belief that so-called *de re* modality is relevant to our understanding of God, in such a way that it is appropriate to speak of a cluster of attributes or properties which God necessarily exemplifies and without which, God would not be God, and of contingent attributes or properties which God has in some but not all possible worlds, as a result of his freedom. God's essential attributes taken together constitute (or are included in) God's *sine qua non*, his *quidditas*, his essence. God's essence and properties are not parts of God, however, but fundamental facts about him. (Of course, it does not follow that we comprehend God's essence. One could claim as I do that we are justified in speaking of God's essence without claiming that we can comprehend it.) The subtext is that our understanding of an essence is closely related to our modal intuitions of necessity, actuality and possibility. I will develop this argument in chapter two.

intend this discussion to be accessible to the reader with no previous exposure to modal logic. While some technical terms are necessary, most of these will recede into the background in later chapters.

In chapter three, I argue that essentialism is not only congenial but also intrinsic to the Christian understanding of God, since it is implied by certain core Christian convictions. It also provides a coherent way of attributing essential properties to God while preserving the contingency of creation and God's relation to the world. In particular it provides a way to express God's real relations to the world and its constituents, without collapsing into panentheism, the idea that the world is one of God's constituents. To achieve these things, we must attribute to God essential and contingent properties, define properties carefully and rebut the charge that this strategy leads to illicit heterodoxy.

One cannot really appreciate the complexity of the problem that besets the classical concept of God or recognize what sort of resolution is needed without considering some concrete contemporary attempts to deal with it, especially among theologians. For that reason, in chapters four through seven, I engage the theological proposals of two important twentieth-century theologians, Karl Barth and Charles Hartshorne. Their views are not simple alternatives to essentialism. In fact, there is some interesting overlap among the various proposals.[2] Nevertheless, Barth and Hartshorne function as the two end points on the spectrum of theological attempts to address and resolve the dilemmas implicit in the classical concept of God. Through detailed interaction with these conversation partners, I seek to show that essentialism can assimilate their best insights and arguments against classical theism while avoiding the problems in their own theological proposals and preserving the classical tradition on the whole.

Barth, for his part, seeks a resolution by reframing the classical concept of God as Being or "Substance," speaking instead of God as being-in-act, or as he often puts it, as the One who loves in freedom. Barth's view is profound and suggestive, but his prose makes it difficult to interpret his argument consistently. Moreover, the classical conception is arguably more firmly grounded in intrinsic Christian belief than Barth recognizes. Thus, while Barth is an insightful and

---

[2]As I define it, Barth's and Hartshorne's doctrines of God are not wholly incompatible with essentialism *simpliciter*—that is, in every sense. They are both deeply critical, however, of the classical use of the notions of substance and essence in theology, as well as various aspects of the classical method for deriving the divine attributes.

usually sympathetic critic of the traditional doctrine of God, an adequate theological proposal should, in my view, do more to accommodate classical theism.

Hartshorne, by contrast, develops an intriguing "dipolar theism," which perhaps has not received the attention it deserves from either mainstream theologians or Christian philosophers. The recent movement within evangelical Christian circles called open theism has significant affinities with Hartshorne. So some of my analysis of Hartshorne will bear on open theism. Unlike most open theists, however, who seek to square their views with Scripture, Hartshorne neither is nor intends to be a Christian theologian. So I take his view as a contemporary natural theology based on pure reason and experience apart from special revelation. Since he attributes to God essential and contingent aspects, his theology may look like essentialism. Hartshorne's argument, however, entails a panentheistic view of God's relation to the world, in which the world is part of a composite God. Since I argue that this contradicts one of the three themes of Christian theology, the Sovereignty-Aseity Conviction, it is crucial to disentangle the claim that God has essential and contingent properties from panentheism.

In chapters eight and nine I take up the doctrines of divine immutability and simplicity. These attributes are central in classical theism, but most twentieth-century theologians have not treated them kindly. They are also the most difficult elements in classical theism to square with certain distinctly biblical and Christian claims. So they present the Christian scholar with a dilemma. On the one hand they seem to derive in large measure from what I call the central themes of Christian theology, which should prevent Christian theologians from abandoning them lightly. In addition, the traditional arguments for simplicity and immutability possess far more substance than many contemporary thinkers seem to realize. For these reasons, the theologian should seek to incorporate not only the traditional convictions that have inspired these doctrines but also much of their content.

On the other hand, the Christian must reject certain forms of these doctrines because they are incompatible with Christian beliefs such as the Trinity, incarnation, divine creative freedom and the divine personality. A chief virtue of the essentialism I propose is that it accommodates these central Christian beliefs while preserving much of the traditional content of the classical attributes, including immutability and simplicity.

I conclude by considering an important problem with essentialism, especially as it bears on God's sovereignty. In seeking to solve this problem, we discover that theism, so far from being inimical to essentialism, provides its best defense, via the ancient doctrine of exemplars or divine ideas.

PHILOSOPHY AND THEOLOGY

You may detect a subtext in this book, so I should probably mention it. For several decades, a number of Anglo-American Christian philosophers have been doing exciting work on subjects relevant to Christian theology.[3] Regrettably, so far few mainstream theologians have utilized their insights. In fact, there has been little interaction in either direction between mainstream theology and contemporary Christian philosophy. What little interaction there has been usually has taken the form of either criticism or insult. Although the biblical theology of the mid-twentieth century encouraged theologians to be suspicious of the philosophical Hellenism of much traditional theology, this more recent rift between theologians and philosophers is not due simply to the theologians' suspicion of the speculations of philosophers. After all, theologians frequently—sometimes too frequently—appropriate the ideas of contemporary philosophers. In contrast to many Christian philosophers, however, who tend to favor the so-called analytic tradition, most contemporary theologians seem more taken with Continental philosophy. But this is not the only barrier between contemporary Christian philosophy and theology.

To generalize, many mainstream theologians see Christian philosophers as uncritically traditional. The philosophers for their part seem convinced that many contemporary mainstream theologians have uncritically adopted non-Christian and anti-Christian philosophy. Whatever truth there is in either of these accusations (and I admit my sympathy with the philosophers on this point), the alienation between Christian theology and philosophy ill serves them both. For that reason, in what follows I attempt to bring these worlds together, not to choose one over the other but rather to mutually enrich the two through cross-fertilization.

---

[3] I am thinking of the work of Richard Swinburne, Alvin Plantinga, Thomas Morris, William Lane Craig, J. P. Moreland, Nicholas Wolterstorff, William Alston, C. Stephan Evans, Eleanor Stump, Basil Mitchell, Diogenes Allen, Robert and Marilyn Adams, Thomas Flint, Dallas Willard and many others.

TRUE HUMILITY

Any book on the doctrine of God merits Augustine's reminder: "To touch God to some extent with the mind is a great blessing, but to comprehend him is entirely impossible."[4] At the same time, if the Christian claim that God has revealed himself has merit, then it warrants our attempt to speak of him and trumps the claim that God is simply ineffable. If God has chosen to reveal himself, we are in no position to deny him that freedom. As Jewish theologian Michael Wyschogrod puts it, "Theologians must not be more protective of God's dignity than he is of his own."[5]

---

[4]*Sermo* 117.iii in Migne, *Patrologia Latina,* 38:663. Quoted in Kelly James Clark, "Hold Not Thy Peace at My Tears," *Our Knowledge of God,* ed. K. J. Clark (The Netherlands: Kluwer Academic, 1992), p. 188.

[5]*The Body of Faith: God and the People of Israel* (Northvale, N.J.: Jason Aronson, 1996), p. 64.

1

CHRISTIAN THEISM
Some Preliminary Issues

Some serious logical dilemmas hide within the traditional doctrine of God. Those dilemmas become most obvious in what is called classical theism, perhaps because in classical theism the Christian doctrine of God becomes most explicit and systematic. Many contemporary theologians seek to resolve the problem by jettisoning classical theism, often claiming it is a holdover from Greek metaphysics that has little or no place in a Christian theology.[1] Despite current fashion, however, simply repudiating classical theism is a mistake, not only because of its predominance in the tradition but also because its underlying motivations are intrinsically Christian. So the Christian theologian who values the tradition should seek to preserve these motivations if at all possible.

So what are those motivations, and why are they intrinsically Christian? If one reads literature from historical theology, it is possible to detect what we might call three themes of Christian theology. Identifying these themes will reveal the source of the conceptual problems that long have plagued the Christian doctrine of God. But besides underlying motivations, there is also a crucial concept to consider. Although it has fallen out of fashion in much contemporary theology, traditionally the concept of essence or nature has been central in Christian theology. In fact, the concept was at the center of virtually

---

[1]Among the most substantive and interesting criticisms are those of Karl Barth and Charles Hartshorne. For that reason, I will consider their views in chapters four through seven. Ironically, although Hartshorne is not a Christian theologian, he still argues that his doctrine of God is more compatible with Christian religious sensibilities than is classical theism, despite the fact that, at least historically, classical theism has been the overwhelming choice in Christian theology.

every christological dispute in the first five centuries of Christian history. Since I will defend a contemporary form of essentialism, it is important to give some account of the classical concept.

CLASSICAL THEISM
The classical method for deriving the divine attributes. No one will be surprised to learn that there are some significant theological disagreements among Catholic, Orthodox and Protestant Christians—as well as between various Protestants—on the nature of the church, its proper authority, and the details of justification and salvation provided by Christ's incarnation, life and crucifixion. Nevertheless, for most of Christian history there has been remarkable agreement on the doctrine of God, at least with respect to God's essence and attributes. While there are discernible differences, there has been a common core of beliefs about God that has stretched from the early church fathers through Thomas Aquinas and the Protestant Scholastics in the West and into the present day. In fact, properly abstracted, this classical theism is also common among the other religions of the book, namely, Judaism and Islam. That common core is often called *classical theism.* Simply put, classical theists understand God to be a supremely perfect, free, transcendent and sovereign Being who freely created the world and upon whom the world depends for its existence. To this, classical Christian theists add the doctrines of the Trinity and the incarnation. This sounds simple enough, but the devil is in the details.

Such agreement extends even to the methods of developing our ideas about God. When they make their method explicit, classical theists typically use three more or less deductive methods to derive the content of God's attributes, called the *via triplex*: the *via eminentiae* (the way of eminence), the *via negativa* (the way of negation) and the *via causalitatis* (the way of causality).

The theologian follows the *via eminentiae* by maximalizing those creaturely attributes taken to be susceptible to perfection, especially those human spiritual attributes like power, wisdom and goodness. These attributes are often called the communicable attributes, since God can share them with creatures, although creatures possess them in their own way, namely, as finite creatures. God, in contrast, possesses them supremely and absolutely. So while these attributes are communicable, they cannot be communicated to creatures as God has them, since he is their unique source.

The theologian follows the *via negativa* by contrasting the transcendent God to all those fleeting aspects of creaturely existence, including the tendency to change or decay, called mutability, as well as finitude, measurability and composition. Although this reasoning can produce an extreme skepticism, which makes it impossible to say anything specific about God, it more typically leads, in a backward sort of way, to a description of God as immutable, infinite, eternal, immeasurable and simple. Since the theologian derives these attributes by negating the created order—which is characterized by succession and the passing of time—it follows from the *via negativa* that divine eternity is not simply everlastingness but rather timelessness. Many classical theists, especially the Reformed Scholastics who followed John Calvin, often call these the incommunicable attributes, since God does not share them with any creatures.

With the *via causalitatis*, or way of causality, the theologian derives the divine attributes by viewing God as the First or Supreme Cause, and all else as effects of that cause. In this way the theologian derives attributes such as necessary existence, self-existence or aseity, and necessary first cause, as well as those derived from the *via eminentiae*, such as omnipotence, omniscience, and the like. This method is apparent, for example, in the famous five ways of Thomas Aquinas, in which Thomas offers five arguments for the existence of God as the First Cause of the universe.

Medieval classical theists also made much of the distinction between actuality and potentiality, which they learned from Aristotle. When annexed to theology, these categories led Thomas and the Protestant Scholastics to conceive of God as *Actus Purus* or *Actus Purissimus*—Pure Act. This means that God is always in a state of pure actuality and realization, and never *in potentia*, with some unfulfilled actuality in his being or essence. In their judgment, to say otherwise would be to imply change or mutability in God, since there would be movement in his essence from potency to actuality. In their view, such movement would contradict God's perfection. In contrast, they insisted that the "inward life of the Godhead is eternally complete and fully realized."[2] This reasoning, which may seem a bit obscure, makes sense

---

[2]"Actus Purus," in Richard A. Muller, *Dictionary of Latin and Greek Theological Terms* (Grand Rapids, Mich.: Baker, 1985), p. 24.

in an Aristotelian framework, in which movement from potency to actuality characterizes how an individual with a common essence is individuated. For example, I as an individual human being actualize the common human essence, which I share with all other human beings. So in a sense I depend upon this common essence in order to exist as a human being. But this is surely an inappropriate analogy for God's existence, since God is the one on whom all things depend. God is not merely an individual instance of some generic essence of divinity. Since God does not share a common essence with another entity, therefore, he does not "move" or change from potency to actuality.[3]

Thomas Aquinas's account. While we can extend the term *classical theism* to cover earlier Christian theologians, early accounts of God's essence and attributes are less systematic and explicit than the account that Thomas Aquinas (1225-1274) provides, especially in his monumental *Summa Theologica*. Partly because he used Aristotle far more than the early church, Thomas was able to extend and systematize the classical tradition. Thomas's thought is the high water mark and *locus classicus* of classical theism. The so-called Protestant Scholastics who followed the Reformation adopted his doctrine of God, whether consciously or unconsciously, almost in its entirety.

Thomas opens his *Summa Theologica* with a brief treatment of God's existence. He denies that God's existence is self-evident to us. This is contrary to Anselm, who had developed the so-called ontological argument for God's existence, in which he attempted to prove God's existence from the idea of a greatest possible being. Nevertheless, Thomas agrees with Anselm's description of God as "something than which none greater can be thought" (1.Q.2.A.1). (The *Summa* is divided into separate books, and each book is divided into questions, with many questions divided into separate articles. Questions are abbreviated as "Q," and articles as "A.") He then summarizes the five ways in which he conceives of God in terms of the four Aristotelian causes (formal, material, efficient and final), with the fourth way drawing on Neo-

---

[3]Presumably this conception provided for the personal and agential aspects of God, even though God's personality per se is seldom articulated as it is in more recent theology. While the classical conception may be inadequate on some accounts, the frequent accusation that it presents an inert God is surely wide of the mark. This is a common accusation in Catherine Mowry LaCugna, *God for Us: The Trinity and the Christian Life* (San Francisco: HarperSanFrancisco, 1991). God in classical theism is "passive" in the sense that he does not "increase," but not in the sense that he is inert.

Platonic themes (1.Q.2.A.2-3).[4] Here as elsewhere we see the relationship between the use of the *via triplex* and the concept of God derived from it, and the traditional arguments for the existence of God.

Next, Thomas treats the divine attributes individually (Q.3-11). While it would be a mistake to assume that order implies a simple ranking of importance, it is significant that he begins his treatment of the attributes (following existence) first with God's simplicity, then his perfection, goodness, infinity, omnipresence, immutability, eternity and unity. These are all incommunicable attributes gleaned from the *via negativa*. Probably because simplicity is not really an attribute but rather concerns the way in which the attributes are related to each other, to God's essence and to God, Thomas treats it first.

After considering divine knowledge and human knowledge of God, Thomas treats God's life, will, love, justice, mercy and power (Q.18-22, 25). This section of the *Summa* seems to be a result not only of the *via causalitatis* but also of Thomas's reflection on the doctrine of creation. He begins to discuss the relations and interactions of the divine persons of the Trinity in question 27 and continues his treatment of the Trinity through question 44. A popular mnemonic device for Catholic students summarizes this section nicely: "God is five notions, four relations, three persons, two processions, and one nature."[5]

One may wonder how Thomas's exposition of the trinitarian relations relates to his treatment of the other divine attributes. His study "Of the One God"—*De Deo Uno*—precedes his treatment "Of the Triune God"—*De Deo Triuno*—and the Catholic and Protestant Scholastics generally followed this order. Even within his treatment of the Trinity, he does not consider the mission of the divine persons until question 43, even though that mission is presumably the basis for our knowledge of the Trinity. Apparently Thomas structures his *Summa* according to the order of being as he understands it, rather than the order of knowing. This need not be inherently problematic. In fact, this

---

[4]Interestingly, his treatment of these proofs is adumbrated in the *Summa*, which may indicate that he does not consider them central for doing theology. He gives them a much greater role in apologetics toward the heathen, treating them at greater length in the *Summa Contra Gentiles*, 1.7-8.

[5]LaCugna, *God for Us*, p. 167. She explains the statement this way: "According to scholastic theology, a notion is what distinguishes each person. The five notions are: innascibility or ingenerateness; paternity; filiation; spiration; procession. Four of the five describe relations; innascibility is the absence of relation. Three of these relations are 'person-constituting': paternity, filiation, spiration. The ternary of relations is derived from the two processions, being begotten and being spirated" (pp. 179-80, n. 133).

order may reflect his apologetic concern, since Christians share the notion of being with Jews and Muslims, but not the concept of God's triunity.

Partly because of this ordering, however, some critics argue that Thomas's entire doctrine of God up to question 27 could stand alone without any modification to account for the trinitarian distinctions. The criticism, strictly speaking, is not that Thomas happens to start with God's attributes, including simplicity and the like, but that his treatment of those attributes is not properly informed by the parts of the doctrine of God that are specific to Christianity. If this criticism is correct, then his doctrine of God fails to attend adequately to the details of God's revelation in Jesus, which is surely the touchstone of any adequate Christian theology. In this way, Thomas may have introduced or perhaps solidified a tension in the classical doctrine of God's essence and attributes, a tension that will need to be resolved.

Protestant Scholasticism. At the beginning of the Reformation, there was little explicit discussion of God's essence and attributes. For example, one searches in vain for a list of divine attributes in John Calvin's *Institutes,* which went through various editions from 1536 to 1559. Perhaps Calvin considered such a project to be unwarranted speculation,[6] or perhaps he took for granted the doctrine of God common in the Christian West. In any case, the attributes quickly reappeared in the writings of Protestant Scholastics and are virtually synonymous with the pre-Reformation understanding. The classical attributes also found their way into Protestant confessions, where they usually enjoy a prominent place. The Presbyterian Westminster Confession, for instance, lists the attributes immediately after *Of the Holy Scriptures* in chapter one. Chapter two, *Of God, and of the Holy Trinity,* states:

> There is but one only living and true God, who is infinite in being and perfection, a most pure spirit, invisible, without body, parts, or passions, immutable, immense, eternal, incomprehensible, almighty, most wise, most holy, most free, most absolute . . . most loving, gracious, merciful, long-suffering, abundant in goodness and truth, forgiving iniquity.

It continues that God is all-sufficient and exists *a se,* having infallible and infinite knowledge "independent upon the creature, so as nothing is to him

---

[6] I owe this insight to a conversation with Bruce L. McCormack.

contingent or uncertain." He is most holy and is sovereign over all.

Clearly the Westminster Confession says a great deal about God's attributes, even before it treats the Trinity. This list of attributes is virtually identical to Thomas's, although the Westminster Confession obviously does not give the explanation that Thomas does in the *Summa,* nor does it give much help in determining the list's origin. The implication seems to be that it is a deliverance from Scripture.

Similarly, Heinrich Heppe, a great summarizer of Reformed Scholasticism, included essentially these same attributes in chapter five of his *Reformed Dogmatics* (1861), after chapter four, "The Existence and Notion of God," and before chapter six, "The Holy Trinity."[7] Heppe describes a minority view in Reformed Scholasticism, which understands the attributes as referring only to how God is revealed to us instead of expressions of how he actually is.[8] This skepticism has some claim to Calvin; but generally the Reformed Scholastics thought the attributes, properly qualified, did tell us something about God and even hinted at a definition of God. So Heppe quotes various Scholastics with approval: "God is a Spirit existing of Himself from eternity, one in essence trine in persons, Father, Son and Holy Spirit"; "God is . . . the *ens perfectissimum*"—the most perfect being. Heppe calls the incommunicable attributes "God's essential properties of the first order . . . predicated as it were a priori, as He is; i.e., they declare the essence of God as it is in Himself absolutely."[9]

By contrast, all parties maintained that finite creatures could never exhaustively define God's nature or essence, since God is incomprehensible to us. Strictly speaking, a definition of God is impossible, since our notion of definition requires a genus, and with it a distinction between species and genus, which would imply an inappropriate distinction in God. This would challenge God's sovereignty by qualifying him with a transcendent category: "for God is not one by genus or species in the philosophical acceptation, but by number or individuality."[10]

At least one source of the Scholastic restraint in speaking of multiple attributes in God was a commitment to the doctrine of divine simplicity. The

---

[7]Heinrich Heppe, *Reformed Dogmatics* (1861), rev. and ed. Ernst Bizer (London: George Allen & Unwin, 1950), pp. 57-104.

[8]Heppe quotes the Reformed Scholastic Polanus as an example (pp. 52-53).

[9]Ibid., p. 63.

[10]Ibid., pp. 52-53. Of course, the scholastic rejection of a definition of God is determined by their definition of *definition* as distinguishing species and genus. Whether there is definition in another sense, they do not consider.

Scholastics warned that the distinction we draw between the attributes of God, and between God's attributes and essence, are due only to the limitation of our powers of comprehension, not to any real distinction in God. It is a *distinctione rationis,* a distinction in thinking. At the same time, a bit obscurely and without further explanation, they insisted that the attributes do denote something objective in God.

The basic problem. This summary treatment suggests that the classical theistic understanding of God may have some problems. The problem, obviously, is that any Christian doctrine of God has to take into account certain biblical claims about God, especially those surrounding Jesus' life, death and resurrection, which were subsequently codified in the early ecumenical creeds at Nicaea (325) and Chalcedon (451). No doubt Thomas Aquinas and the Protestant Scholastics had every intention of doing this. They frequently cite biblical texts as support for the attributes derived from the *via triplex,* even if the biblical texts do not always bear all the weight of the attribute defended. Despite good intentions, however, the three ways can take on a deductive, a priori character. When this occurs, what is ascribed to God seems to result primarily from intuitions about what constitutes maximal greatness or aseity, or what is considered a deficiency in the physical world, with which God must be contrasted. Such a procedure can create a conflict in a Christian concept of God, [11] which derives its content not simply from general metaphysical intuitions but from unique, contingent things that God has done in history and, in particular, in Jesus Christ.

What then is the Christian theologian to do if aspects of classical theism conflict with claims from Scripture and claims about the Trinity, creation, incarnation and the like?

THREE THEMES IN CHRISTIAN THEOLOGY

The themes defined. With any conceptual problem, the easiest solution is to drop one of the sources of the conflict. For instance, three basic beliefs give

---

[11]When I say "the concept of God," I do not mean that God is a concept. In my view the word *God* functions much like a proper name but normally has some implicit connotation. That connotation can be drawn out and formalized into a concept. That connotation is what I mean by the phrase "the concept of God." The word *God* can also refer to or denote God, who revealed himself to Abraham, Isaac and Jacob and is (among other things) the *ens perfectissimum,* Creator of all that is, that than which none greater can be conceived, and the triune God of Christian belief.

rise to the traditional problem of evil: (1) God is all-powerful, (2) God is wholly good, and (3) There is real evil in the world. Any resolution to the problem requires at least analyzing, if not modifying, qualifying or dropping one of these three premises. Similarly, a theologian with a penchant for radical solutions might drop one of the sources of the conflict in the classical concept of God. For instance, if one wants a doctrine of God attentive to the basic claims articulated, say, in the New Testament, Apostles' and Nicene Creeds, and an idea produced by the *via negativa* conflicts with that, then, one might conclude, so much the worse for the *via negativa*. Although the brute simplicity of such a move has its appeal, the solution is a cavalier one, for the sources of the dilemma are intrinsic to Christian belief and not mere dross accreted to the tradition.

To see this, we need to clarify the sources of the conflict, sources easy enough to identify even if they sometimes remain implicit and unarticulated in the literature. Simply put, they seem to arise from certain underlying themes or *regulative principles,* which are almost universal in Christian theology. The first of these must certainly be a commitment to the biblical texts and to certain key events in Jesus' life, which were preserved and enshrined by the early ecumenical creeds. In the Reformed, Lutheran and evangelical traditions, this commitment is often expressed as the principle of *sola Scriptura.* This represents the Protestant conviction that Scripture should have priority for our ideas about God. Thus, ideally, according to *sola Scriptura,* the theologian's metaphysical and ontological commitments should emerge from, or be consistent with, Scripture. The theologian should use philosophical forms that comply with that commitment.

Sola Scriptura has more and less plausible formulations. Protestant theologians have long recognized, for instance, that seeking a pure biblical inductivism or positivism is not only unrealistic but also undesirable. So few modern Protestant theologians interpret the principle in this way. The theological task has never been so simple as compiling various bits of textual data and then arranging them disinterestedly into a theological system. After all, one hopes all theologians will follow valid rules of reasoning, such as Aristotle's laws of thought, even if such rules are merely implicit in the biblical texts. To do so gives us at least the theological equivalent of logical positivism.

Moreover, all theologians appropriate Scripture from within particular intellectual, historical and ecclesiastical settings, and within particular and sometimes peculiar interpretive traditions. This does not mean that the theologian's context determines his or her theological reasoning or that biblical texts have no intrinsic or determinative meaning. It means that theologians should account for their contexts methodologically. That context invariably will include a philosophical milieu, one that can provide philosophical categories useful for filling out the biblical description of God and for working out the implications of Christian belief. The biblical writings, after all, are not texts in systematic theology, philosophy of religion or ethics.

In practice at least, few Protestants have denied any of this. Perhaps the strongest evidence for this is that many Protestant theologians, including Calvin, have recognized the importance of the early ecumenical creeds. Indeed, they see such writings as the Apostles' Creed, the Nicene Creed and Chalcedonian definition of the incarnation, the latter two rich with philosophical terminology, as not only reliable interpretations of Scripture but also necessary safeguards against heresy. Moreover, they normally have not defended these creedal clarifications as independent or extrabiblical sources of authority, for they understand that a plausible rendering of *sola Scriptura* will incorporate the dialectical interplay—in theological reflection—of philosophical, scientific and other sources, even while granting the biblical texts marginal control.

While *sola Scriptura* is characteristically and rhetorically Protestant, commitment to biblical normativity as I am defining it is the norm among Catholic and Orthodox theologians as well. This is evident, for instance, in Thomas Aquinas and Augustine, who believed that, all things being equal, the divine testimony of Scripture trumps other sources of knowledge of God. Of course, Catholicism and Orthodoxy conventionally have been distinguished from Protestantism by their emphasis on tradition in addition to Scripture. However, by acknowledging that biblical normativity includes these nuances and by regarding the early ecumenical creeds as dialectical outgrowths of logic and Scripture, the theme clearly encompasses the Catholic, Protestant and Orthodox traditions. *Sola Scriptura* is best seen, then, as a Protestant emphasis on a universal theme in Christian theology.

Besides this commitment to the witness of Scripture and divine revelation, which I will call biblical normativity hereafter, the other two themes in Christian theology that seem to give rise to problems in classical theism, are the "Principle of Perfection"[12] (PP hereafter) and the "Sovereignty-Aseity Conviction"[13] (SAC hereafter). All three themes[14] motivate the classical use of the *via triplex,* although the themes are more fundamental than the methods themselves.[15] Again, it is probably best to think of these themes primarily as regulative principles rather than specific propositional claims about the nature of God.

Most simply, PP is the conviction that God is perfect or maximally great. He is that than which none greater or better can be conceived, as Anselm ingeniously expressed it. He is that than which none greater is even possible. PP presses theologians on to increasingly exalted claims for God. It is expressed methodologically at least in part with the *via eminentiae.*[16]And it is apparent, of course, in the fact that God's attributes are often described as divine perfections.

SAC is the conviction that God is the one reality that exists *a se* (from and of himself) and is dependent on nothing outside himself for his essence and existence. Though slightly more obscure than PP, this theme manifests itself in a number of ways. It seems to motivate the use of the *via negativa* and *via causalitatis,* underscoring the proximity of God's aseity and the fact that he

---

[12]I do not intend this term to connote "perfect being" theology exclusively, such as that derived from the *via eminentiae.* A contemporary example of such a view can be found in Thomas V. Morris's *Anselmian Explorations* (Notre Dame, Ind.: University of Notre Dame Press, 1987). I see the Principle of Perfection as the motivation that drives the *via eminentiae* and the *via negativa;* however, it does not seem to be the only motivation for the *via negativa,* which also may be inspired by what David Burrell calls the "distinction" between God and the world. However, as I have defined it, the need to make that distinction arises from SAC.

[13]This is a modified version of Alvin Plantinga's notion of the "sovereignty-aseity intuition" which he argues (correctly by my lights) motivates many theologians to posit the absolute simplicity of God's nature or essence. See his *Does God Have a Nature?* (Milwaukee: Marquette University Press, 1980), p. 34.

[14]To avoid overstatement, I prefer to speak here of certain recurrent guiding themes in Christian theology rather than to sources of authority or to nonnegotiable control beliefs.

[15]By mentioning only these three, I am not denying that there are other such guiding themes and commitments in Christian theology, such as the beliefs that God is love or is personal, or the role of personal experience. I highlight these three because they seem to be the themes responsible for the tension in the classical concept of God and also seem to be the themes on which there is significant disagreement in the proposals we consider.

[16]However, PP is susceptible to different interpretations. It is not explicit enough to determine alone whether God is perfect in the sense that he possesses a maximally consistent set of great-making properties, interpreted as *maxima* (or limits *simpliciter*), or whether his perfection is a sort of limit case that merely points toward an indescribable infinity. For example, Morris defines his conception of God in the former way: "God is thought of as exemplifying necessarily a maximally perfect set of compossible great-making properties" (*Anselmian Explorations,* p. 12). Barry Miller describes God's attributes in the latter way. For the distinction between maxima and limit case, see Barry Miller, *A Most Unlikely God* (Notre Dame, Ind.: University of Notre Dame Press, 1996), p. 4ff.

is Creator of all. Various philosophers and theologians express SAC differently. Alvin Plantinga refers to the "sovereignty-aseity intuition,"[17] which includes divine control over all things. He also argues that it motivates the traditional doctrine of divine simplicity. Some speak in more relational terms, insisting on the fundamental "distinction" between God and all created reality.[18] Others prefer to speak (also relationally) of God's "absolute transcendence."[19] These notions seem to be related, while no doubt differing in details. I suspect that SAC rightly defined is implied by PP,[20] as well as by careful attention to the Christian doctrine of creation. Put differently, the Sovereignty-Aseity Conviction seems to be a proper subset of the Principle of Perfection. Some theologians, however, such as Charles Hartshorne, disagree.[21] For that reason, I will distinguish them.

While common in Christian theology generally, the three themes are also three poles around which the most important disputes center in the proposals I consider. In fact, the central differences between them seem to revolve around disagreement on the meaning and relative weight given to these three themes.

In contemporary philosophy of religion these two ways of viewing divine perfection have largely separated into distinct camps, unlike the ancient and medieval theologies. In general the former, often called "perfect being" theologians, distinguish God from the world in modal terms of necessity and contingency, so that God exists and possesses his great-making properties essentially and necessarily, while creatures exist contingently and so do not instantiate any perfections necessarily. The latter tend to distinguish God from creation in terms of finite and infinite, so that they are unlikely to define God's perfections as *maxima*. Recent disputes between the partisans in the debate have gotten quite heated and acerbic. For instance, Leon Pearl accuses those who see God as instantiating a *maxima* of great-making properties of having an "idolatrous concept of God" ("The Misuse of Anselm's Formula for God's Perfection," *Religious Studies* 22 [1986]: 355-65). Despite this contention, all of the disputants seem to share a core conviction about the absolute superiority and perfection of God, even if they cannot agree on what that means.

[17]Plantinga, *Does God Have a Nature?* p. 34.

[18]For example, David Burrell, *Knowing the Unknowable God* (Notre Dame, Ind.: University of Notre Dame Press, 1986), p. 2; David Burrell, "Distinguishing God from the World," in *Language, Meaning and God* (London: Geoffrey Chapman, 1987), pp. 75-91; Robert Sokolowski, *The God of Faith and Reason* (Washington, D.C.: The Catholic University Press of America, 1982), pp. xiii-xiv, 19, 23, 31-34.

[19]Miller, *Most Unlikely God*, p. 13.

[20]As I take him, Anselm conjoins PP and SAC together in *Proslogion* 5, which begins: "God is whatever it is better to be than not to be, and He, the only self-existent being, makes all other things from nothing." In *A Scholastic Miscellany*, ed. Eugene R. Fairweather (Philadelphia: Westminster Press, 1956).

[21]Charles Hartshorne does hold to a (peculiar) version of PP. However, he denies that SAC can be given a determinate sense, and so he denies that it applies to God.

The biblical basis of the Principle of Perfection and the Sovereignty-Aseity Conviction. One might wonder why Christian theologians would use the Principle of Perfection and the Sovereignty-Aseity Conviction, especially if they cause conceptual problems. A simplistic but incorrect argument would be that SAC and PP are mere philosophical speculations that are unrelated to the biblical witness. But there is a strong biblical justification for both themes, although theologians often express them with philosophical concepts. In fact, many biblical texts express PP and SAC, at least in rudimentary forms. God as Almighty (all-sufficient, authoritative) is a common biblical image, especially in Genesis, Exodus and Job. God creates all things without counterpart or challenger (Gen 1; Job 39; Jn 1:3; Col 1:16). He is the Lord, the sovereign King, the Most High, the Mighty One. He reigns forever over all creation, which is his alone, and with which he does according to his will alone.[22] He "accomplishes all things according to his counsel and will" (Eph 1:11). "From him and through him and to him are all things" (Rom 11:36). Even seemingly trivial details fall under his purview: "Are not two sparrows sold for a penny? Yet not one of them will fall to the ground apart from your Father. And even the hairs of your head are all counted" (Mt 10:29-30).

God's sovereignty is never far from his holiness, according to which God is unique, pure and set apart. The Sovereign Lord, Isaiah proclaims, is the Holy One of Israel (Is 30:15). God's holiness connotes that he is separate from the creation, and he acts according to his holiness in separating the night from the day in his first act of creation (Gen 1:4). This holiness separates the biblical God from the other gods of the ancient Near East and the pagan gods of the Greeks and Romans. Because God's holiness means that he is separate and stands apart from the created realm, it is not something that human beings can discover. Rather, God must reveal himself as holy (Ex 3:5; 1 Sam 2:2; Ps 110:3; 111:9; Is 46:8-11).

While less pervasive than the theme of divine sovereignty, Scripture also describes God as perfect (Mt 5:48) in his ways and works (Deut 32:4; 2 Sam 22:31, 33; Ps 18:30), his knowledge (Job 36:4; 37:16), his laws (Ps 19:7; Jas 1:25), his faithfulness (Is 25:1) and his will (Rom 12:2). The bib-

---

[22]1 Chron 29:11; Ezek 17:4; Ps 9; 24:1; 47:2, 7-9; 93; 95:3-5; 104; 115:3; Is 45:9-12; Ex 33:19; Rev 1:8; 4:8, 11.

lical authors imply God's perfection when they praise him superlatively: "Great is our LORD and abundant in power; / his understanding is beyond measure" (Ps 147:5). "Nothing in all creation is hidden from God's sight."[23] God is the exemplar of freedom and resolve (Is 46:10), of power and divinity (Ps 115:3; 135:5-6; Rev 19:16). "For God all things are possible" (Mt 19:26). The sovereign and perfect God is also the standard of justice and faithfulness (Ps 9:16; 33:5; 46:6), great in mercy (1 Chron 21:13), speaking only truth (Ps 33:4; 119:160). He is not limited by time and degradation, as the psalmist says: "you are the same, and your years have no end" (Ps 102:27). He is the exalted One who lives forever, who nevertheless is with the *contrite* and *broken* in spirit (Ps 51:17). In Scripture, these attributes stand comfortably alongside claims that God is the free Creator who has entered freely into covenant with his people. "For the LORD will not forsake his people; / he will not abandon his heritage" (Ps 94:14). In some mysterious way, John even tells us God *is* truth and love (Jn 14:6; 1 Jn 4:8).

Admittedly, historical theological treatments of God's perfection, sovereignty and aseity often outstrip explicit biblical testimony. But they are often an appropriate extension of biblical ideas. For instance, one could argue plausibly that the concept of divine aseity purifies or extends the biblical claim that God is the holy, sovereign Creator of all that is. All things depend on God. God depends on nothing. As such, aseity dovetails with the doctrine of creation *ex nihilo*, a teaching implicit in, or at least consistent with, Scripture.[24] So even though no biblical text explicitly says God exists *a se*, a taproot for the concept of divine aseity exists in the biblical testimony of the self-revealing Creator God. The notion follows much more naturally from the biblical depictions of God than from reflection on the Platonic Demiurge, Neo-Platonic One or other pagan stories of deities who are the top story of a universe ultimately controlled by fate or chaos.

Perhaps the exemplary extension of the Principle of Perfection is Anselm's definition of God as that than which none greater or better can be con-

---

[23]Heb 4:13; Prov 15:3.

[24]For a more detailed argument of the biblical basis for the doctrine of creation *ex nihilo,* see Paul Copan, "Is *Creatio ex Nihilo* a Postbiblical Invention? An Examination of Gerhard May's Proposal," *Trinity Journal* 17 n.s. (1996): 77-93.

ceived.[25] Centuries of Christians have judged Anselm's definition to be a truthful expression of God.[26] While Anselm's claim is not a quotation from Scripture,[27] Paul suggests it when he speaks of Christ's love "that surpasses knowledge," and of him who "is able to accomplish abundantly far more than all we can ask or imagine" (Eph 3:19-20).

Such extrapolated interpretations of PP and SAC exercise enough control that theologians, including staunchly biblical ones, sometimes use them, in a sort of hermeneutical feedback loop, to interpret Scripture. For example, when Calvin or Augustine disallows the most anthropomorphic interpretation of passages that speak of God walking in the garden or having an arm or changing his mind, they betray their commitment to the Principle of Perfection.[28] We must judge the legitimacy of such use case by case; but this is a widely accepted practice when attributing an action or characteristic to God— such as literal repentance—would contradict his aseity or perfection.

Other sources for the Principle of Perfection and the Sovereignty-Aseity Conviction. The extension of the Principle of Perfection and the Sovereignty-Aseity Conviction beyond explicit biblical language also has a fairly obvious doxological motivation. That is, something intrinsic to how Christians worship and praise God rightly creates the need to ascribe to God the most exalted terms. In fact, Scripture suggests as much. Thus David prays: "Yours, O LORD, are the greatness, the power, the glory, the victory, and the majesty; for all that is in the heavens and on the earth is yours" (1 Chron 29:11). Ironically, the philosopher J. N. Findlay describes this commitment well in an essay attempting to disprove the existence of God:

Now it is contrary to the demands and claims inherent in religious attitudes that

---

[25]Or alternatively, "A being than which none greater can be thought" (*Proslogion* 2). Of course, the principle of perfection is not necessarily the only thing that motivates Anselm's definition; I claim only that it is one motivation. Further, it does not necessarily entail the conception popular among contemporary "perfect being" theologians.

[26]For example, Thomas Aquinas defends divine perfection in *Summa Theologica* 1.Q.4.

[27]It may be implied by Scripture, particularly the biblical claims of God as Creator and the God-world distinction. For argument, see Robert Sokolowski, *The God of Faith and Reason* (Washington, D.C.: Catholic University of America Press, 1995), pp. 1-11, 21-29, 111.

[28]Of course, this is not to claim that such exegetical explanations are motivated exclusively by commitment to divine perfection. In the case at hand, for instance, the conviction that God does not have a body is also important. However, this belief in God's immateriality itself issues from commitment to PP, since materiality would imply change and therefore imperfection.

their object should exist "accidentally"; it is also contrary to these demands that it should *possess its various excellences* in some merely adventitious manner. It would be quite unsatisfactory from the religious stand point, if an object merely *happened* to be wise, good, powerful, and so forth, even to a superlative degree. . . . And so we are led on irresistibly, by the demands inherent in religious reverence, to hold that an adequate object of our worship must possess its various excellences in some necessary manner.[29]

What Findlay calls "religious attitudes" and "the demands inherent in religious reverence" seem to be clear expressions of the Principle of Perfection.[30]

The attributes that a theologian may believe the principle implies in a particular intellectual context are distinct from commitment to the principle. Our intuitions about what constitutes perfection vary widely and will unavoidably be influenced by our intellectual context. An important contemporary example of this is the differing assessments of divine suffering. Classical theists saw suffering as a deficiency that besets finite beings like ourselves. To attribute suffering to God would violate his absolute immutability and impassability and hence would imply imperfection in God. So, not surprisingly, they denied that God suffers. In contrast, many modern theologians and philosophers view suffering as a necessary condition for love. Since God is love, divine suffering is now frequently made a central motif in Christian theology.[31] This debate is best seen not as a dispute about whether God is perfect but about what properly constitutes God's perfection. So one can approve of the "religious attitude" Findlay describes without automatically deciding what attributes God does in fact possess, the content of those perfections, how he possesses them or even of the propriety of speaking of God as possessing attributes.

When we consider the wealth of direct if rudimentary scriptural support, the doxological motivation attested to by Scripture and reason and the near universality of the PP and the SAC in the Christian tradition, it is plausible to

---

[29]J. N. Findlay, "Can God's Existence Be Disproved?" *Mind* 57 (1948): 108-18, quoted in Alvin Plantinga, *The Nature of Necessity* (Oxford: Clarendon, 1974), pp. 229-30.

[30]Findlay thought these "religious attitudes" summoned a God that necessarily does not exist, since he thought all existential claims are contingent. I disagree with this assumption.

[31]For example, see Jürgen Moltmann, *The Crucified God* (London: SCM Press, 1974) and *The Trinity and the Kingdom* (San Francisco: HarperSanFrancisco, 1981), pp. 21-60.

conclude that they are essential for developing a Christian concept of God.[32] Certainly for the traditional Christian, the specific way in which God has revealed himself must constrain the content of the PP and the SAC. Nevertheless, if extrabiblical extrapolations of these themes have no legitimate role to play in Christian theology, then their ubiquity in the history of Christian theology would make that history theologically suspect.[33]

The problem restated as an interaction of the three themes. Now that we have the three themes clearly before us, we can restate the problem that seems to beset the classical concept of God. But we must be careful not to misidentify the nature of the conflict. Strictly speaking, the problem is not that classical theists have employed a philosophical construct, using philosophical terminology built up from a pretheoretical and even extrabiblical concept of God. After all, there is a sense in which even Scripture appeals to a pre-Christian, and even pre-Israelite, concept of God. Thus the Old Testament texts—perhaps most importantly, the Pentateuch—retain the ancient Near Eastern terms *El* and *Elohim* in reference to the God worshiped by the Jews. The biblical "conscription" of these words and the identification of *Elohim* with the self-revealing Yahweh of Jewish history imply this.[34] English translations of these passages often retain this distinction by switching between the words *God* and "the LORD" to denote the same

---

[32]Moreover, if they are intrinsic to the Christian concept of God, then it seems that the Christian theologian is warranted in adopting them. As an argument for this, it is plausible to suppose that if God has chosen to reveal himself determinately in history, he would superintend some process or community that would preserve at least the bare essentials of that revelation. This does not require that one accord infallibility to every historical development in Christian doctrine. This is impossible in any case, since not all such developments are compatible. The fact that I place a high authority in the ecumenical councils relative to the authority of Scripture itself betrays my conviction that God superintends the church's history. Functionally, this amounts to the conservative principle that Christians should treat ecumenical councils as proper extrapolations and interpretations of Scripture, unless it is demonstrated otherwise.

[33]To entertain a bit of speculation, perhaps PP and SAC begin more as biblically informed intuitions than as fully formed conceptions, although they are always expressed with some positive content. (They have *some* content, such as "God is perfect" and "God is sovereign and exists *a se*." But these propositions can be developed in diverse ways.) In this form, they constitute a potential source for natural theology. If this is the case, then Christian theological reflection would be a process whereby these intuitions are shaped, corrected and, in extreme cases, repudiated in light of God's special acts of revelation in history and Scripture.

[34]This is an interesting and complicated topic, one that is tangential to my argument here. For an especially insightful and adept treatment, see Wolfhart Pannenberg, *Systematic Theology*, trans. Geoffrey Bromiley (Grand Rapids, Mich.: Eerdmans, 1991), vol. 1, chaps. 2-4.

deity.[35] And the words *theos* and *God* had pre-Christian meanings as well. After all, Yahweh did not reveal himself to a people devoid of theological context, any more than he revealed himself in the person of Jesus to a theologically neutral civilization. So the problem is not simply that the classical theist employs extrabiblical or philosophical notions of divinity.

Put baldly, the problem is that such expectations and intuitions fed by a pre-Christian concept of God can sometimes contradict what Christians believe God has revealed about himself in salvation history and the biblical narratives. And deductions from such intuitions will be equally problematic.

Similarly, when the PP and the SAC become a priori principles for articulating God's nature or essence, outside the influence of Scripture, they can generate concepts of God incompatible with each other as well as with important biblical assertions. For example, the PP can render a "perfect being" theology that contradicts biblical claims about a God who becomes incarnate in history as a human being, suffers and even dies on a cross.

Equally problematic, the SAC can generate either a highly agnostic negative theology or a conception of God as an undifferentiated Absolute that contradicts the claims that God exists as a Trinity, has revealed himself in human history, became incarnate, has moral attributes and has freely created the universe.[36]

In response to such problems, twentieth-century theologians generally have not treated classical theism sympathetically. They often have accused it of being a residue from an antiquated and even unbiblical Greek metaphysics, which has created irreconcilable problems for Christian theology.[37] In natural theology, so their argument goes, classical theists develop a concept of God as

---

[35]A most instructive passage in this regard is the account of the divine epiphany to Moses in Exodus 3.

[36]In fact, a large swath of English-speaking Christian philosophers could be roughly divided into three camps, depending on which of these principles they tend to emphasize. So-called Anselmians and "perfect being" theologians include Thomas V. Morris, Alvin Plantinga, Nicholas Wolterstorff, Kelly James Clark, Edward Wierenga, perhaps Richard Swinburne, Anthony Kenny and, to a lesser degree, William Alston. (Morris even refers to himself as an Anselmian.) Process theologians also tend to grant priority to the PP but come close to rejecting SAC. Contemporary Thomists and classical theists tend to emphasize divine aseity, absoluteness and distinction from the world. Examples include David Burrell, Robert Sokolowski, Brian Davies, Barry Miller, Eleanore Stump, William Mann, Norman Kretzmann and James Ross. Many mainstream theologians, who intend to be more kerygmatic and biblical, often dismiss all these groups as unduly philosophical and insufficiently biblical.

[37]Moltmann even goes so far as to criticize the Christian tradition for adopting monotheism. See *Trinity and the Kingdom*, pp. 129-37.

he is in himself using the *via triplex*. Then, in revealed theology, they try but fail to reconcile that concept with God as revealed in Scripture.

There is some truth in this accusation. It is surely undeniable, for instance, that Thomas's account of the divine attributes in questions 3-11 (from divine simplicity to unity) of the *Summa Theologica* exhibits the influence, perhaps even the determinative influence, of Aristotle and Plotinus. Moreover, many portions of Scripture, including ones whose plain sense seems nonnegotiable for Christians, ascribe to God somewhat surprising characteristics and actions that do not seem to comport well with PP and SAC. Particularly striking is Paul's claim that in Christ God took on the form of a servant, "being born in human likeness . . . he humbled himself and became obedient to the point of death—even death on a cross" (Phil 2:7-8). These and many comparable texts remind us that we are not free to fill the notions of divine sovereignty and perfection with meanings that contradict God's acts as revealed in Scripture. In particular, no Christian theologian can tolerate definitions of God's perfection or sovereignty that contradict the claim that God became incarnate as the man Jesus, who mourned, suffered and died. If we find this counterintuitive, then so much the worse for intuition, at least on these points.

The proper Christian response to the PP and the SAC, therefore, involves a yes and a no. On the one hand, these themes have substantial biblical warrant and issue from genuinely Christian motivations. So Christian theologians are not free to abandon them in favor of biblical normativity. Accordingly, they should avoid hastily contrasting, say, the attributes of classical theism and the proper attributes that should derive from a biblically grounded doctrine of God, whether the contrast is framed as a conflict between natural and revealed theology, Athens and Jerusalem or philosophy and theology.[38]

On the other hand, the Christian tradition is marked by extensions of these themes beyond biblical warrant. When conflict results within a doctrine of

---

[38]By framing the three themes as I have, I hope to avoid postulating an unnecessary conflict between biblical and philosophical sources. I also hope to account for the presence of PP and SAC even among theologians who criticize classical theism. Two examples of this are Moltmann in *Trinity and the Kingdom* and LaCugna in *God for Us*. While Moltmann and LaCugna criticize the Thomistic attributes for being motivated by philosophical convictions of what constitutes perfection, they clearly have their own preferences for the divine perfections, which also have philosophical affinities. The contemporary "open theists" also tend to criticize classical theism for undue Hellenistic influence. See Clark Pinnock et al., *The Openness of God* (Downers Grove, Ill.: InterVarsity Press, 1994).

God, theologians must seek a resolution by modifying PP and SAC to conform to biblical normativity.

The value of treating the PP and the SAC as legitimate themes in Christian theology, as we have done here, is that we can preserve them as motivations or regulative principles while allowing room for criticism of their positive content in particular doctrinal formulations. For instance, later I argue that certain formulations of some divine attributes, such as immutability and simplicity, can introduce a conflict into the concept of God, which must be resolved in light of the biblical witness.

THE CONCEPT OF ESSENCE IN THE CHRISTIAN TRADITION

Besides these underlying themes, from the earliest days of Christian doctrinal reflection, theologians have used certain terms that carry ontological implications, usually drawn from current philosophy. The needs of Christian theology often have required significant modification of these terms and the concepts they connote, but the procedure is unavoidable in any attempt to make theological language more precise. The most important is probably the Greek term *ousia* (being or substance), as well as its partial equivalents *hypostasis*, *physis* and *hyparxis*. These terms functioned differently at different times, different authors used them differently, and the same authors sometimes used them differently in different writings. They were translated variously into Latin as *essentia*, *substantia*, *existentia* and *natura*. *Hypostasis* and *prosopon* were often translated as *persona* (person). English translations include *substance*, *essence* and *nature*. Understandably, such variation makes historical analysis of this concept, or cluster of concepts, a daunting task.

Plato may be the first to have used *ousia* in a philosophical sense, using it to refer to such concepts as being, existence, unchanging reality and constitution.[39] Aristotle's use of *ousia*, however, and his distinction between primary and secondary substances profoundly influenced medieval and later theology. Primary substances are the persisting individuals of which things are predicated but which are not predicates themselves. Secondary substances are what are predicated of primary substances and of which accidents may be predi-

---

[39]See Christopher Stead, *Divine Substance* (Oxford: Clarendon, 1977), pp. 29-30, the best single book on the topic.

cated. The use of these notions is complicated and goes beyond our concerns here.[40] Note, however, that among ancient writers the use of *ousia* et al. invariably had the connotation of reality, so that "to designate x as an *ousia* in the sense of 'substance' was *both* to declare that x is more truly real than states, processes, etc., *and* to give x an initial classification in the scheme of things."[41]

Heretical developments among the ranks of the early church leadership encouraged careful distinctions and terminological precision. The initial trouble was a theological opinion prevalent among Arians that Jesus was not of the same ontological status as the Father. To say otherwise, thought the Arians, would compromise God's sovereignty as well as monotheism itself. So Arians understood Christ not as God but as a sort of pre-eminent creature. The need to preserve Jesus' full deity against this Arian heresy required precision, an ample motivation for adopting philosophical terms. The Nicene Fathers' insistence on the complete equality of the Father and Son was codified in 325 with the term *homoousios* (same substance). The Nicene Creed says that they are consubstantial; they are of the same substance (as opposed to being merely "of like substance," *homoiousios*). At Constantinople (381) it becomes clear that Father, Son and Spirit are three *hypostases,* three subsistent realities of the same *ousia.* The Nicene Fathers introduced these terms over the objections of the Arians, who claimed that the terms were unbiblical. The Nicene Fathers, who prevailed in the controversy, contended that the terms, although drawn from philosophy, provided certain ontological distinctions necessary to draw out biblical claims and preserve the implications of the faith. Ironically, if the Nicene Fathers were correct, then the biblicist Arians were less faithful to Scripture than the Fathers who introduced extrabiblical terminology.

---

[40]See Stead, *Divine Substance,* chaps. 2-5 for such details. Aristotle mentions ten categories in his *Categoriae,* in *The Basic Works of Aristotle,* ed. Richard McKeon (New York: Random House, 1941), pp. 7-37. Besides primary substance, nine secondary substances can be predicated of primary substances: quantity, relation, quality, place, time, posture, having, acting and being acted upon. In *Topics* 1.5-6 (ed. McKeon, pp. 191-93), Aristotle says five things may be predicated of a primary substance: definition, property, genus, differentia and accident. A definition signifies the essence of a primary substance. Genera and species tell us the kind of primary substances, which are defined by their essential attributes. Primary substances also have accidents, which are nonessential attributes. It does not seem possible to reconcile completely everything Aristotle says on these matters in all his works, although his general views are clear enough. For discussion, see Diogenes Allen, *Philosophy for Understanding Theology* (Atlanta: John Knox Press, 1985), chap. 4.

[41]Stead, *Divine Substance,* pp. 131-32. Stead includes among the senses of *ousia* as substance the following: existence, category or status, substance, stuff or material, form, definition and (somewhat differently) truth.

The Chalcedonian formula in 451 again appropriates these terms, claiming that Christ is one *hypostasis* and *prosopon* (or person) and two *physes* (natures, roughly synonymous with *ousia*). These claims, along with the Apostles' Creed, are the most ecumenical of all official Christian documents, giving them a central place in the Christian tradition. Even the most biblicist theologians usually have accepted them.

Essence, substance and related concepts had other theological implications in the early church. There was no clear delineation in antiquity between God's substance on the one hand and his unchanging or essential attributes on the other,[42] although an attempt to guard God's transcendence led to a distinction between God's *ousia* and his *energia,* which emanated from his *ousia*. This distinction became common stock in Eastern Orthodoxy.

The desire to preserve divine unity led some in the early centuries toward subordinationism, which portrayed the Son and Spirit as subordinate to the Father, in order to reconcile christological claims with monotheism. This strategy often betrayed a material influence from Neo-Platonism, with the Father, Son and Spirit looking suspiciously akin to the Plotinian ontological levels of the One, Nous and Soul. Nicaea and Chalcedon ended the viability of such an approach for the orthodox. Scruples over God's transcendence, aseity and unity, however, led many to deny a distinction between God's attributes, as well as a distinction between God's attributes, his nature and God himself. Therefore theologians as early as Irenaeus argued not only for divine unity and oneness but also for the related notion of divine simplicity. Irenaeus claimed that God is "simple and not compounded, uniform and wholly alike in himself, being wholly mind and wholly spirit . . . wholly hearing, wholly sight, wholly light and wholly the source of all good things."[43] And Augustine said of God, "He is what he has."[44] Athanasius argued for similar reasons that God did not possess multiple accidents or contingent properties.[45] Unlike subordinationism, the notion of divine simplicity was retained and developed in the tradition, receiving its strongest formulation from Thomas Aquinas. Here and elsewhere we can detect not only the presence but also the pressures of philosophical concepts on theological concepts.

---

[42]Stead, *Divine Substance,* p. 166.

[43]Irenaeus *Adversus Haereses* 2.13.3.

[44]Augustine *City of God* 9.10.

[45]See quotes and citation in Stead, *Divine Substance,* pp. 187-88, 109.

In theology, it is notoriously difficult to separate legitimate from illegitimate uses of philosophical concepts and terms. This is especially true with respect to fundamental concepts like *ousia,* which different theologians took in almost opposite directions. Whichever direction a theologian took, however, an uncharitable critic could accuse him of being unduly influenced by Hellenistic modes of thought. For instance, if a theologian identified God as a substance, one could take that as evidence of the determinative influence of Greek philosophy. In such a case, so the accusation might go, God is treated as any other creature, being placed under the category of substance.

In contrast, if another theologian said God is beyond substance, one could deem this as evidence of overweening Hellenistic influence, since Neo-Platonists said similar things of the One. Since Hellenistic categories could be used in such different and even contradictory fashions, it is easy to misconstrue their influence. In any event, we should not make such accusations glibly. The fact that early theologians appropriated "substance" language does not determine its propriety in speaking of God either then or now.

More theologically problematic senses of *substance* and *essence* emerged in later Western philosophy. The rationalist René Descartes (1596-1650) conceived of God and created minds as substances, but he distinguished created substances from the one strict, self-existent substance, namely, God. For Descartes, the principal attribute of mind was thought and the principal attribute of body was extension. Benedict de Spinoza (1632-1677) was stricter than Descartes, insisting that there can be only one substance, which he defined in his *Ethics* as that which exists "in itself, and is conceived through itself." This understanding was not Spinoza's creation, since this was one sense of *ousia* in late antiquity.[46] For Spinoza, however, that one substance, which he called *Deus, sive Natura (God, or Nature),* had infinite attributes, including mind and extension.[47]

Spinoza's definition of substance thus entailed pantheism or metaphysical

---

[46]Stead defines a typical sense of *ousia* as substance in this way:
  (i) *Ousia* does not exist in, or as an aspect of, something else; anything else exists in, or as an aspect of, it.
  (ii) Consequently *ousia* is the most permanent form of being; it is what persists through change and makes it comprehensible (*Divine Substance,* p. 138).

[47]See "Spinoza, Baruch," in *The Cambridge Dictionary of Philosophy,* ed. Robert Audi (Cambridge: Cambridge University Press, 1995), pp. 759-60.

monism. Perhaps in Spinoza we see most clearly that how one defines substance, essence, being and other ontological terms determines how useful and
congenial they will be for Christian theology.[48] But the mere use of a term tells
us very little. So we must evaluate the theological use of philosophical concepts case by case, in light of the central themes of Christian theology and, in
particular, the biblical witness.

My purpose in what follows is not to take over these ancient terms but
rather to preserve the realist theological conviction that inspired their adoption in the early, medieval and Reformation church, by means of a viable contemporary essentialism. In this way, I hope to accommodate this dominant
part of the Christian tradition while correcting some residual confusions.

CONCLUSION

While the three themes of Christian theology clearly informed the classical
theistic method, they are also central themes by which my proposal may be
compared with the proposals of Barth, Hartshorne and classical theism. The
themes can function as a taxonomy for evaluating various twentieth-century
attempts to resolve the tensions in classical theism. For instance, kergymatic
theologians such as Karl Barth and Jürgen Moltmann opt, at least rhetorically,
for the priority of biblical normativity over either PP or SAC, while Charles
Hartshorne prefers PP to either biblical normativity or SAC. And some contemporary Thomists, such as David Burrell, Barry Miller and James Ross, have
an obvious affinity for SAC over biblical normativity or PP. The great strength
of Anglo-American Christian philosophy for theology is the tools it offers for
articulating a doctrine of God that effectively honors the Principle of Perfection, the Sovereignty-Aseity Conviction and biblical normativity without
slighting any of them.

The essentialist model I introduce in chapters two and three continues this
tradition. At the very least, the use of the term *essence* is an important point of
contact and continuity between the Christian tradition and contemporary es-

---

[48]In the early Christian centuries, theologians who used *ousia* in one sense often judged some under-
standings of substance completely inadequate for theological use. For instance, the Stoic conception,
which understood matter as the primary reality (see Stead, *Divine Substance,* pp. 118-25, 138), was
contrary to the Christian conviction of God's immateriality. So early Christian theology was more
akin to the Platonic rather than the Stoic understanding of substance, insofar as the latter had a consistent definition of *ousia*.

sentialism. My goal is to preserve as much as possible in the classical concept of God, qualifying it only when the demands of logic and Christian particularity require it. Since theologians have taken the notions of divine simplicity and immutability to be the most difficult aspects of classical theism to reconcile with the relational, trinitarian God of Christian belief, I will consider these in the concluding chapters.

2

From Modal Speech to Essentialism

While language about essences, essential and contingent properties, and the like has a long and substantial history in Western thought, it has become virtually orthodox opinion in theological circles that essentialist language should be overcome rather than preserved or defended.[1] This view seems to derive from the assumption that some development in philosophy has made such language obsolete. In contrast, in recent years philosophers have successfully defended essentialism, building on logicians' careful analyses of concepts such as necessity and possibility. A number of philosophers have in turn applied these insights to various metaphysical and epistemological issues. With some adaptation, these insights can also be used for theology. That is the work of chapter three.

In this chapter, I introduce modal logic and then adopt what is called the S5 model as the one that most adequately captures the notions of logical necessity and possibility. I then add quantification and the possible worlds semantic interpretation of quantified S5. Armed with this form of possible worlds semantics, I then discuss its merits for our understanding of essentialism. This requires the introduction of a few distinctions, between *de re* and

---

[1]Far too often, theologians take for granted contentious philosophical conclusions, often claiming that an irreversible historical process somehow makes it impossible to hold a previously held view. Jürgen Moltmann is somewhat typical when he declares, "A return to the earlier Trinity of substance is practically impossible, if only because the return to the cosmology of the old way of thinking has become impossible too, ever since the beginning of modern times" (*The Trinity and the Kingdom* [San Francisco: HarperSanFrancisco, 1981], pp. 18-19). Regrettably, such assertions frequently take the place of argument.

de dicto modality, actualism and possibilism, and contingent and essential properties. Finally, I consider the most important criticisms of this type of possible worlds semantics, none of which constitute insuperable difficulties for the essentialist.

Having read that compact summary, you might be getting worried. In the interest of full disclosure, I admit that this is the most difficult chapter of this book. Unless you are already familiar with modal logic and possible worlds semantics, you will have to grapple with new arguments, learn the meaning of a few symbols and the definitions of several new concepts. But take heart: The purpose of modal logic and possible worlds semantics is to capture and clarify deep and well-founded intuitions that we already use every day. For that reason, these topics are not nearly as difficult as they first appear. And if you persevere, I promise you will reap a great intellectual reward.[2]

THE DEVELOPMENT OF MODAL LOGIC

The beginnings. Modal logic has its origin in the common use of certain modal terms such as *might, must, possibly, necessarily, ought to, have to, could not be otherwise, would have been,* and the like. There are several distinct types of modality. Deontic modalities such as *should have to* and *ought to* concern moral obligation and permission. Assertic modalities, which express natural or causal "necessity," concern matters of fact, such as *It is impossible for a cow to jump over the moon* (I doubt whether such natural modalities are in any sense necessary, but since that is not the subject of this book, I will let that pass). Epistemic modal terms are those such as *knows that* and *believes that.* The modalities most frequently debated in the last half-century or so, however, are those concerned with logical possibility, impossibility, necessity and contingency. Since they concern the ways a proposition can be true or false, these are called *alethic* modalities.[3] Necessity et al. also can be used to modify the way a certain truth, attribute or property attaches to an entity. (This is

---

[2]I have put technical background issues in the notes. For ambitious readers who desire still more background in these topics, I recommend the following books, which I follow liberally in this chapter: Alvin Plantinga, *The Nature of Necessity* (Oxford: Oxford University Press, 1974), and Kenneth Konyndyk, *Introductory Modal Logic* (Notre Dame, Ind.: University of Notre Dame Press, 1986).

[3]See "Alethic Modality" in *The Cambridge Dictionary of Philosophy,* ed. Robert Audi (Cambridge: Cambridge University Press, 1995), p. 17.

so-called *de re* necessity, which we will discuss below.) These are the modalities of interest here.

Modal logic is the study and formalization of pretheoretic statements and
inferences that employ such phrases as *it is possible that* and *it is necessary that*
as well as their negations, such as *it is impossible that* and *it is not necessary
that*. It builds on what logicians call first-order and second-order logic.
When formalized these phrases are converted to operators, which can be attached to sentences and predicates. To make things especially difficult, logicians often designate these operators with symbols. Perhaps the most popular symbol for necessity is □, which we can translate as *it is necessary that* or
necessarily. The symbol ◇ is the common symbol for possibility. We can
translate it as *it is possible that* or *possibly*. When attached to predicates, □
may be translated roughly as *necessarily*, and ◇ as *possibly*. These operators
as well as propositions and predicates are subject to negation, which I will
symbolize with ~. So ~□ may be translated as *it is not necessary that* and ~◇
as *it is not possible that*.[4]

In *De Interpretatione*, Aristotle did the first work of formalizing our use of
terms connoting necessity and possibility when he analyzed the syllogism.
(Syllogisms are nontautological arguments in which conclusions follow by necessity from premises.) In doing so, he discovered that *possibly* and *necessarily*
can be translated into each other.[5] A system can take one of these as primitive
and define the other in light of it. So, $\Box p = \sim\!\Diamond\!\sim\!p$, and $\Diamond p = \sim\!\Box\!\sim\!p$. In English,
these would be, *Necessarily p = it is not possible that not p,* and *possibly p = It is
not necessary that p not be the case.* Since Aristotle did not always distinguish

---

[4]Since modal logic builds on first-order logic, other symbols turn up. Here are the formalisms I prefer.
I adopt the operations of conjunction, symbolized by "&" and translated by "and," and inclusive dis-
junction, symbolized by "∨" and translated by "or." For implication or logical consequence I adopt
the symbol →, which I interpret as strict implication or entailment. We can usually translate this with
a conditional *if . . . then . . .* , or more precisely by *entails*. It is roughly equivalent to Bertrand Russell
and A. N. Whitehead's material implication (⊃) with a necessity operator attached to it. So $p \to q =$
$\Box(p \supset q)$. Material equivalence and biconditionality, which can be symbolized by ↔, can be trans-
lated by *if and only if*. So, $(p \to q) \leftrightarrow (\sim\!p \lor q) \leftrightarrow \sim\!(p \,\&\, \sim\!q)$. Rather than use these symbols in the text,
I will normally use their approximate English translation (on my interpretation), with the exception
of "&," since its meaning is intuitively obvious.

[5]Konyndyk, *Introductory Modal Logic,* p. 1. I follow this text at certain points in this section. I recommend Konyndyk's clear introduction to this subject. Less current but also popular is G. E. Hughes
and M. J. Cresswell, *An Introduction to Modal Logic* (London: Methuen, 1968). See also their supple-
ment, *A Companion to Modal Logic* (London: Methuen, 1984).

between mere possibility and contingency, however, his treatment was incomplete. Contingencies are those possibilities that are not necessary. Possibilities include both contingent and necessary states of affairs, since a necessary truth is also a possible truth. So the set of contingent truths is a subset of all possible truths. Incidentally, a contingent truth can be expressed by $\Diamond p$ & $\Diamond \sim p$ *(possibly p & possibly not p)*, but no truth can be expressed by a simple p & $\sim p$, which plainly violates the law of noncontradiction.

Although Aristotle made a start at formalizing the concepts of necessity and possibility, for most of Western history philosophers and everyone else had to rely on intuition in evaluating claims of necessity and possibility. The central formal breakthroughs did not occur until the mid-twentieth century, and it led to many different systems of modal logic.[6] The details are complicated, but modal logic can be supplemented with a certain possible worlds interpretation, which is not only less technical but also makes intuition a more reliable guide.

Necessity. To get to essentialism from modal logic, we first have to understand *logical necessity.* We may understand truths that possess "broadly logical necessity"[7] as all those truths whose denials are not self-consistent (whether we can determine self-consistency is another matter).[8] That is, if a proposition p is necessarily true, then denying p will produce a proposition that denies its own truth. Given the plausible premise that any self-denying proposition can-

---

[6]Some work toward formalization finally began in the nineteenth century; and in the 1930s C. I. Lewis developed several axiomatic systems that formalized modal inferences. He began to study modal logic because he thought the notion of material implication, "⊃," proposed in Russell and Whitehead's *Principia Mathematica,* was inadequate as a formalization of the concept of implication. (See discussion in Konyndyk, *Introductory Modal Logic,* pp. 65-66.) Lewis's work led to several systems, including what are called systems S4 and S5. Although many systems have been proposed, the ones most discussed and adopted are the system T, the "*Brouwersche,*" S4 and S5. The simplest of these is T, since it has the fewest axioms. Robert Feys studied it, as well as a version of it called M by G. H. von Wright in 1951. For details, see G. H. von Wright, *An Essay in Modal Logic* (Amsterdam: North Holland, 1951). Although Lewis did not propose T, it fits well with his modal systems, and so it is considered a Lewis system (in Lemmon, "New Foundations for Lewis Modal Systems," *The Journal of Symbolic Logic* 24 [1959]: 1-14). See Konyndyk, *Introductory Modal Logic,* p. 31.

[7]"Broadly logical necessity" is a phrase coined by Plantinga in *Nature of Necessity,* p. 2. My defense of the term, however, goes beyond anything Plantinga has explicitly claimed for it.

[8]Such logical necessity should not be equated with or reduced to other epistemological notions such as self-evidence, apriority or even "ungiveupability" or "unrejectability." For arguments for the non-equivalence of logical necessity with each of these concepts, see Konyndyk, *Introductory Modal Logic,* pp. 14-16. Fuller discussion is found in Plantinga, *Nature of Necessity,* pp. 2-9.

not be true, come what may, then the denial of p will never be true; so p will always be true.[9]

Regrettably, this explanation amounts to little more than the claim that a necessary truth is just any truth whose denial is logically impossible. This is blatantly circular, since I am using a concept of necessity, namely, impossibility, in the explanation. The problem is that necessity is so fundamental to our ways of thinking that it is difficult to get an adequate analysis of the concept. Probably for this reason, philosopher Alvin Plantinga, in his playfully but aptly titled study *The Nature of Necessity,* begins his first chapter with a section called *Necessity Circumscribed.*[10] We can get some general pretheoretic idea of what necessity is, but we cannot expect to attain a list of necessary and sufficient conditions of the concept. As Plantinga says, "We must give examples and hope for the best."[11]

Paradigmatic examples of necessary truths include the truths of mathematics and set theory, as well as claims that are true by definition, such as *All bachelors are unmarried males,* and perhaps *All material objects are extended.* There are other more debatable claims that seem susceptible to necessity, even if their truth is disputed, such as *Every human person has a body*

---

[9]When I say "broadly logical necessity" I mean to deny the strong bifurcation some make between logical necessity and ontological or metaphysical necessity. Usually someone who maintains such a bifurcation is implying a Kantian distinction, contending that mere logical truths, while no doubt truths, apply only to the realm of our perception, to the phenomenal realm. By extension, so the argument goes, they have no application to the so-called noumenal realm, to the way things are apart from our perception.

Now arguments to establish such a bifurcation are rare. Kant's antinomies in the *Critique of Pure Reason* may be relevant, but they do not establish it. In any case, by speaking of broadly logical necessity (I will delete "broadly" in the future) I do not mean to deny all distinction between, say, logic and reality; still less do I mean to idealize reality, so that reality is just defined as that which we perceive. Nor do I mean that reality is always how we expect it to be or that it is constrained by our conceptual categories, whatever that means. What I am denoting by "broadly logical necessity" is that way we all speak when we say something *is* possible or *is* necessary. Our use of modal terms, as well as their meaning, have ontological implications. We might say this implies that there is a modal structure to reality. This is no argument from the way we speak to the way things are. It is an encouragement to recognize our ontological commitment to such a modal structure when we participate in such discourse. Everyday modal speech of this type is virtually impossible to excise, and it does not easily tolerate a bifurcation between mere logical necessity and ontological necessity. We seek a way to accommodate this way we speak, not to dismiss it. For these reasons, when we contemplate modal logic, it is a short step to modal metaphysics. All this will merit a revisiting when we enter the realm of systematic theology below.

[10]Plantinga, *Nature of Necessity,* pp. 2-9.

[11]Ibid., p. 2.

at some time or another, God exists necessarily or *Matter exists necessarily.* Let us consider necessity and possibility as they apply first to propositions, so-called *de dicto* modality, and then to the way in which entities may possess properties, so-called *de re* modality.[12]

Formal systems. In the middle of the last century, logicians developed lots of axiomatized systems of modal logic. But such riches presented a dilemma, since they suggested there was no single correct system. Syntaxes for systems were available, but not semantic interpretations. As Michael Loux puts it, the early logicians had failed "to identify models for those systems, sets of objects in terms of which the formulas of the systems could be interpreted. The result was that modal logicians were incapable of defining the notion of a valid formula of a modal system and so were incapable of providing completeness proofs for the systems."[13]

So perhaps instead of correctness in the abstract, we should ask what exactly a given system captures. In particular, which system best formalizes the pretheoretical notion of logical necessity? The clear answer is a system called S5. This system is "most complete" because it includes all the axioms of the other systems, but it can prove more than the others. So S5 "contains" the other systems.[14] The characteristic axiom of S5 makes the modal status of all

---

[12]There are also claims that are no doubt necessarily true, such as *Everything either is an odd number or is not an odd number.* Such claims have an air of triviality, however, since they depend upon logical truths, in this case, the principle of excluded middle (a or ~a).

[13]Michael J. Loux, "Introduction," in *The Possible and the Actual,* ed. Michael J. Loux (Ithaca, N.Y.: Cornell University Press, 1979), p. 19.

[14]Perhaps the three most important systems are T, S4 and S5. T is the simplest of the three, having the fewest axioms. Its characteristic axiom is this:

(T) $\Box p \rightarrow p$.

This is uncontroversial for anyone who enjoys at least a rudimentary apprehension of necessity. If it is necessarily true that $2 + 2 = 4$, then it is true that $2 + 2 = 4$. In addition to this T includes the axioms that anything that follows or is entailed by a necessary truth is itself a necessary truth, and that all tautologies are included in the set of necessary truths. So T maintains a close affinity to most people's modal intuitions.

While T does not generate any falsehoods, it fails to capture all that is inherent in the notion of logical necessity. Moreover, when the system is used (along with certain introduction, reiteration and elimination rules), it can generate irritating *iterated modalities,* such as $\Box\Box\Diamond\Box p$ and $\Diamond\Diamond\Box\Diamond\Box p$, which do not allow for reduction into simpler forms. These constructions quickly outstrip our modal intuitions and become difficult to distinguish from each other. We can reduce any pair of $\Box$'s to a single $\Box$ and prove the equivalence of $\Diamond p$ and $\Diamond\Diamond p$ by adding another axiom, which is the characteristic axiom of S4:

(S4) $\Box p \rightarrow \Box\Box p$.

propositions necessary—either necessarily necessary, necessarily possible, necessarily contingent or necessarily impossible. This is just what we want as a model for logical necessity; but the virtue of this axiom is easier to grasp when S5 is interpreted with possible worlds semantics. So, rather than spending time with complicated and arcane systems of modal logic, let's add possible worlds, which is much easier to follow.

POSSIBLE WORLDS SEMANTICS

Possible worlds. In developing the notion of necessity and the doctrine of creation, Gottfried Wilhelm Leibniz (1646-1716) suggested the notion of *possible worlds*. In the last few decades, this idea has borne fruit as a semantic interpretation of modal logic. Not only does this method offer an easier and more intuitive way of discussing modal problems, but also it provides a way to decide which system most adequately formalizes the notion of logical necessity. While philosophers have proposed various interpretations of possible worlds, I favor Alvin Plantinga's description of possible worlds as maximally consistent states of affairs.

I will take the concept of a state of affairs as primitive. That is, I will assume that you have some grasp of the concept of a state of affairs apart from definition. Of course, we can offer what philosophers call an ostensive definition of a state of affairs as well as a few examples. Unfortunately, it is partially circular, since it uses modal notions. The entry for "state of affairs" in *The Cambridge Dictionary of Philosophy* is perhaps as good as it gets:

> a possibility, actuality, or impossibility of the kind expressed by a nominalization of a declarative sentence. (The declarative sentence 'This die comes up six' can be nominalized either through the construction 'that this die comes up six' or through the likes of 'this die's coming up six.' The resulting nomi-

---

This axiom may seem less intuitive than the previous one. In fact, philosophers hotly contested its acceptability until developments by Saul Kripke, Jaako Hintikka and others in the 1960s. Once we add the possible worlds interpretation, however, its truth will be apparent as an implication of the notion of logical necessity.

We reach S5, which has the broadest applicability of all the systems, by adding one more axiom to S4:
(S5) $\Diamond p \rightarrow \Box \Diamond p$.

(See Plantinga, *Nature of Necessity*, p. 48, for more discussion.) The addition of this axiom makes the modal status of all propositions necessary—either necessarily necessary, necessarily possible, necessarily contingent or necessarily impossible. There is also a system intermediate between T and S4, also contained in S5, which adds the *Brouwersche* axiom, $p \rightarrow \Box \Diamond p$.

nalizations might be interpreted as naming corresponding propositions or states of affairs.)[15]

Socrates' teaching Plato in Athens and *Jay's writing a book in 2002* are examples of nominalized declarative sentences that express states of affairs. They may be specified to time and place, like the above examples, or be more general and range over numerous discrete events in many possible worlds, such as *having a headache*. States of affairs may obtain, or they may occur, like events. Necessary and actual states of affairs are truths.[16]

As I mean it, a proposition[17] is a "meaning," which can be true or false (except perhaps in some vague terms and contexts), which one may express by a statement, sentence or utterance. It is the object of intentions, which a person may express by a propositional attitude statement such as *I believe that . . .* or *I think that . . .* A proposition may express some state of affairs, whether necessary, contingent, possible or impossible, but a proposition is not identical with a state of affairs. An approximate synonym of a state of affairs that obtains is the usual notion of a *fact*.

Possible worlds that are not actual are *ways things could have been;*[18] they are states of affairs other than the one that obtains. The actual world, the one that obtains, is also a possible world, given the eternal verity that anything that is actual is possible. It is the one that is actual.

At the same time, let us not designate every isolated possible state of affairs as a possible world—otherwise, they will merely be synonyms. Let's reserve that honorific "possible world" for worlds that are maximal or complete. If a state of affairs is maximal or complete, then it either contains or precludes every other state of affairs. So a maximal state of affairs is a conjunction of states of affairs. If a state of affairs S obtains in a world w_1, then the state of affairs $\sim S$

---

[15]*Cambridge Dictionary of Philosophy*, p. 765.

[16]Some philosophers claim that states of affairs are propositions; see Roderick M. Chisholm, "Problems of Identity," in *Identity and Individuation*, ed. Milton K. Munitz (New York: New York University Press, 1971), pp. 25-27. To be frank, however, I find this obscure, so I distinguish the two.

[17]For an analysis that exhibits the difficulty of defining a proposition precisely, as well as the troubles that attend attempts to reduce propositions to other entities such as sentences or utterances, see Richard Cartwright, "Propositions," in *Analytical Philosophy*, ed. R. J. Butler (Oxford: Basil Blackwell, 1962), pp. 81-103.

[18]This is how Plantinga interprets them in *Nature of Necessity*, p. 44. This interpretation seems to best approximate our pretheoretic modal intuitions. I borrow heavily from Plantinga in this section; in fact, the model adopted here is essentially his proposal from *Nature of Necessity*, plus a few qualifications.

does not obtain at w_1.[19] If w_1 is the actual world, and in the actual world Plato is the teacher of Aristotle, then in w_1 the state of affairs expressed by *It is not the case that Plato is the teacher of Aristotle* does not obtain. Most concisely, a possible world is a conjunction of a maximally consistent state of affairs or a maximally consistent set of states of affairs.

The account is complicated slightly by the fact that states of affairs are often tensed, so that a state of affairs may obtain at one time and not obtain at another time. Such states of affairs are expressed, obviously enough, as tensed expressions. *Jay's writing a book about God on October 19, 2002* is a nontransient state of affairs, if it ever obtains. *Jay's writing a book about God,* however, obtains at some times but not at others. It is therefore a transient state of affairs.[20] To keep things simple, think of possible worlds as maximal sets of nontransient states of affairs.[21]

Problems with the interpretation of possible worlds. We will consider several common criticisms of possible worlds semantics below. But first let us clarify the status of possible worlds. Frequently objections arise not from any intrinsic problem with the concept of possible worlds but from certain images that the term is likely to engender in the fertile mind.

Perhaps the fundamental worry, if not argument, is that possible worlds seem so metaphysically prodigal or extravagant. For those fed empiricism with their mothers' milk, possible worlds may appear to be excessive in extremis, a paradigmatic violation of Ockham's razor that one should not multiply entities without

---

[19]In quantified form, every world is such that [where S designates a single state of affairs] $(S)(S \lor \sim S)$.

[20]John Pollock adds this nuance to Plantinga's theory in "Plantinga and Possible Worlds," in *Alvin Plantinga,* ed. James E. Tomberlin and Peter Van Inwagen (Dordrecht: D. Reidel, 1985), pp. 121-22. See also Plantinga's "Self-Profile" in this collection, pp. 90-91. With considerable complication, we could construe possible worlds as linearly ordered, causally related maximally consistent sets of states of affairs. This will commend itself to anyone who denies the viability of tenseless or temporally invariant states of affairs. But this scruple has no negative implications for this model. See Plantinga, "Replies," in *Alvin Plantinga,* pp. 327-29.

[21]Although not essential to this model, to distinguish propositions from states of affairs, we might conceive of the book on a world as being the set of propositions true at that world had that world been actual. Propositions and states of affairs are no doubt related. But whereas states of affairs obtain or are instantiated or actual, propositions are true or false. Plantinga judges that since propositions have at least these properties in distinction, they should be distinguished, in "Actualism and Possible Worlds," in *The Possible and the Actual,* ed. Michael J. Loux (Ithaca, N.Y.: Cornell University Press, 1979), pp. 258-59. The state of affairs *Bill Clinton's being president in 1997* obtains. The proposition that *Bill Clinton is president in 1997* is true. So the book on the actual world is the set of all propositions that are in fact true. The books on all other possible worlds are the propositions that would be true in their respective worlds were those worlds actual.

need. For this reason, it is important to realize how congenial possible worlds are to our usual ways of thinking and speaking. Michael Loux puts it well:

> The trouble with possible worlds, we want to say, is that they represent an exotic piece of metaphysical machinery, the armchair invention of a speculative ontologist lacking what Bertrand Russell called 'a robust sense of reality.' But the fact is that some of our most deep-seated intuitions suggest that the appeal to possible worlds is nothing more than a formalization of generally held philosophical views about matters modal. All (or at least most) of us think that things might have gone otherwise, that there are different ways things might have been, alternative ways things might have gone; and we tend to think that these different ways things might have been constitute the touchstones for determining the truth value of sentences prefaced by modal operators.[22]

Philosopher David Lewis, in his section on "Possible Worlds" in *Counterfactuals,* does a masterful job of commending possible worlds talk based on its sheer ordinariness. To speak of possible worlds in his view is to paraphrase the claim in ordinary language that "there are many ways things could have been besides the way they actually are." Some may call this "ways things could have been." Lewis and others prefer to speak of possible worlds.[23] He argues that one need not always take such claims at face value, but he does recognize a presumption in favor of doing so unless "(1) taking them at face value is known to lead to trouble, and (2) taking them some other way is known not to."[24]

Now as Lewis takes them, they do lead to trouble, since his interpretation seems committed to nonexistent existents.[25] On this interpretation, possible worlds are just as real in some sense as the actual world. Lewis seems to argue that the primary difference between this world and other possible worlds is merely that this world is graced with our presence.

Adopting possible worlds semantics in general, however, does not commit us to this most realist interpretation. That is, we need not (indeed, should not) think of possible worlds as an infinite set of worlds floating around out there somewhere, just as actual as our world but inaccessible to us. Possible worlds

---

[22]Loux, "Introduction," p. 30.

[23]David Lewis, *Counterfactuals* (Cambridge, Mass.: Harvard University Press, 1973), p. 84.

[24]Ibid.

[25]"Realism about unactualized possibles is exactly the thesis that there are more things than actually exist," ibid., p. 86.

are not other places where things are going on in more or less different ways
from the actual world. On the model adopted here, there is exactly one actual
world, namely, the one we are at.

There are several modest ways to interpret possible worlds. If one's purpose
is to paraphrase or accommodate ordinary modal discourse (talk of "ways things
might have been"), however, then it's reasonable to define them as states of affairs.[26] This seems to be the least farfetched of the various options, since it remains closely tethered to the way most people talk. So in a sense, this account
is reductive, since it does not interpret possible worlds as literal objects. It is not
reductionist in any strong sense, however, since it preserves the conviction that
possible worlds discourse has referents and is not merely a figure of speech.[27]

Adding quantification. To capture the notion of logical necessity, particularly when it applies not only to propositions (*de dicto*) but also to the way an
entity possesses a property (*de re*), we must add what logicians call "quantification" to the propositional modal logic already introduced. Quantifying can
be difficult to grasp in modal logic, but it is much more accessible when put
in terms of possible worlds.

For quantification, we add two operations to normal propositional logic,

---

[26]It seems to me there is general agreement between Plantinga's interpretation of possible worlds as
maximal states of affairs and Robert Stalnaker's "ways things might have been." See Stalnaker's "Possible Worlds" in *The Possible and the Actual*, ed. Michael J. Loux (Ithaca, N.Y.: Cornell University
Press, 1979), pp. 225-34. However, Stalnaker understands properties in set-theoretical terms, arguing that they are "functions from worlds to sets of *n*-tuples and that propositions are functions from
worlds to truth values" (Loux, "Introduction," p. 51). Plantinga finds this problematic.

[27]There are other interpretations than the one I have chosen. Other "potential world-surrogates" include
linguistic entities such as Rudolf Carnap's "state descriptions," propositions, properties, set-theoretical
combinatorial constructs of all the basic elements of the actual world, and mental entities of various
sorts. (For discussion, see William Lycan, "The Trouble with Possible Worlds," in *The Possible and the
Actual*, ed. Michael J. Loux [Ithaca, N.Y.: Cornell University Press, 1979], pp. 302-12.) Some of these
might do just as well (in fact, I prefer theistic mental entities in the conclusion), although I think the
model I have chosen overcomes problems with most other options. For instance, linguistic and mental
entities are problematic because modal talk implies that there is an immense number of possibilities
that no one ever has or ever will consider, or speak of. (As we will see, however, this all changes in a
theistic context, which most theorists do not consider.) Combinatorial constructs of all the entities in
the actual world do not allow for the possibility that there could have been more things or other things
than the things that actually exist. So this option does not really accommodate modal discourse. Propositions are similar to states of affairs but are susceptible to all the semantic paradoxes that plague philosophers of language. The books on worlds mentioned in the previous section are books of true propositions at worlds, and so they do not contain paradoxical or contradictory propositions. But even if we
repair this problem, possible worlds as maximal states of affairs—and not as propositions—still captures more fully what most of us mean when we speak of "ways things might have been."

called universal and existential quantification (plus some other rules for introduction and elimination of operations). Universal quantification attempts to
formalize the common use of the words *all* and *every.* Existential quantification
attempts to capture our use of "some," although it is more accurately translated
as "at least one." Logicians often symbolize these operations with parentheses
around a variable, (*x*), to symbolize universal quantification, and ∃ attached to
a variable to symbolize existential quantification. So, if we read lower case letters as variables, and upper case letters as predicates, we could translate (*x*)(*Ax*
→ *Hx*) as *For every object x, if x is an American, then x is a human* (where *A* is the
symbol for the predicate *is an American* and *H* is the symbol for the predicate *is
a human*). Most simply, this formalizes the claim that all Americans are human.
For existential quantification we could translate (∃*x*)(*Ax & Hx*) as *There is at
least one American that is human,* or *Some Americans are human.*[28]

I interpret the quantifiers in the substitutional and not the objectual way,
which means I do not understand the use of existential quantifiers as implying
that certain objects exist.[29] This requires that when one is quantifying, one must
stipulate the range of the quantifiers. This is not something we normally do in
everyday conversation. Normally, the domain of such terms as "everything" and
"some" is provided by the context. For example, if in 1980 Tom Landry's assis-
tant football coach takes a head count and then tells Landry before practice, "Everyone is here," the domain over which "everyone" ranges in this statement is
probably the set consisting of all the current players, coaches and trainers of the
Dallas Cowboys. It does not range over, say, all Texans or even all football players. Since quantifiers are taken to have a domain, that is, since quantifiers must
range over some set of objects, quantification in possible worlds semantics is
taken to range over the domain of possible worlds. Thus we are confronted with
the task of determining the status of possible worlds. This requires not only that
we have some feeble grasp of, but also that we distinguish between *actuality* and

---

[28]To be complete, we can take the following so-called equivalence relations as valid:

$$(\exists x)Ax \leftrightarrow \sim(x) \sim Ax$$
$$(x)Ax \leftrightarrow \sim(\exists x) \sim Ax$$
$$\sim(\exists x)Ax \leftrightarrow (x) \sim Ax$$
$$\sim(x)Ax \leftrightarrow (\exists x) \sim Ax$$

Like the modal operators, the quantifiers are interdefinable. See Konyndyk, *Introductory Modal Logic,* p. 71.

[29]There are some technical complications here, but I will not go into them, since I do not think they
are crucial to my argument.

existence. So besides states of affairs, existence and actuality are fundamental to this possible worlds semantics (see below).

Translating necessity and possibility into possible worlds terminology is now intuitively easy. A necessary truth *t* is any proposition that is true in every possible world. There is no possible world at which *t* fails to be true. A possible truth is a proposition that is true at one or more possible world. It describes a state of affairs that obtains at some possible world. That is, if *t* is possible, then there is some world *w*, such that, if *w* had been actual, *t* would be true. A contingent truth is true at some possible world(s) and false at others. And an impossibility is any state of affairs that obtains at *no* possible world and by extension any proposition affirming such a state of affairs.

In possible worlds semantics, then, logical necessity is really the operation of universal quantification, and possibility is the operation of existential quantification ranging over all possible worlds. Combining the quantifiers and the possible worlds semantics to modal logic gives us a fairly accessible way of formalizing some of our discourse concerning necessity.[30]

---

[30]The breakthrough in the addition of quantification to modal logic came with the publication of a paper by Saul Kripke in 1959, "A Completeness Theorem in Modal Logic," *The Journal of Symbolic Logic* 24, no. 1 (March 1959): 1-14. In this paper, Kripke "attempts to state and prove a completeness theorem for the system of S5 . . . supplemented by first-order quantifiers and the sign of equality" (p. 1).

Others, such as Stig Kanger, Dana Scott and Jaako Hintikka, developed work more or less simultaneously on related issues. See, for example, Hintikka's *Models for Modalities* (Dordrecht: R. Reidel, 1969). One of the first philosophers to explore the implications of combining quantification with modal logic was Ruth Barcan Marcus. See Robert Stalnaker, "The Interaction of Modality with Quantification and Identity," in *Modality, Morality and Belief,* ed. W. Sinnott-Armstrong, D. Raffman and N. Asher (Cambridge: Cambridge University Press, 1995), p. 12. Certain problems, however, led to a revision and improvement of Kripke's proposal in 1963. See Kripke's "Some Semantical Considerations on Modal Logic," reprinted in *Reference and Modality,* ed. Leonard Linsky (Oxford: Oxford University Press, 1963). Kripke uses the notions of a model structure, invoking sets of n-tuples. For a fairly accessible summary of Kripke's procedure, see Plantinga, *Nature of Necessity,* pp. 123-31. This proposal has problems as well, which are repaired with the additional premise of actualism (see below).

In short, Arthur Prior argued that a certain objectionable formula, called the Barcan Formula (after logician Ruth Barcan Marcus), could be deduced from a quantified S5. Kripke claimed in the later paper that this was incorrect and was able to avoid the infelicitous deduction by using a stricter form of a rule of necessitation, called universal closure: "A universal closure of a formula is obtained by binding all free occurrences of variables in the formula with universal quantifiers prefixed to the formula." The effect of this strategy was to prevent the Barcan and Converse Barcan Formulas, as well as the Buridan formula, from being included in the system, although they can be added without inconsistency. These are as follows:

Barcan Formula:	$(x)\Box Ax \rightarrow \Box(x)Ax$
Converse Barcan Formula:	$\Box(x)Ax \rightarrow (x)\Box Ax$
Buridan Formula:	$\Diamond(x)Ax \rightarrow (x)\Diamond Ax$
Converse Buridan Formula:	$(x)\Diamond Ax \rightarrow \Diamond(x)Ax$

See Konyndyk, *Introductory Modal Logic,* pp. 94, 98. See also Ruth Barcan Marcus, Modalities: *Philosophical Essays* (New York: Oxford University Press, 1993). These formulas, if allowed, make *de re* and *de dicto* necessity equivalent. The Buridan Formulas also do the same for possibility (see Konyndyk, ibid., pp. 92-101). However, by excluding the Converse Barcan Formula, Kripke's interpretation seems to have excluded too much. The problem with this will become clear below, when I introduce the distinctions between *de re* and *de dicto* modality.

Although it is a bit technical for a brief introduction, one can explain the superiority of S5 for capturing logical necessity with Kripke's notion of accessibility between possible worlds, which has become a standard formulation in the field (see "Kripke Semantics," in *The Cambridge Dictionary of Philosophy,* pp. 413-14). Accessibility is the relation of necessity and possibility between worlds, a relation being "a two-or-more place property . . . or the extension of such a property" ("Relation," ibid., pp. 688-89), which holds between given entities. Examples include loves, is the father of, and next to. The entities related are called the terms of the relation.

In possible worlds semantics, accessibility is a relation that holds between possible worlds. The degree of accessibility one world has to another is different in the different systems (T, S4, S5, etc.). Accessibility is weakest in T and strongest in S5. In T, the accessibility relation is only reflexive. In S4, the relation is reflexive and transitive but not symmetrical. And in S5, it is reflexive, transitive and symmetrical.

Reflexivity is a relation that anything has to itself (aRa). The paradigmatic reflexive relation is identity, a = a. a is identical with a. In a transitive relation, a relation is transferred across a middle term. If a has some relation R to b and b has some relation R to c, then if a has the same relation R to c, then that relation is transitive (aRb & bRc) → aRc. More perspicuously, consider the transitive relation of height. If Darcy is taller than Jane, and Jane is taller than Elizabeth, then Darcy is taller than Elizabeth.

In a symmetrical relation, the order of terms is reversible, which is not the case in a merely transitive relation. So, aRb → bRa. The relation of spouse is symmetrical (but the relation denoted by husband or wife is not). If Jay is the spouse of Ginny, then Ginny is the spouse of Jay. Keeping these three relations in mind, we can now consider the accessibility relation, or relative possibility between worlds, that holds for the different models.

In system T, recall that the characteristic formula is $\Box p \rightarrow p$. For a world w_1, $\Box p$ means that p is true in one world accessible to world w_1. The minimum model to map this axiom is one possible world, w_1, accessible to itself, where the antecedent of this conditional (the left side) is true. Such a model would have only one world, and so to all appearances, p would be equivalent to $\Box p$, and T would be indistinguishable from propositional logic. This would allow us to eliminate all modal distinctions, in which case we would not need possible worlds semantics in the first place. (I am following several features of Konyndyk's treatment of accessibility, *Introductory Modal Logic,* pp. 55-60.)

So in T, all worlds are accessible to themselves. There could be a world w_1 accessible to itself, in which both p and $\Box p$ are true, and a world w_2 in which p but not $\Box p$ is true. In another world w_3, accessible to w_2 but not accessible to w_1, ~p is true. So $\Box p \rightarrow p$ holds in w_1, and p holds in every world accessible to w_1. Even though ~p is true in w_3, this does not contradict the truth of $\Box p$ in w_1, since w_3 is not accessible to w_1, and in this model, "$\Box$" means true in every accessible world. So the relation in T is reflexive but not transitive or symmetrical.

If the accessibility relation is transitive as well as reflexive, then the characteristic formula of S4, $\Box p \rightarrow \Box\Box p$, will not fail to hold, as will the characteristic formula of T. The characteristic formula of S5, $\Diamond p \rightarrow \Box \Diamond p$ does not hold, however, because $\Diamond$~p could hold in w_3 while $\Box \Diamond p$ does not. The accessibility relation does not hold symmetrically between w_2 and w_3 or between w_3 and w_1.

Now imagine the accessibility relation between our three possible worlds is reflexive, transitive and symmetrical. In such a scenario accessibility will be an equivalence relation between all possible worlds. We will have a model in which the S5 formula, $\Diamond p \rightarrow \Box \Diamond p$, will not fail to hold. In S5, every possible world is accessible to every other. So S5, in which the accessibility relation is reflexive, transitive and symmetrical, and the modal status of propositions is the same in every possible world, best captures the concept of logical possibility and necessity.

The operators □ and ◇, however, can be interpreted differently in different systems. In fact, for purposes other than capturing logical necessity, a system other than S5 might be better. For example, some have argued that the S4 system best maps temporal or tense modalities, since it captures the asymmetry of the relation of the present to the past and future.[31] That is, it is plausible to suppose that certain events are possible from the present to the future, which are no longer possible from the present to the past. The future is open in a way in which the past is not. S4 captures this very asymmetry.

For the notion of logical possibility, however, this asymmetry would imply something like "relative possibility," which is exceedingly odd. For when we say that something is, say, logically impossible, we do not normally mean that it is impossible in this world but that it might be possible or even actual or necessarily true in some other world. Rather, we mean that if something is logically impossible, then it cannot be true in any possible situation. And if something is contingently true, then it could not be logically impossible in some other possible world. It could only be false, and contingently so. Logical necessity and possibility, unlike probability, do not come in degrees.[32] When one says that $1 + 1 = 2$ is a necessary truth, one cannot also say (consistently) that there could be some other world where $1 + 1 = 19$.[33] Quantified S5 with possible world semantics accommodates these clear intuitions, making it the model most appropriate for our purpose, namely, to increase our understanding of essences and essential and contingent properties.[34]

---

[31]Hintikka argues this in the "Modes of Modality," in *Models for Modalities*, p. 82. He may not still agree with this conclusion.

[32]Alan R. White, *Modal Thinking* (Oxford: Basil Blackwell, 1975), p. 39.

[33]For a clear treatment of these matters, see also Loux's "Introduction," pp. 16-30.

[34]Lots of philosophical problems stem from misunderstanding modal notions (White, *Modal Thinking*, p. 6). So possible worlds semantics promises theoretical payoff in the analysis of logical consequence and implication, the truth value of counterfactuals (see, for example, Lewis, *Counterfactuals*, p. 57, n. 24), the function of proper names and the nature of linguistic meaning and reference. See, for example, Casimir Lewy, *Meaning and Modality* (Cambridge: Cambridge University Press, 1976), M. J. Cresswell's "The World Is Everything That Is the Case," and David Kaplan's "Transworld Heir Lines" and "How to Russell a Frege-Church" in *The Possible and the Actual*, ed. Michael J. Loux (Ithaca, N.Y.: Cornell University Press, 1979). It also aids our understanding of natural kinds and the identity of persons and artifacts through time and change. Arthur N. Prior is the "key player" in developing modal concepts with respect to time. See, for example, his *Time and Modality* (Westport, Conn.: Greenwood, 1957), *Past, Present and Future* (Oxford: Oxford University Press, 1967) and *Papers on Tense and Time* (Oxford: Oxford University Press, 1968). A more recent work in the field is David S. Oderberg, *The Metaphysics of Identity over Time* (New York: St. Martin's Press, 1993).

ESSENTIALISM

After this whirlwind tour of modal logic and possible worlds semantics, we are now ready to consider essentialism. So far, I have focused on necessity and possibility as they apply to propositions. Although I have hinted at another type of modality, I have waited until we had the entire apparatus before us to consider the type of modality that bears directly on properties and essences.

Modality *de* re *and* de dicto. As I have suggested already, there are two types of modality, traditionally called modality *de re* and *de dicto*.[35] *De dicto* refers to the modality that attaches to a proposition or dictum, such as

Necessarily five is prime.

Here necessity is predicated on the proposition that five is prime. Modality *de re* concerns modality as it relates to an entity, in particular, to the way a property attaches to or is exemplified by an entity, such as this:

Five is necessarily prime.

Here we assert that the property of being prime is necessary to the number five. Five necessarily exemplifies the property of being prime, or primehood. It is not possible that five could have been other than a prime number.

We might also claim that some entity has a certain property contingently or accidentally (that is, actually but not necessarily), for example,

Leibniz is (contingently) a philosopher.

That is, Leibniz has the property of being a philosopher only contingently. He might never have been a philosopher. He might never even have read a book.

In theology specifically, possible worlds semantics can be brought to bear on the problem of evil, the soundness of the ontological argument for the existence of God (see, for example, chapters 9 and 10 of Plantinga's *Nature of Necessity*), and the compatibility of divine foreknowledge and human freedom. Thomas Aquinas used a rough version when he distinguished between the necessity of the consequent $[p \rightarrow \Box q]$ and the necessity of the consequence $[\Box(p \rightarrow q)]$ in *Summa Contra Gentiles,* book i, chapter 67, and *Summa Theologica,* I.14.13. A more precise contemporary strategy is Alvin Plantinga, "On Ockham's Way Out," in *The Concept of God,* ed. Thomas V. Morris (Oxford: Oxford University Press, 1987), pp. 171-200. The gist of this argument is that God's foreknowledge does not entail determinism, because

(A) $\Box$(God knows that Ginny is sitting $\rightarrow$ Ginny is sitting) [necessity of the consequence] does not entail

(B) God knows that Ginny is sitting $\rightarrow$ $\Box$Ginny is sitting [necessity of the consequent].
The truth of (B) is required for determinism, but foreknowledge only requires (A).

[35]Although philosophers have recognized this distinction at least since Aristotle (*Prior Analytics* 1.9), and it was quite common in medieval philosophy, many modern philosophers have avoided it.

These sorts of distinctions are the stuff of everyday conversation. Most of us suppose that certain things could have existed but had properties quite different from the ones they actually have. We also suppose that some things could not have existed if they had lacked certain properties. For instance, perhaps Socrates could never have existed if he had never been a human being. There might be strident debate over whether some particular property is essential or contingent, or whether we know how to settle such questions. But most of us take for granted that such a distinction exists. So, although assertions of modality *de re* may appear suspect to some philosophers, they are common in normal language.[36]

Essential and contingent properties. Modality *de re* is closely related to essentialism. By essentialism, I mean the thesis *that persons, objects and entities have some of their properties necessarily or essentially, and others accidentally or contingently.* In addition, the essentialist contends that *entities have essences,* which we can tentatively characterize as (at least) *a set of essential properties that an entity exemplifies.* The concepts of essence and property have a long and controversial history. Are properties metaphysical parts of an entity? Are there eternal Platonic Forms or Universals, abstract objects like Goodness or Knowledge, which contingent objects somehow participate in by possessing goodness or knowledge? Do properties exist, but only in concrete entities, which become universals by an act of abstraction by a mind? To answer yes to any of these questions is, in my view, to accept a realist interpretation of properties and essences, real in the sense that we can refer to them and properly attribute them to entities within the world (but we should note that the last view, called conceptualism, is often called anti-realism). In contrast to these interpretations, however, is a reductionist view, called fictionalism or nominalism, that holds that essences and properties are merely fictions, linguistic artifacts that we mistakenly project onto reality, that we reify. They may help us to talk and get on in the world, but they do not express anything true about the world.

The virtue of the method I am proposing here is that it allows us to capture the intuition that essences and properties are somehow part of reality (contrary to fictionalism)—that we need them to describe the world adequately—and to accommodate the essentialist speech embedded in everyday language,

---

[36]For more on this distinction, see Alvin Plantinga, "De Re et De Dicto," *Nous* 3 (1969): 235-58.

without requiring that we choose one or the other of these realist theories. So, a property as I mean it is at least some fact about an entity in the world, some truth about it. For example, if I exemplify the property of patience, that means (at least) that I am patient, that it is a fact about me that I am patient, that the proposition *Jay is patient* is true. We can affirm this without getting into difficult debates about Platonism, universals, and so forth. This modest understanding of properties will be extremely important to remember when we apply essentialist language to God.

Although many philosophers have presented arguments against essentialism generally, probably the most persistent recent critic of modality *de re* and its attendant essentialism was the philosopher W. V. O. Quine. The arguments he offered against essentialism and related concepts all seem to emanate from his fictionalist belief that "necessity resides in the way we say things, and not in the things we talk about."[37] Quine could barely tolerate modality *de dicto* as an interpretation of analytic truth—such as *all bachelors are unmarried*—and perhaps as an analysis of C. I. Lewis's concept of strict necessity. But to trade in quantified modality, he warned, "leads us back into the metaphysical jungle of Aristotelian essentialism."[38] By "Aristotelian essentialism" he meant at least the distinction between essential and contingent properties, and probably also the notion of common essences. Presumably Quine thought the disrepute into which Aristotelian essentialism had fallen would be enough to ward off potential traders.[39] To Quine essentialists erroneously bestowed certain traits on ob-

---

[37]W. V. O. Quine, "Three Grades of Modal Involvement," in *The Ways of Paradox and Other Essays* (New York: Random House, 1966), p. 174.

[38]Ibid.; also, Konyndyk, *Introductory Modal Logic*, p. 86.

[39]W. V. O. Quine, "Reference and Modality," in *Reference and Modality,* ed. Leonard Linsky (Oxford: Clarendon, 1971), p. 30. To force the point, Quine offered a celebrated argument concerning the number of planets in the solar system. The gist of Quine's argument is this. The quantified modal logic partisan should be able to get

(1) ($\exists x$) (Necessarily, x is greater than seven)

by existential generalization from

(2) Necessarily, nine is greater than seven.

And since

(3) Nine is the number of planets

he argues one should be able to instantiate (1) by

(4) Necessarily, the number of planets is greater than seven.

However, if we assume, as he does, that necessity is merely a linguistic function of sentences we use to pick out objects for consideration, then (4) is false. The only way to preserve the truth of (4)

jects without recognizing that judging any trait as essential depends merely on the way we pick out that object for consideration.[40]

An extensive literature developed in response to Quine.[41] Since his objections have ceased to play a central role in the field, however, I will not offer an analysis of them here. As Loux notes,

> Initially, Quine's criticisms were taken very seriously, and a large number of philosophers tried to show that quantified modal logic does not commit its proponents to Aristotelian essentialism. But with the development of a semantics for modal logic, attempts to answer Quine became less and less frequent. Philosophers came to see . . . that if we take a realistic interpretation of possible-worlds semantics, we have a perfectly coherent framework for expressing the content of an essentialist metaphysics.[42]

So we should remember that the type of essentialism we are defending here was forged in the face of strident opposition and is formulated to overcome such opposition.[43]

So how do we understand necessary and contingent properties in terms of possible worlds? Initially, we might suppose an entity, say, Socrates, necessarily has some property P_n just in case[44] he exemplifies P_n in every world. Here we run into trouble because on this account Socrates will not have any essential properties unless he exists in every possible world. That is, if Socrates did not

---

is to commit to Aristotelian essentialism. See Loux, "Introduction," p. 24, n. 7. This is a good argument only for someone who refuses to consider the viability of essentialism. To work, it requires that one refuse to accept the distinction between *de re* and *de dicto* modality, a refusal for which there is no good argument.

[40]See W. V. O. Quine, *From a Logical Point of View* (New York: Harper & Row, 1961), pp. 155-56. Quine offered several different arguments against essentialism. A justly famous one is the problem of the mathematical cyclist. See his *Word and Object* (Cambridge, Mass.: MIT Press, 1960), p. 199. Plantinga gave one resolution to the problem in *Nature of Necessity*, pp. 23-26.

[41]See the anthology *Reference and Modality*.

[42]Loux, "Introduction," p. 25, n. 7.

[43]In 1988, Ruth Barcan Marcus said of Quine's shift in his treatment of quantification into modal contexts: "Over the years, some criticisms have been withdrawn or tempered, new criticisms have emerged, and finally the whole thrust shifts from a concern with motivation, paradoxes, puzzles, and the senselessness of interpretations of modal logic to claims about modal logic's repugnant essentialist commitments." In "A Backward Look at Quine's Animadversions on Modalities," in *Modalities*, 1 n. 34. So his criticisms seemed to move from positive arguments to mere assertions of his nominalistic prejudices. At that point, taking account of his criticisms is pressing only to nominalists.

[44]"Just in case" is a synonym for "if and only if."

exist necessarily, he would have no essential properties. To avoid this problem, we should distinguish three propositions:

(A) Socrates has *P* in every world;

(B) Socrates has *P* and has it in every world in which he exists;

(C) Socrates has *P* and there is no world in which Socrates has the complement ~*P* of *P*.[45]

(B) and (C) seem to capture what we mean by having a property necessarily, without committing us to the implausible implication that Socrates and other contingent beings exist in every world. If we had to adopt (A) as an adequate formulation of *de re* modality, we would be committed to the claim that only necessary beings—that is, beings that are actual in every possible world—have essential properties. To avoid confusion on this point, let us say that when an entity has a property *P* necessarily, whether or not that entity exists necessarily, then that entity will exemplify *P* essentially. So, if Socrates has some property *P* in every world in which he exists, then he will exemplify *P* essentially. *P* will be an essential property of Socrates. (This follows from property actualism, which means that Socrates will have no properties in worlds in which he does not exist. See below.) Similarly, a contingent or accidental property *P* of Socrates will be any property Socrates exemplifies in some possible worlds, and exemplifies its complement ~*P* in others.[46]

Finally, this definition of an essential property implies that if existence is a property, then everything exists essentially. But this is different from saying that everything has necessary existence, which an entity will have only if it ex-

---

[45]Plantinga, *Nature of Necessity*, p. 56.

[46]Because I endorse actualism, I do not allow the presence of nonexistent existents. This implies that an entity will have no properties in worlds in which it does not exist. We might call this property actualism. Plantinga has elsewhere called this view "serious actualism," but this is less descriptive (Alvin Plantinga, "On Existentialism," *Philosophical Studies* 44 [1983]: 1-20). For an argument from actualism to serious or property actualism, see Plantinga's reply to Pollock in Tomberlin and Van Inwagen, *Alvin Plantinga*, pp. 321-25. We can symbolize property actualism thus:

$$\Box(x)(P(x) \rightarrow E(x)),$$

where *E* means "exists" (see Graeme Forbes, *Languages of Possibility* [Oxford: Basil Blackwell, 1989], p. 45). Since Socrates exemplifies no properties in worlds in which he does not exist, he exemplifies neither *P* nor ~*P* in such worlds. So, if that common Socratic attribution *snubnosedness* is a property Socrates does have in the actual world, it will be contingent or accidental just in case there is some other world in which Socrates both exists and is not snubnosed.

ists in every possible world.[47] On our account, there may be necessarily and contingently existing entities. However, if one agrees with Immanuel Kant that existence (or at least existence other than necessary existence) is not a property, then one can construe existence not as a property itself but as a necessary condition for an entity to exemplify properties. Either way, existence clearly functions differently than other run-o'-the-mill properties, whether necessary or contingent.[48]

Haecceities and individual essences. Perhaps the capstone of essentialism is not merely the thesis that entities can exemplify essential and accidental properties but also the thesis that there are essences of kinds (or natural kinds) and of individuals. The conjunction of whatever essential properties go into the kind *human* will be the human essence. Ideally this set would be necessary and sufficient to determine if an entity is or is not a human. (This is different from the matter of whether we have access to this set, or whether we can discern whether a particular individual exemplifies that set.) So, for example, if we assume Aristotle's definition that a human is a rational animal, then all humans are essentially rational animals: $(x)(Hx \leftrightarrow (Rx \,\&\, Ax))$. This would be a summary definition, since what is deemed "rational" and "animal" would again be determined by the essential properties that go into "rational" and "animal." So at least part of an individual's essence will consist in the kind of individual it is. "Kind" on this rendering is some specified set of essential properties.[49]

In addition to kind essences, however, there are also individual essences,

---

[47]Ibid., p. 61. See also Plantinga, "Actualism and Possible Worlds," pp. 261-62.

[48]So far this account is arid and formal and does not help us decide which properties are essential to an entity and which are accidental. But the fact that such details are often a matter of dispute does not discredit essentialist distinctions. Even if we are rarely able to specify essential properties of an entity, this does not mean that entities do not exemplify them. Someone may object that the notion of essential properties is incoherent unless some examples can be cited. And some examples can be cited. For there are any number of trivial essential properties that everything has, as well as so-called world-indexed properties. *Being three or three diverse, being self-identical, being married if a husband,* and *being related to God* are all examples (assuming God's existence). And given that I am American in the actual world w_a, *being American in w_a* is one of my essential properties. These may not be very illuminating examples, but examples they are. So the notion of essential properties is coherent. We will discuss these types of properties below. See ibid., pp. 60-69, for more on such properties.

[49]This procedure does not entail, by the way, that we accept Aristotle's thesis of the immutability of species. A kind essence need not be synonymous with the delineations that humans propose such as those between species, many of which may be artificial. That said, there are many complicated matters here, perhaps the most pressing being the irritating presence of vague and partially defined predicates.

and their partial synonym, *haecceities*. Loosely, a haecceity is a "thisness" of an individual, that which individuates the person from all other entities. There is a long-standing dispute in the history of philosophy concerning haecceities. For Duns Scotus and Thomas Aquinas, a haecceity is "the fundamental actuality of an existent being." It is a "positive perfection that serves as a primitive existence and individuation principle for concrete existents."[50] In this sense, a haecceity is irreducible and not synonymous with any set of properties, essential or not. Perhaps we should think of a haecceity in this sense as whatever underlies those properties. Whether there is a haecceity in this sense is a matter I will not dispute.

For my purposes here, however, I need only the weaker sense (associated with Leibniz, but I will not accept his entire definition—see below), which I will refer to as an individual essence rather than a haecceity to avoid confusion. An individual essence is (at least) that cluster of properties an entity exemplifies essentially, including not only its kind-essential properties (whenever the entity is a kind of some sort), but also all those essential properties that distinguish it from every other entity or object. One might call the individual essence a property itself, meaning that it is conjunctive property of all the essential properties, although I will continue to call it a *set* of essential properties. Still, it should be clear that an essence entails each of its properties.[51] More formally, following Graeme Forbes, we might put it as follows: "An individual essence of an object *x* is a set of properties *I* which satisfies the following two conditions":

(1) **Every property *P* in *I* is an essential property of *x*.**

(2) **It is not possible that some object *y* distinct from *x* has every member of *I*.**[52]

Assuming the truth of actualism (see below), no entity will have an individual essence unless it exists in some possible world *w*. For any individual essence *I*, *being instantiated in a possible world* is essential to *I*,[53] so essences themselves have essential properties.

---

[50]"Haecceity," *Cambridge Dictionary of Philosophy*, p. 308.

[51]See, for example, Alvin Plantinga, "World and Essence," *Philosophical Review* 79 (1970): 482ff.

[52]Graeme Forbes, *The Metaphysics of Modality* (Oxford: Clarendon, 1985), p. 99.

[53]Plantinga, *Nature of Necessity*, p. 77.

Now while there are no individual essences unless the essence is instantiated in some possible world, clearly there could be objects that happen not to be instantiated in the actual world. This implies that there must be uninstantiated essences, essences that could be instantiated but in fact are not. This notion is troubling to many. Some complain that it gives the possible priority over the actual, whatever that means. Nevertheless, our discourse about the actual world often implies the existence of uninstantiated essences (or clusters of properties that could be but are not uniquely possessed by some individual), however counterintuitive they may appear at first blush. Their existence follows from the claim that at least one individual in the actual world, say, Socrates, might not have existed. If this is so, then there is some possible world $w_{\sim S}$ where Socrates does not exist. So, if $w_{\sim S}$ had been actual, then

(S) Socrates does not exist

would have been true. (S) is true-at-$w_{\sim S}$. But even if $w_{\sim S}$ had been actual, Socrates might *possibly* have existed, as he would at every possible world. This is true just in case there is some essence (call it Socrateity) that, if Socrates had existed, he would have exemplified. But the property of *being identical with Socrates* would not have been instantiated in $w_{\sim S}$, even though it is possibly exemplified there. In $w_{\sim S}$,

(Socrates-identity is not exemplified) & $\Diamond$(Socrates-identity is exemplified)

is true. So although uninstantiated essences might initially seem distasteful, they follow from the plausible claim that some objects in this world exist contingently. If we wish to accommodate this claim, then we will include uninstantiated essences in our ontology.[54]

This is true quite apart from the difficulty of asserting propositions such as (S). Depending on how proper names refer, it might be impossible for any contingent individual existing in $w_{\sim S}$ to state (S) or any proposition with "Socrates" in it. For example, in $w_{\sim S}$ the requisite referential chain (on Saul Kripke's account in *Naming and Necessity*[55]) would not have developed for re-

---

[54]I do not mean to imply that they should cease to be troubling. More needs to be said. I will argue in the conclusion that understanding abstract entities like properties and uninstantiated essences becomes most sensible in a theological context, in which they are conceived as objects of divine thought.

[55]Saul Kripke, *Naming and Necessity* (Cambridge, Mass.: Harvard University Press, 1972).

ferring to Socrates. If this were the case, then (S) might be "unstatable" in $w_{\sim S}$. And then an inhabitant of $w_{\sim S}$ would be unable to refer to Socrates. But this is a different matter from (S)'s truth or falsity. We should not confuse statability with truth conditions. For example, if I lose my voice, I will be unable to state "I have lost my voice." But someone else could state the truth that I lost my voice. No doubt, there are countless other truths and falsehoods which one may be unable to express. This does not affect their truth or falsity.[56]

Actualism. There are two primary criticisms against talk of possible worlds. Interestingly, both lead us to draw out their ontological implications. One of these criticisms, the so-called problem of transworld identity, leads straight to a discussion of the merits of essentialism. It underscores the importance of distinguishing between essential and contingent properties and the need to posit individual essences or haecceities.

The other perennial criticism against quantified modal systems in general, especially when given the possible worlds interpretation, is that they seem to posit nonexistent entities, or, when necessity is applied to properties, to imply that things could have properties in worlds in which they do not exist. We may call this the problem of nonactual objects. It amounts in its most immodest form to affirming that there exist some things that do not exist. The problem is not that we would be quantifying over abstract objects in such a system; rather, it is that such items are contradictions. When we try to quantify over "things that do not exist," we get

$$(NA)(\exists x) \sim(\exists y)(y = x).^{57}$$

In plain English, this means something like, *For some x, there is some nonexistent y, such that y equals x,* or, *There is something that is identical to something that does not exist.* Most discerning souls will suspect that (NA) should count decisively against any theory that entails it.

Kripke's formulation, if not modified, may suggest just this idea, often called possibilism. The difficulty emerges from a certain way of taking quanti-

---

[56]This point is necessary to block a certain argument against the possibility of future or possible but nonactual individuals, as well as haecceities, such as the argument by Barry Miller, *From Existence to God* (London: Routledge, 1992), pp. 40-63. We return to this topic in the conclusion.

[57]Lycan, "Trouble with Possible Worlds," p. 283.

fication in the context of possible worlds. Although some unflinchingly accept these unsavory consequences,[58] few philosophers will defend something so implausible as the thesis that nonexistent objects exist.

The problem may infect more than the theories of a few logicians, however, since it seems to be implied from the plausible idea that there could be objects distinct from every object that does exist in the actual world. Most of us suppose that there could be more objects than there actually are and that there could have been, or could be, objects distinct from every actual object. Otherwise, it would be a necessary truth that there are just the number and type of objects there are. For example, if there are 10^{79} elementary particles in the universe, then *Necessarily, there are 10^{79} elementary particles*. But this obliterates our most basic modal intuitions.

We also think that many claims about counterfactual situations have truth conditions—that is, they could be true or false. So we want, if available, a theory that accommodates these common sense claims, allows us to use possible worlds semantics and does not posit nonexistent entities. These are the aspirations for actualism.[59]

The actualist seeks to ground modal discourse in the actual world while still

---

[58]Meinong, for instance, is reputed to have taken the existence of such entities to be intuitively obvious ("The Theory of Objects," in *Realism and the Background of Phenomenology,* ed. Roderick M. Chisholm [Glencoe, Ill.: The Free Press, 1960]). This is how Lycan interprets him in "The Trouble with Possible Worlds," pp. 275-77. Apparently he tolerated in his ontology even nonexistent impossibles, like square circles, since these things must exist in some sense, since we are able to refer to them.

David Lewis is renowned for his defense of nonexistent possibles as well (in *Counterfactuals*). Lewis does have a defense, which appears by my lights to make his view at least intelligible. Most simply, he argues that the possibilist uses "exists" in two different ways (David Lewis, "Possible Worlds," in *The Possible and the Actual,* ed. Michael J. Loux [Ithaca, N.Y.: Cornell University Press, 1979], pp. 225-34). This may be expressed by using the normal quantifier sign in an unrestricted sense, to range over all possible objects. Then we use a quantifier with a modifier attached to capture "exists" with respect only to actual objects. Then, instead of the contradiction generated above, we have something like $(\exists x) \sim(\exists_a y)(x = y)$ where $\exists_a$ is the restricted quantifier. According to Loux, Lewis is taking the unrestricted quantifier as primitive and defining the restricted quantifier in terms of it: $(\exists_a x)(\phi x)$ = df. $(\exists x)(\phi x \,\&\, x$ is actual) (Loux, p. 46). While this may preserve consistency, it is hardly illuminating. His theory also requires world-bound individuals and counterparts that fail to accommodate modal intuitions and seem to result principally from his possibilism. So most—including me—judge that if another, namely actualist, interpretation is possible, it is to be preferred.

[59]Thomas Jager provides a semantics for actualism combined with quantified modal logic in "An Actualistic Semantics for Quantified Modal Logic," *Notre Dame Journal of Formal Logic* 23 (1982): 335-49.

accommodating our modal intuitions. Actualism is the view that there neither are nor could be any nonexistent objects.[60] Actualists who deny the viability of modality are usually nominalists or conceptualists who insist that only individual objects exist. The actualism referred to here, however, is the modal variety. So when I say actualist, I mean "modal actualist"[61] unless otherwise indicated. Such an actualist hopes to preserve the logical distinctions required for modal reasoning while avoiding positing or implying the existence of nonexistent entities. So the actualist attempts to steer between the Scylla of extreme modal realism or possibilism (as in the theories of Meinong and David Lewis) and the Charybdis of reductionistic nominalism or fictionalism (as in the early Quine). The actualist takes actuality as an absolute, not merely as a relative property of possible worlds.[62] I have betrayed my commitment to a type of actualism by defining possible worlds not simply as other worlds that we do not inhabit, or as literal objects, but as maximally consistent states of affairs. This does not entail commitment to nonexistent existents.

Actualism is not the thesis that whatever is is actual, since there are states of affairs that are not actual.[63] It is the thesis that there are no things that do not exist. Possible worlds are states of affairs that are among the constituents, so to speak, of the actual world, all of which are obtainable. That is, they could be or could have been instantiated. The contents of the actual world cannot be described without the use of modal terms and concepts. Nevertheless, the only possible world that is concrete, which obtains, which is actual, is the actual world, a world that nevertheless calls for the use of modal terms and concepts. This position bears clear affinities to common sense, because we all engage in talk about ways things might have been.[64]

Actuality is closely linked to truth, so that when a state of affairs is actual—

---

[60]This phrasing is originally ascribed to Robert M. Adams in "Theories of Actuality," in *The Possible and the Actual,* ed. Michael J. Loux (Ithaca, N.Y.: Cornell University Press, 1979), pp. 190-209. One should note that essentialism and actualism, as we have defined them, are not contradictory notions. Rather, actualism qualifies essentialism. Essentialism as defined here may conflict more clearly with what is usually called existentialism, at least in its stronger forms. But I suspect a *rapprochement* is possible even between moderate existentialism and the essentialism I am defending.

[61]As Loux calls Stalnaker and Plantinga, in his "Introduction," p. 49.

[62]Robert M. Adams, review of *Nature of Necessity, Nous* 11 (1977): 175-90.

[63]See Plantinga, "On Existentialism," pp. 1-20.

[64]Stalnaker, "Possible Worlds," p. 230.

when it obtains—it is a fact. When we assert that some actual state of affairs is actual, we speak a truth. This link between actuality and truth helps us see the fundamental difference between a merely possible world and the actual world. It is true that each world is actual at itself. This just means that for every world w it is not possible that w be actual and that w not be actual.[65] That is, for every possible world w_p, w_p has the property of being actual at w_p. David Lewis infers from this that the actual world is not significantly different from all the others.[66] But Lewis concludes more than he ought, for this inference ignores the yawning difference between a proposition being true and being false, or between a state of affairs obtaining and not obtaining. The fact that in some world w_p, George H. W. Bush is elected president of the United States in 1992 does not change the fact that in 1992, Bill Clinton and not George H. W. Bush was in fact elected president. All the *possibilia* do not change that.

The problem of transworld identity. Theories such as one sketched above, if successful, would allow us to speak of objects and persons who can retain their identities through time and through various states of affairs—that is, across possible worlds. Consider the truth of the following disjunctive claim. Tomorrow at 8:00 A.M., I will either be sleeping or not sleeping. Or to put it as a conjunction,

> (S) *Possibly* (I am sleeping at 8:00 A.M.) & *possibly* (I am not sleeping at 8:00 A.M.).

But clearly these are not compossible (simultaneously possible) states of affairs; that is,

> (NS) *It is not possible that* (I am sleeping at 8:00 A.M. & I am not sleeping at 8:00 A.M.).

At most only one of these conjuncts will be actual. So the left conjunct of (S) (the part to the left of the "&" symbol) is part of a different possible world than the right conjunct. Nevertheless, clearly, when I speak thus, I mean that *I* can exist in either of these worlds.

But this so-called transworld identity troubles some critics, such as Leibniz and David Lewis, who claim that it fails to preserve the identity of individuals.

---

[65]Plantinga, *Nature of Necessity*, pp. 48-49.
[66]David Lewis, "Anselm and Actuality," *Nous* 4 (1970): 186-87.

Since laws of identity, such as $a = a$, are fundamental to our ways of speaking and thinking, any theory that violated them would be in serious trouble. Such critics have offered several arguments against the theory of transworld identity, all centering on the problem of identity, often called the problem of transworld identity. Such critics charge that transworld identity (1) makes it impossible to identify individuals from world to world, (2) does not preserve so-called transitivity of identity and (3) violates Leibniz's "Law of the indiscernibility of identicals."[67] (1) is the least compelling, so let us treat it first.

Consider the individual in this world whom we call Winston Churchill. In this world—the actual world—he had certain identifying characteristics. He was portly, smoked long cigars, served as prime minister of Great Britain during World War II and gave a speech about the Iron Curtain at Westminster College. Most proponents of transworld identity, however, will contend that these are all contingent attributes of Churchill. He might never have been prime minister of Great Britain. He might have been a clerk in the British patent office. He might have been allergic to tobacco smoke, subsisted on a low-fat diet and maintained a strict bodybuilding regimen, been named John Major and died at the age of forty-two. But in this case, the opponent of transworld identity may ask, how are we supposed to identify him? What "empirically manifest"[68] property or criterion can we offer to pick Churchill out in a world in which he is so different from our own?

This problem is more apparent than real because it presupposes a questionable picture of possible worlds. For it is not as if anyone is claiming that there is such a world actually playing itself out in some dimension parallel to our own. There is not another Churchill living his life in this way. Moreover, we do not have to be able to identify Churchill in that world, since we do not have to peer into these different worlds to locate him. Rather, in possible worlds discourse, we stipulate certain possible characteristics of an individual in this world, whom we can identify, namely, Winston Churchill. It is that individual

---

[67]For a fuller discussion of the problem, see Roderick M. Chisholm, "Identity Through Possible Worlds," Kaplan, "Transworld Heir Lines," and Alvin Plantinga, "Transworld Identity or World Bound Individuals?" in *The Possible and the Actual,* ed. Michael J. Loux (Ithaca, N.Y.: Cornell University Press, 1979); also, Jaako Hintikka, "Individuals, Possible Worlds and Epistemic Logic," *Nous* 1 (1967): 33-63, and Alvin Plantinga, "World and Essence," *Philosophical Review* 79 (1970): 477-82.

[68]This is Plantinga's term from *The Nature of Necessity,* p. 93.

we intend to speak of, only it is that individual in a different situation.

But even if this picture of concurrently running parallel worlds made sense, our inability to identify Churchill in another world is really an epistemological problem—a mere lack of knowledge—which does not bear on the question of whether Churchill exists in that world. Being incognito does not negate identity.

Perhaps the best analogy for this is a temporal one. We all assume that some things, including humans, retain identity across time, even if it is difficult or impossible to identify discrete individuals at different times. Plantinga's example of Brentano is as good as any. He mentions two pictures of Brentano included in one of Brentano's books, one picture at age twenty, the other at age seventy: "The youthful Brentano looks much like Apollo; the elderly Brentano resembles, instead, Jerome Hines in his portrayal of the dying Czar in Boris Godounov."[69] Plantinga's point is that our inability to establish criteria to identify the two does not mean that it is not the same individual in both pictures. This argument also applies to the same individual existing in different maximal states of affairs. Of course, there are differences between identity across time and across possible worlds, but those differences do not refute the point. As we speak of individuals persisting in different times, so we speak of individuals persisting in different states of affairs.[70] Unless such discourse is utterly confused or obviously incoherent, then that is all we need to preserve transworld identity.[71]

There are two more substantial arguments against transworld identity. Answering them requires that we appeal to the existence of individual essences and haecceities and to the distinction between essential and contingent properties. One argument asks us to imagine a succession of similar worlds $w_1 \ldots w_n$ in which two individuals exchange one property after another as we move from

[69]Ibid., p. 94.

[70]Not accepting identity across different possible worlds leads to theoretical grief. Baruch Brody, who finds essentialism to be plausible, nevertheless is convinced that there is some problem with transworld identity. At the same time, he thinks that Leibniz's law is rightly modified to preserve identity through time. Combining these elements, his theory has counterintuitive implications, such as making properties attained in the past essential to an entity. For instance, *eating Malt o'Meal on October 18, 1997* is now one of my essential properties. The dilemma is generated because Brody perceives a problem where one does not exist. See his *Identity and Essence* (Princeton, N.J.: Princeton University Press, 1980), pp. 84-134.

[71]For more indications that the so-called problem of transworld identity is not much of a problem, see Peter Van Inwagen, "Plantinga on Trans-World Identity," in *Alvin Plantinga*, ed. James E. Tomberlin and Peter Van Inwagen (Dordrecht: D. Reidel, 1985), pp. 101-20.

one world to the next. So in w_1, the actual world, Smith is a red-headed banker married to Susan and living in Sacramento, and Jones is a black-haired drug dealer, three times divorced and living in Miami. As we move along the succession of possible worlds, Smith and Jones exchange these properties, including their names, with each other until at some world w_n, they exchange places completely. If such a scenario were possible, then Smith at w_1 = Jones at w_n, and Jones at w_1 = Smith at w_n, even though they are distinct individuals at w_1 (the actual world). This violates the principle of the transitivity of identity; that is, if a is equal to b and b is equal to c, then a is equal to c. And since we are much more certain of this principle than of the highfalutin' doctrine of transworld identity, the latter must go. Or so argues the opponent of transworld identity.

Now defenders of transworld identity are duty bound to deny that such a scenario is possible. But how? They will have to argue that while Smith and Jones can exchange[72] many properties in different possible worlds, some properties, namely, those constituting or included in their individual essences, cannot be exchanged in any world. In other words, they will appeal to the individual essences of individuals to preserve identity across worlds. Contingent properties can be exchanged. Individual essences cannot. Again, we may be unable to identify certain individuals in these alternate worlds. But as I have already argued, this is a false dilemma because it presupposes an incorrect picture of the status of possible worlds.

The third argument against transworld identity is also the strongest. According to this argument, transworld identity violates the principle of the indiscernibility of identicals, also called Leibniz's law, which states:

> **(LL) For any objects x and y, if x is identical with y, then for any property P, x has P if and only if y has P.**

We should not confuse this principle with any of various versions of the identity of indiscernibles, only one of which is likely to be necessarily true:

> **(IdIn) If any objects x and y have all properties in common, then x and y are identical.[73]**

---

[72]"Exchange" in the sense that Smith could have had many of the properties Jones does have, and vice versa.

[73]See, for example, "Identity of Indiscernibles," *Cambridge Dictionary of Philosophy*, pp. 359-60 for discussion.

Now if (LL) is necessary to preserve identity then the notion of transworld identity is lost. For clearly, Smith in w_1 will differ from Smith in w_2 in some way, even if the only difference between w_1 and w_2 is that, whereas in w_1, there are 10^{79} fundamental particles of matter, in w_2, there are $10^{79} + 1$ particles of matter. So Smith in w_1 will be such that there are 10^{79} fundamental particles, and Smith in w_2 will be such that there are $10^{79} + 1$ fundamental particles; and sure enough, these are different properties. So Smith's identity (given the truth of (LL)) will dissolve from w_1 to w_2.

Not surprisingly, philosophers who find (LL) to be intuitively obvious deny that individuals can exist in more than one world. Thus they ascribe to some theory of world-bound individuals. This tactic has two problems. First, defenders of world-bound individuals do not avoid the claim that there are individual essences. Rather, they must claim that individuals have all their properties essentially, a position sometimes called mereological essentialism. So for Smith in w_1, the fact that there are 10^{79} fundamental particles in the universe is one of his essential properties. Such a claim dissolves most of the reasons for considering alternative worlds in the first place.[74]

Second, (LL) proves too much. If (LL) were necessary to preserve the identity of individuals, then change through time, no matter how trivial, would destroy identity.[75] For again, Smith at time t will differ in some way from Smith at $t+1$. Whereas Smith at t will be identical with Smith, Smith at $t+1$ does not enjoy this property. The proponent of (LL), then, seems committed, not only to world bound individuals, but to "instant" or time-bound individuals as well. Even the most skeptical of philosophers, such as Quine, take it for granted that there is such a relation as transtemporal identity for at least some individuals.[76] Surely this is more intuitively plausible than (LL).

The clearest way through the problem is to qualify (LL) so that it does not

---

[74]As Plantinga notes, the theory of world-bound individuals has other unhappy consequences. For example, to deny any truth about Socrates, say, to deny that Socrates is wise, will be to assert a necessary falsehood. And given one of the paradoxes of strict implication (which is not really a paradox but a question of relevance between premises and conclusions in certain conditionals), a proposition such as *Socrates exists*, since necessarily true, will entail every true proposition (see pp. 108-15). This grants too much modal weight to items that seem clearly contingent.

[75]I have followed Plantinga in ibid. closely in this section, pp. 92-98.

[76]Of course he denied the existence of an analogous relation across worlds. See Forbes, *Metaphysics of Modality*, p. 52.

rule out a priori identity across times and worlds (maximally possible states of affairs). This means adding time and world quantifiers to (LL):

(LLtw) **For any object, x, and any object, y, if x is identical with y, then for any property, P, any world, w, and any time, t, x has P in w at t if and only if y has P in w at t.**[77]

This formulation accommodates the fact that we speak of individuals as persisting through different times and states of affairs. Thus it more closely formalizes our ordinary understanding and discourse about identity. And given LL_{tw}, this argument against transworld identity evaporates.

Counterpart theory. Defenders of transworld individuals do seem to equivocate, however, when they use the word *exists*. Such equivocation may be one of the sources of the dispute. So let us clarify. When one says that an individual, say Socrates, exists in more than one world, one does not mean that Socrates is actual in more than one world. There are not, say, 10^{100} different Socrates, differing only on contingent matters, living parallel lives in their respective worlds. To say that Socrates exists in a possible world w_p other than the actual world is just to say that, if w_p had been actual, then Socrates *would* have existed. On the other hand, to say he exists in the actual world is to say that he exists in the most basic sense.

It is no surprise, then, that philosophers like David Lewis—who tend to grant nonactual possibles a stronger status than the modal actualist—suspect that the notion of transworld individuals compromises identity. Lewis's possibilism, yoked with an understanding of identity similar to (LL), requires that individuals exist in only one possible world. (This is similar to Leibniz's case. If [LL] is a correct rendering of identity, then transworld individuals are unthinkable.)

As already noted, the doctrine of world-bound individuals makes nonsense of our most stable modal intuitions. Lewis hopes to repair this by proposing an alternate theory for interpreting our speech concerning ways individuals and entities might have been. Instead of saying that the same individual can exist in different possible worlds, he proposes that individuals exist in only one world, but many of them have counterparts, which are very much like them, in other possible worlds. An entity's counterparts resemble it "closely in

---

[77]See Loux, "Introduction," p. 42.

both content and context in important respects"; they resemble it "more closely than do other things in their worlds." So "the counterpart relation is a relation of similarity" but not normally an equivalence relation.[78] On this view, when I say *I could have been a rock star,* I am referring to a different possible world, stipulated to contain one of my counterparts, who is a rock star. This theory allows us to avoid the implausible implication that my failing to be a rock star is one of my essential properties (since I really could have been a rock star!). As long as I have a counterpart in some possible world who enjoys rock-stardom, then I am not shackled with essential nonrockstardom.

This theory has more to commend it than is apparent from this bare sketch. Nevertheless, many philosophers have subjected it to severe criticism, mostly because it fails to accommodate prephilosophical modal intuitions.[79] Perhaps Lewis could protect the theory by insisting that it has some other use. But such a strategy would contradict a great deal else that he says. In short, counterpart theory does not seem to be a plausible interpretation of counterfactual and modal discourse. When I say that I could have been a rock star, I mean me, not some other strikingly similar counterpart. Lewis might be able to map normal discourse, including my claim, into counterpart theory; but his interpretation affirms a different proposition from the one I am affirming.[80]

I will not survey other related criticisms[81] because I have not adopted the premises that seem to generate the need for counterpart theory. Those premises are an excessively stringent criterion of identity such as (LL) and a possibilist interpretation of possible worlds semantics. Without these motivations, we do not need counterpart theory.

CONCLUSION

While modal logic and possible worlds semantics may appear to be ivory-tower creations of tenured logicians with too much time on their hands, their motivation resides in our common use of modal terms and ideas. Rightly ap-

---

[78]David Lewis, "Counterpart Theory and Quantified Modal Logic," in *The Possible and the Actual,* ed. Michael J. Loux (Ithaca, N.Y.: Cornell University Press, 1979), p. 112.

[79]See Loux, "Introduction," pp. 39-42.

[80]See Plantinga, *Nature of Necessity,* p. 117; "Transworld Identity or World Bound Individuals," pp. 157-65; and Saul Kripke, "Identity and Necessity," in *Identity and Individuation,* ed. Milton K. Munitz (New York: New York University Press, 1971), pp. 147-49.

[81]See ibid., pp. 102-20.

plied, these tools have remarkable applications, especially as a means for defending essentialism. At this point I have considered essentialism only as it applies to individuals and entities in the created universe. My purpose is to use essentialism to attribute properties and perfections to the triune God. This will require some tinkering. It will also reveal ways in which a Christian theistic context can help fortify essentialism. Christian theism needs a well-formulated essentialism. Conversely, essentialism needs theism for its final justification.

3

THEOLOGICAL ESSENTIALISM

The previous chapter provided little more than an introduction to the issues surrounding modal logic and possible worlds semantics. Still, I hope that it is enough to dispel the nagging suspicion that these topics are somehow defunct. Moreover, I hope it will allow me to assume the value of these tools for defending essentialism, which is, after all, our purpose here. Therefore, in this chapter I will apply some of the conceptual tools introduced in chapter two to the Christian doctrine of God.

It should become clear in the following that Christian theologians and philosophers are well within their rights in extending essentialism to theology. The notion of possible worlds is at home in a theistic conception of reality. Essentialist distinctions emerge naturally from the things Christians say about God. In fact, essentialism is rooted in pretheoretical Christian discourse, most importantly in Scripture. These facts, as well as the fact that essentialism clarifies many important intuitions about the doctrine of God, suggests that an account of God that builds on this approach is well warranted.

THE THEOLOGICAL BASIS OF ESSENTIALISM

Possible worlds semantics, modal logic and essentialism are viable in our contemporary setting. There are no impenetrable barriers outside Christian theology to prevent us from using essentialist language. But coherence is merely a necessary but not a sufficient condition for its use in Christian theology. If possible, we would like to have specifically theological reasons for using it. So what do possible worlds semantics and modal metaphysics have to do with the Christian doctrine of God?

Possible worlds in Leibniz. Perhaps surprisingly, the concept of possible worlds has its home and its historical antecedent in a theological frame of mind. While speculation about multiple worlds may be as old as philosophy itself, the concept of possible worlds as alternative ways the world might have been originated in the Christian thought of Gottfried Leibniz (1646-1716). Not surprisingly, he develops it in his reflection on the doctrine of creation, in which he imagines God in the creative act as having before his mind an infinite set of worlds which he could have created, choosing—as befits his perfect goodness—to create the one best in total.[1] For Leibniz, there are an infinite number of Adams that God could have created[2] and even an infinite number of natural laws that he could have actualized.[3] Since God had such alternatives available to him, Leibniz argues that God is free in creating the world. Therefore, the world is contingent.[4]

Leibniz's is a specifically Christian argument—*via* the doctrine of creation—for the idea that (at least some) counterfactuals have truth conditions. If they do not, Leibniz argues, then we must deny that this world is contingent. It seems unlikely that this understanding of possible worlds could have emerged in a context in which the world was understood as the product of an impersonal and ironclad cosmic necessity. Thus, it's not surprising that the concept of possible worlds has its wellspring in the conviction that the actual world is contingent—contingent because it has its sufficient cause in the free choice of a Creator.

Leibniz's key insight here is that freedom and contingency are interdependent concepts. If there is *no* sense in talking of possible worlds, then there is no sense in talking about the contingency of creation and the necessity of

---

[1]Robert Merrihew Adams, in his entry "Possible Worlds" in *The Cambridge Dictionary of Philosophy,* ed. Robert Audi (Cambridge: Cambridge University Press, 1995), p. 633, credits Leibniz with the concept of possible worlds.

[2]"Correspondence with Arnauld," in *Philosophical Writings,* ed. G. H. R. Parkinson (London: Everyman's Library, n.d.), p. 51. Notice that Leibniz's discussion of different "Adams" results from his argument that individuals are world bound. Presumably Adam had many counterparts, also named "Adam," in other possible worlds. But Leibniz does not speak of one Adam existing in different worlds.

[3]Ibid., p. 54.

[4]"For when I speak of possibilities, I am quite satisfied that it should be possible to form true propositions about them. . . . And if we absolutely reject pure possibilities, this means that there is no contingency; for if nothing is possible except what God has in fact created, what God has created would be necessary, supposing he had once decided to create anything." Ibid., p. 59.

God's existence. If the only world God could have created is the actual world, then his only free choice would be whether or not to create this one world. But even this modest picture presupposes that there is more than one possible world. If God could choose to create or not to create, then there are at least two possible worlds: the world in which God does create this particular universe and the one in which he does not (remembering that possible worlds are maximally consistent states of affairs). To excise *possibilia* completely, one must remove even this choice. But then the actual world would be the only possible world, and as such, it would be necessary. At the very least, its modal status would be the same as God's. This is surely not compatible with God's creative freedom.[5]

The concept of intelligence. Philosopher and mathematician William Dembski has recently made a related argument. Dembski points out that contingency and choice are implicated in the very concept of intelligence. Even the etymology of the word illustrates this point. The word *intelligent* comes from the Latin preposition *inter,* meaning "between," and the Latin verb *lego,* meaning "to choose or select." To act intelligently or to be an intelligent agent is literally to be able to choose between competing options. It is to select from among contingent possibilities, not all of which are compatible with each other.

The choices of an intelligent agent differ from other events and forms of causality. Within nature, if an event occurs regularly under similar conditions, we normally attribute it to an impersonal or unintelligent cause such as natural law. (Dembski puts such explanations under the category of "necessity."[6]) And

---

[5]Commitment to divine freedom in creation does not oblige one to accept all the details of Leibniz's conception, even if one defends the cogency of possible worlds semantics. One might suspect, as I do, that what Leibniz preserves of divine freedom with the idea of infinite possibilities, he spoils by insisting there is only one world God could have created consistent with his moral nature. Leibniz argued only that God could logically have created a different world, but not morally. To succeed, however, his argument requires the additional premise that there is only one best world consonant with God's nature. Leibniz did not accept that many worlds could equally satisfy God's moral nature, despite the fact that one could easily conceive of many equally good worlds that God could create. For an argument that God need not have created the best world in either sense, see the reprint of Robert Merrihew Adams, "Must God Create the Best?" in *The Concept of God,* ed. Thomas V. Morris (Oxford: Oxford University Press, 1987), pp. 91-106.

[6]It is doubtful that events that occur as a result of natural law should be described in terms of necessity. But Dembski is simply describing how such events are often described within the scientific community, which is often not careful in distinguishing between natural law and logical necessity.

a contingent event not caused by an agent we normally attribute to chance. But it is the unique domain of intelligence to select from among contingencies, not randomly but freely.[7]

This is relevant to theism because God is the paradigmatic intelligent agent. God's freedom is preeminent. It is the archetype for intelligent agency generally. Whatever paltry intelligent agency we enjoy is a mere shadow of divine intelligence. If intelligence generically implies the choosing between competing, contingent possibilities, then that implication is even stronger with respect to God, who creates without a preexisting universe or substratum, unlike all merely human agents. If human beings exercise intelligent agency despite being shaped, conditioned and circumscribed by time, place, environment and happenstance, then how much more does God exercise such agency? Dembski's analysis of the notion of intelligence provides additional support to Leibniz's argument for the legitimacy of using possible worlds discourse in theology.

Biblical intimations. Besides the fact that the notion of possible worlds emerges within the Christian tradition as an analysis of God's creative activity and intelligent agency,[8] its pretheoretic intuition—that there are ways things might have been, that counterfactuals have truth conditions—is embedded in the biblical narratives themselves. This is most explicit in the Old Testament narratives, which treat God's covenant with Israel and his promises (especially) to the Davidic monarchy. These usually consist of a divine promise of blessing to the king or to Israel, a promise that is contingent on the king or the covenant people following the Lord's commands and decrees (see, for example, 1 Kings 2:4; 6:12; 1 Sam 12:15; 2 Chron 7:17-22). These promises often include a contingency with respect to how God will act in the future, stating that God will tailor his re-

---

[7]See William Dembski, *Intelligent Design: The Bridge Between Science and Theology* (Downers Grove, Ill.: InterVarsity Press, 1999), pp. 227-29.

[8]Moreover, the possible worlds model adopted here was developed by (among others) a Jewish theist, Saul Kripke, and a Christian theist, Alvin Plantinga. Their projects emerged from theistic intuitions and have been constructed in the face of philosophical hostility from physicalists such as W. V. O. Quine. The reductionist spirit that animates materialism is hostile to theism and to possible worlds for similar reasons; not surprisingly, materialists and physicalists everywhere continue to wage war with possible worlds conceptions. This does not guarantee that any such conception will in fact be compatible with full-fledged Christian belief. There are specifically theological criticisms to confront as well.

sponse to the actions of the covenant people. The Lord's appearance to Solomon after Solomon completed the temple in Jerusalem is a fitting example: "If my people who are called by my name will humble themselves, pray, seek my face, and turn from their wicked ways, then will I hear from heaven, and will forgive their sin and will heal their land" (2 Chron 7:14). Such interactions between God and the Israelites are common fare in the Old Testament.

Two popular biblical examples that imply God's knowledge of future counterfactuals are 1 Samuel 23:11-28 and Matthew 11:21. In the first, David decides to flee Keilah after the Lord tells him that if he stays, the citizens of the city will surrender him and his men to Saul. By fleeing, this event does not occur. Similarly in Matthew 11:21, Jesus mourns for the unrepentant regions to which he traveled, declaring, "Woe to you, Chorazin! Woe to you, Bethsaida! For if the deeds of power done in you had been done in Tyre and Sidon, they would have repented long ago in sackcloth and ashes." These passages appear frequently in the medieval debates between Molinists and Thomists over divine sovereignty and human freedom, especially concerning God's knowledge of "counterfactuals of freedom."[9] But the issues are not limited to these isolated passages. Counterfactuals, conditionals and other modal language permeate the Bible. Such speech even introduces the canon in the narrative of God's dealing with Adam and Eve ("but of the tree of the knowledge of good and evil you shall not eat, for in the day that you eat of it you shall die," Gen 2:17).

We find another telling counterfactual on the lips of Samuel, the Lord's mouthpiece to Saul. According to 1 Samuel, when Saul was fighting the Philistines, he waited for Samuel seven days at Gilgal. Growing impatient when his men began to scatter, he offered sacrifices contrary to Samuel's instructions. When Samuel arrived, he rebuked Saul, declaring, "You have not kept the commandment of the LORD your God, which he commanded you. The LORD would have established your kingdom over Israel forever, but now your kingdom will not continue; the LORD has sought out a man after his own heart; and the LORD has appointed him to be ruler over his people, because you have not kept what the LORD commanded you" (1 Sam 13:13-14).

---

[9]Karl Barth refers to this discussion in *Church Dogmatics* 2/1 (Edinburgh: T & T Clark, 1957), p. 571.

In this text, we seem to have the imprimatur of the Lord testifying that counterfactual states of affairs have truth conditions.[10] If Saul had been obedient, the future of the monarchy would have been quite different. As it was, Saul incited divine judgment. If possible worlds semantics is a sensible paraphrase of this way of speaking, then it is compatible with the letter and the spirit of the biblical texts.

Some versions of a possible worlds conception may conflict with Christian commitments. If we want philosophy to serve as a handmaiden to theology, then we will seek a possible worlds model that is compatible with and even implied by those commitments.

The implicit essentialism of theological claims. So the biblical narratives contain much modal discourse, and the implications of divine freedom and intelligence give the Christian theologian some claim to speak of possible worlds. However, the essentialist project is less modest than simply an appeal to alternative maximal states of affairs in order to explain divine freedom in creation. The essentialist also seeks to use the language of possible worlds and the essentialist concept developed from it to speak of the divine essence.[11]

The most obvious if uninspiring justification for such an endeavor is that Scripture and Christians as a matter of fact do aspire and intend to speak of God, of what he does and of what he is like. Surely such intentions, while no doubt informed by theoretical conceptions of various sorts, are pretheoretic in the sense that they precede explicit theoretical formulations. However uncon-

---

[10]Note that this is not an airtight argument for some other things, such as God's knowledge of the future or of counterfactual situations involving free acts of agents other than God. Although this biblical passage implies both these things, the skeptic concerning God's knowledge of these items will be quick to point out that the truth of Samuel's claim requires only that God know what God would do in a counterfactual situation. And God could know what he would do freely in a counterfactual situation without knowing what other free agents would do in the same situation. None of this is directly relevant to the present discussion. Possible worlds semantics does not stand or fall on God's knowledge of counterfactuals of any sort but only on their susceptibility to truth conditions. On this question the biblical witness, including this instance, clearly inclines toward the affirmative.

[11]Normally I will say simply that I wish to speak of the divine essence. I do not imply that I intend to speak exhaustively or comprehensively of God's nature, something impossible for finite creatures. So most precisely, I intend to use essentialism armed with possible worlds semantics to articulate those aspects of the divine nature that Christians know something about, or at least claim to know something about.

sciously, the theoretician builds on this pretheoretic practice.[12] Thus we seek a notion of essence adequate to how Scripture and the church speak of God.[13]

Moreover, as detailed in chapter one, the concept or rather cluster of concepts of essence or nature (*essentia, natura, substantia, physis, ousia*) is embedded in the Christian creeds and scholarly tradition, however subject such speech is to qualification. The Nicene Creed and Chalcedonian definition officially codified the propriety of using *ousia* and *hypostasis* in theology. That Christians have spoken of God's nature or essence from the earliest times is undeniable.[14] This is a brute fact and lends a prima facie warrant to theological use of contemporary essentialism.

Also as noted in chapter one, traditionally the use of essentialist terms was closely related to the Christian desire to express the supreme reality of God.[15] While some traditional appeals to Scripture to justify this strategy now look somewhat strained exegetically, at least one biblical theme does support this procedure. This is the theme of God's name. The Tetragrammaton, the primary proper name of God in the Old Testament, is related to the Hebrew word *hayah*, "to be." The divine epiphany to Moses at Horeb is a popular traditional locus and the canonical introduction of this divine self-designation, although it is used in the biblical texts prior to this narrative. When God calls Moses at Horeb to return to Egypt, Moses asks God, "'If I come to the Israelites and say to them, "The God of your ancestors has sent me to you," and they ask me, "What is his name?" what shall I say to them?' God said to Moses, 'I AM WHO I AM. . . . Thus you shall say to the Israelites, "I AM has sent me to you"'" (Ex 3:13-14). The

---

[12]Christian claims were most clearly pretheoretic in the early church, prior to official doctrinal formulations such as the Nicene Creed and the Chalcedonian definition. In the life of the church since then, the interaction between theoretical and pretheoretical discourse is more dialectical. That is, after creedal formulations became part of the liturgy and catechism, they shaped and informed the actual intentions and beliefs of Christians. I am not contending that there is a simple asymmetrical relation between pre-theoretical intentions and beliefs on the one hand and theoretical doctrinal formulations on the other. I am arguing only that official formulations are parasitic on the actual beliefs of the church.

[13]Given this priority, the mere presence of essentialist or substantialist language in a theological explanation is not enough to impugn it as tainted by Aristotelianism, an accusation all too common among critics of essentialism. See, for example, Colin Gunton, *Becoming and Being: The Doctrine of God in Charles Hartshorne and Karl Barth* (Oxford: Oxford University Press, 1976), pp. 143, 170.

[14]See Heinrich Heppe's examples from various Reformed Scholastics in his *Reformed Dogmatics* (1861), rev. and ed. Ernst Bizer (London: George Allen & Unwin, 1950), pp. 52-56.

[15]See Christopher Stead, *Divine Substance* (Oxford: Clarendon, 1977), p. 166: "Christian conceptions of God's substance depend largely on biblical texts of the form 'God is . . .' or 'I am . . . ,' particularly where the predicate lends itself to philosophical development."

Septuagint translates this divine appellation suggestively as "I am he who is," although the precise connotation of this name is disputed among biblical scholars. More recently, some have suggested "I WILL BE WHAT I WILL BE."

> Despite disagreement over the translation of the name, a clear burden of the passage is to identify this God who identifies himself thus as the same God who revealed himself to Israel's ancestors. So the Lord continues, "The LORD, the God of your ancestors, the God of Abraham, the God of Isaac, and the God of Jacob, has sent me to you":
>
> This is my name forever,
>   and this my title for all generations. (Ex. 3:15)

Moreover, the name is laden with the connotation that being itself is fundamental to this God. The passage probably cannot bear the weight that the Septuagint gives it, which implies that we are given here a definition of God's nature in terms of his absoluteness or aseity. Nevertheless, given the significance attached to the giving of a name in the Bible and the ancient Near East generally, we hardly can overestimate the importance of this passage. As Gerhard von Rad expresses it, "According to ancient ideas, a name was not just 'noise and smoke': instead, there was a close and essential relationship between it and its subject. The subject is in the name, and on that account the name carries with it a statement about the nature of its subject or at least about the power appertaining to it."[16]

We should not expect these texts to establish all the detailed precision of later Christian theological formulations; but the concern with being is surely congenial to this important theme in the Old Testament. When God offers his name in this way, we discover that his self-designation carries the connotation of being and existence. This lends an essentialist project some biblical warrant.[17]

---

[16]Gerhard von Rad, *Old Testament Theology*, 2 vols. (New York: Harper & Row, 1962), 1:181-82.

[17]Admittedly, when we speak of God's essence we enter a hornet's nest of difficulties in attempting to relate the status of universals to God. However, these complications are another argument for the utility of the possible worlds construal of essentialism. For it allows us facility to speak of properties and essences without committing us to a more specific theory about the precise status of universals, properties, etc. It provides a moderately straightforward way of conceiving of them, even if we find no way of deciding if, say, an essence is a substrate that underlies all particular properties, or is more or less the sum of essential properties constituting an entity (a bundle). And formulated actualistically, we should be able to mark off a fairly defensible territory that avoids the excesses of extreme realism on the one hand and nominalism on the other.

Theological arguments for the essentialist distinction between essential and accidental divine properties. These considerations alone are still not enough, however, since theological essentialism concerns not only general speech about God's essence but also encourages the distinction between essential and contingent properties or attributes for speaking of God. Here, the Christian essentialist seems to depart from the tradition, for classical theists have hesitated to endorse this distinction with respect to God. I will suggest later that this departure from the tradition is more apparent than real, because of the different ways of understanding properties in the medieval and contemporary essentialist contexts. But let us let that pass for now and consider how the distinction between God's essential and contingent properties is suggested by biblical and Christian discourse. Indeed, each of the three themes of Christian theology mentioned in chapter one seemed to support the distinction.

Biblical normativity justifies several claims. For instance, Scripture describes God as the source for creation, which is the product of God's free choice (Gen 1; Jn 1:3; Col 1:16). God is also free to enter into that creation and to interact with his creatures. The supreme act of this entry and interaction was incarnation, an event that, upon reflection, gives rise to an understanding of God as triune.[18]

Given the Principle of Perfection (PP), we want to affirm among other things that God's existence is profoundly different from the creation and its constituents. Whereas the creation and its members are contingent—that is, it is possible that they not exist—God exists necessarily. The creation does not exist as it is in every possible world,[19] and in many it would not exist at all. God exists in every possible world, whatever creation there is, and whether or not there is a creation.

Given the Sovereignty-Aseity Conviction (SAC), we wish to maintain that God is not dependent on anything outside himself for his existence. And intuitively, if God's existence is necessary and eternal[20] and the creation's exis-

---

[18] "In the beginning was the Word, and the Word was with God, and the Word was God. He was in the beginning with God. . . . He was in the world, and the world came into being through him. . . . And the Word became flesh and lived among us, and we have seen his glory, the glory as of a father's only son, full of grace and truth" (Jn 1:1-2, 10, 14).

[19] If this world is w_1, then, if another possible world, w_2, had been actual, then w_1 would not have been actual.

[20] I am using *eternal* here to mean that God's existence had no beginning, and it will have no end. I am not endorsing either the thesis that eternity is timeless or that it is rather duration without beginning or end.

tence is finite and contingent, then God's existence cannot depend on the existence of the creation. Thus we conclude that a necessarily existing Creator has entered into relations with contingent creatures, even becoming one of those creatures while nevertheless remaining God. These are at the core of Christian belief. But how are we to reconcile them?

Think of properties, again, as states of affairs concerning entities of different types; as truths or facts about such entities. An entity is anything or anyone that exists and can be denoted by a noun or pronoun in a sentence. Crudely put, any essential property concerning a contingent person such as, say, Joan of Arc, will be a truth that obtains for her in every world in which she exists. More precisely, it will be a truth about the way she exists, about her being in the world. It will be a truth about her. Perhaps one such property for Joan of Arc is being a human being. That is, in every possible world in which Joan of Arc exists[21] she is a human being. If this is correct, then there are no worlds in which Joan of Arc exists but is the set of even integers. Other facts about her do not obtain in every world. It is possible that she could have been born in, say, Wales. So being from the area we now call France is a contingent fact about her. While in the actual world she was from France, in other possible but nonactual worlds she would be from Wales. So having her birth in France is not an essential property for Joan of Arc. And being called *Joan of Arc* for posterity and *being burned at the stake* one may assume are also contingent properties for her. So her accidental properties are contingent; but as a contingent being, while her essential properties are essential to her, they are contingent on her existing in the actual world.

With respect to God, when we say certain things are true of him, we seem to be making certain "ontological commitments" about him as well.[22] (To say

---

[21]She actually exists only in the actual world—a seemingly obvious but crucial point.

[22]This is a self-conscious reference to Quine's term "ontic commitment" in *Word and Object* (Cambridge, Mass.: MIT Press, 1960), in his chapter "Ontic Decision." The term arises in his discussion of realism and nominalism and refers to the fact that certain ways of speaking can "commit" us, so to speak, to certain ontological entities. His worry is that a way of speaking of properties may imply something about their ontological status to which one may not want to commit. Similarly, in "Three Grades of Modal Involvement," in *The Ways of Paradox and Other Essays* (New York: Random House, 1966), pp. 156-74, Quine detects (I think correctly) that one's way of viewing and speaking of modality also brings with it certain ontological commitments, certain "degrees of involvement" in the existence of the entities implied by the discourse employed. He warned that making of necessity anything more than a "semantic predicate" "leads us back into the metaphysical jungle of Aristotelian essentialism" (p. 174). For Quine the nominalist, this bit of question begging was a stinging criticism of an ontological commitment he considered imprudent.

one is ontologically committed to certain objects or properties means that certain assertions and affirmations cannot be true unless the objects or properties of that kind exist.[23]) Since Christians affirm that God has necessary existence (he does not just exist essentially, as does everything; rather, he has necessary existence essentially), the way we negotiate essential and contingent properties in God will differ from the case of Joan of Arc. For one thing, God's essential properties are essential to him, but they are also necessarily exemplified since he exists in every possible world. His accidental properties are contingent since they do not obtain in every possible world. Notice that the seemingly modest things we are already claiming about God draw us naturally into this way of speaking. While additional nuance and philosophical distinctions will be required, the procedure so far is uncontrived.

Now consider

(1) That God created the world.

On the account sketched above, this expresses a true but contingent state of affairs. If Christians are correct, then (1) expresses a fact. What that truth includes and what it entails is vast and beyond our ken. But surely among those things, it entails[24] the truth of

(2) God's having created the world,

(3) God's choosing to create the world,

and

(4) this world's having been created.

Such pedantic entailments are logically trivial but ontologically significant. (1)-(4) are all the result of God's free choice. While (2), (3) and (4) are clearly related, (2) and (3) seem principally to do with God, and (4) with the world. More precisely, they relate God and the world in some way and also seem to entail certain properties both of the world and of God. God and the world appear to be terms related by the asymmetrical relation of creation. God has the relation or the relational property *being Creator of the world*. The world has the relation *having been created by God*. But does this mean there are two relations, corresponding to the two terms? That does not sound quite right.

---

[23]See Graeme Forbes, *Languages of Possibility* (Oxford: Basil Blackwell, 1989), p. 108.

[24]That is, (1) is true if and only if (2), (3) and (4) are true, and false otherwise.

Rather, these are truths about the relation between the world and God. So, on the essentialist understanding of properties, these truths, these states of affairs that the Christian believes obtain in the actual world, either entail or perhaps presuppose that God has certain properties and that the world has certain properties.[25]

Whether we like it or not, these simple and intrinsically Christian claims thrust us quickly into sticky essentialist questions, such as, how do these properties relate to the essence of the world and of God? Which such properties are essential and which are contingent? How do possible worlds relate to God's choice? Do divine choices range over possible worlds? What implications does this have for divine sovereignty and aseity (SAC)? We have commitments that seem to attribute some essential characteristics to God, which will go into our understanding of his essence. Some such essential characteristics are perfections, such as necessary omniscience and perhaps necessary existence. In possible world terms this translates into the claim that God is omniscient and exists in every possible world.[26]

We also attribute to God characteristics that are contingent, such as *God's having created the world*. The doctrine of creation suggests the need for the distinction between necessary and contingent divine properties. How do these characteristics relate to God's essential properties and to his essence generally? How do we decide?

At this stage, we do not have a general theory of being, or of how being generically relates to God and the world, although what we say about God clearly has some implications for such a theory. Happily, we need not decide what God's essence is in order to proceed. Biblical and Christian discourse virtually demands some sort of distinction between God's essential and contingent properties (on the definition of properties offered above), and that will be

---

[25]For ease of use I say that God and the world have certain properties. At this point, however, I do not intend to favor one or another view of how properties relate to the identity or the essence of either God or the world.

[26]Although strictly speaking, we should not imply that God is a mere member of these worlds. To avoid this implication, we might say that it is true at every world that God exists and that that world is created by God; for every world *w*, if *w* were actual, God would exist. Moreover, there is no world *w*, such that had it been actual, God would not have existed. Since this way of speaking is unwieldy, I will forego it. Note that it implies that God's existence is a state of affairs. No doubt it is the supreme state of affairs, but if it is a truth that obtains, it is a state of affairs nonetheless.

our focus. First let us develop this conception of God; then we can consider the significant objections leveled against it.

A PRELIMINARY ESSENTIALIST CONCEPTION OF GOD

Divine essential properties. We need to modify the everyday distinction between essential and contingent properties when applying it to God. Perhaps the most obvious difference between the mundane and theological use of the distinction is that unlike individuals in the created realm, if God exists necessarily, then God's essential properties will converge with his necessary properties. The possible worlds picture sketched in chapter two makes this clear. As we noted, contingent entities such as Socrates will have an essential property *P* just in case there is no world in which Socrates both exists and lacks *P.* An essential property of Socrates, then, is captured by both

(B) **Socrates has *P* and has it in every world in which he exists,**

(C) **Socrates has *P* and there is no world in which Socrates has the complement ~*P* of *P.***

But Socrates' possession of an essential property is not captured by

(A) **Socrates has *P* in every world**

since this would require that Socrates exist in every world in order for *P* to be an essential property. And since he does not exist in every world he would have no essential properties on (A).

A divine essential property, however, is captured by something like (A), since God does exist in every possible world. (B) and (C) are also truth preserving in God's case, but they are redundant and do not express the fact that God exists in every possible world. So every essential divine property is also a necessary property. That is, if God has any essential property *P,* then *P* will be necessarily exemplified. *Necessarily, God has P and has P essentially* will be true since it is true in every possible world. So a modified version of (A) captures an essential divine property:

(A_d)**God has *P* in every world.**

Even if one views properties, numbers, sets, propositions and the like as necessarily existing abstract objects, it does not follow that they enjoy the same sort of necessary existence as God does. For God's essence, as distinct from all such abstract entities and from all merely contingently instantiated individual essences, is concretely instantiated in every possible world.[27] God is the one necessarily existing, personal, concrete being and causal agent. The notion of uninstantiated essence, while applicable to contingently existing things, does not apply to God. There is no uninstantiated divine essence. There is no abstract essence that in any way precedes God's concrete actuality. This follows from the Principle of Perfection. For if God exists in only some worlds, then it is possible that God not exist. And surely it would be greater to exist in every possible world than in merely some.[28] This entails (if true) that God's essence is not uninstantiated in any possible world. He exists concretely and actually in every world. It is difficult to know what mode of existence could exceed this.

Of course, (A_d) is merely formal at this point and does not help us much in identifying God's essential properties.[29] (A_d) does not presuppose a specific material content for the divine attributes. Although it is not devoid of content, what attributes Christians believe God has are not determined by the essentialist distinction alone.

So every attribute of which (A_d) is true will be included in the divine essence or nature.[30] It does not follow that we comprehend or exhaustively define God in this way, even if we named or knew that certain properties were included in

---

[27]Again, I am assuming for the moment that it is appropriate to say that God instantiates properties. This may not be quite right; but I delay consideration of this matter until chapter nine.

[28]Notice that this claim is not the same as Anselm's argument, which Kant criticized in his *Critique of Pure Reason*. At least one version of Anselm's ontological argument for God's existence included the premise that it is greater to exist than not to exist. This premise assumes it is meaningful to compare things that actually exist with things that do not. Whether or not this is a meaningful assumption, the above claim does not presuppose it. It asserts only that in terms of greatness, it is greater to exist in every possible world than in only some.

[29]No doubt God will have certain trivial properties, such *as being divine or not being divine, being self-identical,* and the like (assuming for the moment that God has properties at all). And short of a great argument indicating otherwise, God seems to share these properties with everything that exists. Those other things undoubtedly exist because of his good pleasure. Nevertheless, in choosing to create other things, God has bestowed on them the honor of sharing some trivial properties with God. Of course, we could multiply such properties all day, without getting any nearer to a Christian doctrine of God or any apprehension of the divine perfections.

Still more inconsequential are the many so-called Cambridge properties that God has, such as *being thought of by Augustine in* A.D. *400* and *being referred to by Jonathan Edwards in many sermons.* These are no doubt truths involving God, but they seem so extrinsic as to be frivolous. They do not tell us anything more about God than could be deduced by any village atheist.

[30]Such expressions as "included in" should not be taken as a ruling against the doctrine of divine simplicity, which we consider below.

his essence. Still, there is no reason not to apply the concept of haecceity or individual essence to God. God's haecceity is at least God's concrete reality or those divine aspects that are the same in every possible world. In God's case, however, it is difficult to get any space between God's essence and his haecceity. Since God exemplifies his essence in every possible world, his haecceity does not distinguish him from a generic divine essence, in the way that, say, my haecceity distinguishes me from generic humanness. Moreover, the doctrine of the Trinity, which we will consider below, complicates things considerably.

Divine perfections. Essentialism provides a framework for organizing, conceptualizing and relating the divine essence and properties to God, to each other and to created entities. But it leaves most of the content of these things unspecified. At the same time, essentialism does have certain implications for that content. As mentioned, God has any number of trivially essential attributes. In the doctrine of God, however, the attributes normally discussed are perfections. The Principle of Perfection leads us to place the perfections among God's essential properties, since it is obviously greater to exemplify things like perfect knowledge, power and love in every world in which one exists than to exemplify them accidentally, that is, in only some worlds in which one exists. And since God exists in every possible world, he possesses or exemplifies all his perfections in every possible world. So not only are they his essential properties, but he also exemplifies them necessarily. The perfections include all those properties susceptible to perfection, such as knowledge, goodness, presence, freedom, power, love, mercy, justice and holiness. If we take necessary existence as a perfection of existence, it will be included as well. If not, then, in order to be maximally great, God still must exemplify the perfections in every possible world. So he exemplifies them and thus exists in every possible world, whether or not necessary existence is itself a perfection. Let us call the conjunction of these perfections the property of omnicompetence, which God necessarily exemplifies.

While infinity and eternity usually are placed among the incommunicable attributes, aspects of these properties are implied here as well. If divine eternity entails at least the property that God always has and always will exist, then necessary existence certainly entails it. For if it is impossible that God not exist, then there is no time at which God could not exist. The possible worlds apparatus enables us to conceptualize this. Assume that S5 best accounts for logical modality. Then, at any time t at which God exists, or—to avoid implying divine temporality—at any possible world w_p at which God exists, there is no other possible world at which he does not exist. (Existing at any time t will be a proper subset of all possible worlds, or perhaps one conjunct of a possible world, if we conceive of God as temporal in some sense.) So there is no time and no state of affairs at which he does not exist, if he is maximally perfect in any possible world. And obviously enough, there *will* be no time at which he does not exist. So this aspect of eternity is provided simply by the truth of God's necessary existence. Similarly, necessary existence may imply that God is temporally infinite (if there is a coherent concept of temporal infinity); deciding this, however, would require a lengthy discussion of eternity. Whether or not God is eternal in another sense, such as being timeless, is another matter.[31]

Of course, in naming the divine perfections, we speak only of properties that are susceptible to perfection. Some properties are not so susceptible, for instance, *being North Korean*. It is difficult to imagine what the perfection of such a property would be. Moreover, to say that God has such perfections is quite different from giving precise content to the implications and meaning of them individually or severally. This latter task has proven difficult in the history of theology. For instance, what does omnipotence or perfect power come to? Does it require the ability to sin or commit suicide, or to square a circle? Certain formulations notoriously generate paradoxes, such as the inference that if God is omnipotent, then he must be able to create a rock he cannot lift. There also are issues of compossibility, such as the classic dilemma of God making either an irresistible force or an immovable object, but not both simultaneously.[32] These are all complications

---

[31]I will mention divine eternity in more detail in chapter eight, in relation to immutability.

[32]The paradoxes of omnipotence are probably the most popular conundrums generated by traditional attempts to define omnipotence precisely. For recent discussion see Richard Swinburne, *The Coherence of Theism* (Oxford: Clarendon, 1977), pp. 149-61; Alvin Plantinga, *God and Other Minds* (Ithaca, N.Y.: Cornell University Press, 1967), pp. 168-73; Anthony Kenny, "The Definition of Omnipotence," and Thomas P. Flint and Alfred J. Freddoso, "Maximal Power," in *The Concept of God,* ed. Thomas V. Morris (Oxford: Oxford University Press, 1987), pp. 125-33, 134-67; Peter Geach, "Omnipotence," in *Providence and Evil* (Cambridge: Cambridge University Press, 1977). A classic modern statement of the paradox is J. L. Mackie's "Evil and Omnipotence," *Mind* 64 (1955): 200-212. I will not discuss the merits of different proposals, since it is not my purpose to offer a detailed analysis of the definition of the divine perfections. Nevertheless, Anthony Kenny's definition seems close to an accurate analysis of omnipotence. He defines God as omnipotent if he has every power that is logically possible for a being with God's other attributes to possess ("Definition of Omnipotence," pp. 131-32). This leaves many questions unanswered, including the precise definition of power and the nature of the other divine attributes.

with the content of the perfections. Such complications of analysis do not imply
that the concepts themselves have no denotation; that is, complications do not
imply that the perfections do not refer to anything. Complexities confront the
analysis of all concepts, including the notions of truth, sentences and persons.
Nevertheless, we still think all three exist and understand most discussions that
include them. Thus, just as we continue to speak of truth, sentences and persons,
so we properly continue to speak of the divine perfections.

The classical theists from Thomas Aquinas to the Protestant Scholastics in-
ferred most of these attributes either from the Principle of Perfection, the Sovereignty-Aseity Conviction, or both, filtered through the methods of the *via triplex*. They often cited biblical passages as evidence for many of the perfections,
although such passages usually underdetermine the content of the perfections.
For example, consider Heppe's biblical citations in defense of Heidegger's definition of divine immutability, "by which [God] alone is *per se* and *a se,* in actuality and in potency, devoid of all succession, change or variation, remaining
the same eternally without even the faintest shadow of transmutation." He
mentions Isaiah 46, Romans 11 and Hebrews 6:17-18.[33] These passages indeed
declare that God is resolute, unswerving in his purposes and always faithful in
his promises. These claims certainly relate to immutability. But do they demonstrate that God is "devoid of all succession," that none of his properties could
change across time? We will try to answer that in chapter eight.

Of course, just because no biblical text directly determines Heidegger's definition of immutability does not mean that it is wrong. But his definition undoubtedly draws on sources other than Scripture. We may suspect those
sources include certain intuitions about what constitutes God's perfection and
what is required to preserve God's sovereignty. If we want the biblical texts to
function normatively in such matters, however, then this aprioristic tendency
will be inappropriate in cases where conflict with biblical claims arises. We
want Scripture to exercise normative influence on our understanding of the divine attributes. I will scrutinize this matter in chapters four and five, when I
consider Barth's critique of what he often calls the "older theology."

Divine accidents. Besides perfections, it seems that God has accidents or
contingent properties as well. These are those things true of God in some pos-

---

[33] Heppe, *Reformed Dogmatics,* p. 67.

sible worlds but not true in others. A principle (A_c), which is parallel to (A_d) above, expresses a contingent property of God:

(A_c) God has *P* in at least one world and has ~*P* in at least one other world.

Since God exists in every world, the principle for his contingent properties is simpler than it is for contingent beings.[34] For example, *having created Jay* and *choosing to create Jay* are two of God's contingent properties for which I should be eternally grateful. They are relational properties and are true in the actual world w_a. There is some other possible world, $w_{\sim j}$, in which, if it had been actual, I would not have existed. If God had made $w_{\sim j}$ actual, then *having created Jay* would not be one of God's contingent attributes. This seems to follow quite naturally from the fact that God created me and I am a contingent being.

While not prejudging the relation of God's will and choice to his essence, all of God's contingent properties seem to issue from his choice. While God has the property *having created Jay,* the fact that he created me is the result of his free choice. He does not have this property imposed on him from without. This contrasts with many of the contingent properties of contingent created beings, which are not the result of their bearer's choice. For instance, *being born in Texas* is one of my contingent properties. I could have been born in Oklahoma or New Jersey. Nevertheless, I had no choice whatsoever in bearing this property.

Among God's contingent properties will be all those properties that include contingent states of affairs, such as those concerned with creation. If this world is w_a, then all God's properties, which include his relations to constituents of w_a, will be contingent properties, truly predicated of him in the actual world, and so, truly predicated of him. None of these, however, will be part of his essence, since an essence is a set of all essential properties or at least includes that set.[35] So there is no problem concerning the contingency of creation or God's aseity with respect to it.

---

[34]God will not have the attribute *(P and ~P)* in any world, but he could have *(P and $\Diamond$ ~P)* if *P* is a contingent or accidental property. If *P* is a contingent divine property in w_p, however, then the world-indexed conjunctive property *(P-in-w_p and ~P-in-$w_{\sim p}$)* would be one of God's essential properties. But this seems trivial.

[35]Although again, world-indexed versions of these properties will be somewhat trivial essential properties. The properties amount to nothing more than the claim that, say, the conjunctive property *(If God created Jay, then God created Jay)* & *(It is possible that God created Jay)* is an essential divine property.

Although world w_a is contingent, every state of affairs in w_a need not be contingent in order for God to exist *a se,* since at least one state of affairs necessarily obtains. That is the state of affairs in which God exists, assuming his existence is a state of affairs.[36] Every possible world includes this state of affairs as one of its constituents. But this does not compromise God's ontological sufficiency, since that state of affairs is not outside him in the same way that, say, I am. So we must be careful to avoid understanding a possible world on a par with the actual world as a contingent creation. While the actual created world is contingent, there are things that are necessarily true in the actual world, such as God's existence. Dilemmas still lurk in the neighborhood, but I will postpone them until later chapters.

Also among God's contingent properties will be such items as his *being Creator of* w_a, *being Creator of Socrates* and *being Creator of Mt. Rainier.* But clearly such properties imply or presuppose some other divine property, perhaps a dispositional property, such as a divine creative ability that ontologically precedes such discrete acts. But if God had not created this or any other contingent world, would not such a property be only potential, since God would not exercise it in this way? Already we see an apparent conflict with classical theism, which claims that there is no potentiality in God. Whether it is a real conflict remains to be seen.

The trinitarian distinctions. So God has his perfections in every possible world and has various accidents in some possible worlds but not others. Aside from the traditional perfections, however, what about those properties that might never occur on an intuitive treatment of divine properties based on perfection and aseity derived from the *via triplex?* For example, what about the claim that God became human? How do we construe this? Clearly the property of (I) *becoming incarnate as the man Jesus* is a contingent property of God, or more precisely, of God the Son, since God might not have created material beings or any beings, thus obviating any need to become incarnate. This does not imply, however, that (I) is somehow unimportant or irrelevant to God or his purposes. It means that God could have remained fully himself even if he had never become incarnate.

---

[36]Some contemporary proponents of simplicity in fact argue that God's existence is not a state of affairs. We deal with this contention in chapter nine.

But if our grounds for distinguishing Father, Son and Spirit is the incarnation, then that distinction might itself be contingent. Important Christian practices prohibit this claim, however, such as praying to Jesus and calling him "Lord," as do many biblical texts, such as John 1:1, 1 Corinthians 8:4-7, Colossians 1:15-21, 2:9, Philippians 2:6 and Hebrews 1:3. The theologian who takes these as normative will argue that in Scripture we are confronted not with a generically theistic God but with the triune God for whom the incarnation, while itself contingent, reveals a preexisting capacity in God, namely, his trinitarian essence. So it is important to distinguish between (I) and trinitarianism.

While there is some diversity of trinitarian theories in the tradition, there is a cluster of identity claims that constitute the conceptual core of the doctrine, articulated in verses 16 and 17 of *Quicunque:* "Thus the Father is God, the Son God, the Holy Spirit God; and yet there are not three Gods, but there is one God."[37]

With this assertion, we enter the most peculiar aspect of the Christian doctrine of God. No Christian theology can bypass or softsell it.

Building on these identity claims is the Nicene formulation, implied in Scripture but explicitly formalized and dressed in philosophical garb in A.D. 325, that God is Father, Son and Holy Spirit, three persons (*hypostases*) and one essence (*ousia*). If one judges Nicaea as a legitimate development from Scripture, then one will join the Nicene fathers in insisting that the trinitarian distinctions are eternal and essential to God. To make the trinitarian distinctions contingent—or to relegate them to God only in his operations *ad extra,* that is, outside himself—would be to remove them from God's essence. This would land us precariously close to the ancient heresies of Arianism or Sabellianism, which inspired the Nicaean formulation. In these heresies, the Trinity tells us not about God in himself (*in se*) but about how he has appeared in history. So the essentialist committed to trinitarianism must place the trinitarian distinction(s) among God's essential properties.

Now things get complicated. On the one hand, if any perfection is an essential divine property, then, in order for a divine person such as the Son to be divine, he must possess that property and share it with the Father and Spirit.

---

[37]See also Augustine *De Trinitate* 8.1.1; 5.8-11; Gregory of Nyssa, "An Answer to Ablatius: That We Should Not Think of Saying There Are Three Gods," in *Christology of the Later Fathers,* ed. Edward R. Hardy (Philadelphia: Westminster Press, 1954), pp. 256-67.

Whatever the essence of divinity is, the divine persons of the Trinity share it.

On the other hand, while we can attribute the perfections to God and to all three persons without discrimination, this is not the case for all the trinitarian properties. For if the trinitarian distinctions are essential, then there will be essential properties that one person has which the other two lack. To be sure, they will all share some essential trinitarian properties, for example, *being a divine person, being essentially related to two other divine persons* and *being a member of the Holy Trinity.* And God in three persons will be essentially triune. At the same time the Father has the essential property of begetting the Son, whereas the Son has the essential property of being begotten by the Father. The Spirit has the essential property of proceeding from the Father and perhaps the Son, whereas the Father has the essential property of being the Source of the Spirit's procession, and so on. So should we conclude that each of the divine persons has an essence different from the other three? But then, what has become of the claim that there is one God with one divine essence?

A fully satisfying resolution to these problems would require a lengthy foray into trinitarian doctrine. Still, there is no reason to fear that essentialism puts God's unity uniquely at risk. In any analysis of the Trinity, there is always the danger of either tritheism, which posits three gods, or modalism, according to which the divine persons are merely historical modes of the same undifferentiated God.

The essentialist in particular must be careful not to construe the shared divine essence as a so-called kind essence analogous to, say, the human kind essence. The human kind essence signifies those things all human beings hold in common and that make them human. Natural kinds are not necessarily instantiated or exemplified. For instance, there are many possible worlds in which the natural kind "human" is not exemplified. There are also many possible worlds in which the individuals who exemplify the human essence in the actual world do not do so. So it is possible that the human kind essence not be exemplified, and it is possible that my unique individual essence not be exemplified. So there is a sense in which the generic human "kind essence" is detachable from all individual human beings and also that my individual essence or haecceity is detachable from me. This is not the case with the divine persons of the Trinity. Each exemplifies the divine essence essentially and necessarily. It is impossible for there to be either an unexemplified divine essence or for any of the divine persons to fail to instantiate the divine essence. It is also impossible for the individual essences of the divine persons to be uninstantiated. There is no possible world in which they fail to exemplify the divine essence, and there is no possible world in which any other entity does so. Even the very ways in which the divine persons are differentiated, namely, by their essential relations to each other, underscores their unity in differentiation.

There may be more than one orthodox way for the essentialist to articulate the Trinity. Some might be tempted to say that, in a sense, the category of haecceity or individual essence could apply to God as Trinity and to the individual persons, although in different ways. Alternatively, one might seek to distinguish the concept of individual essence from the concept of haecceity, applying the former to the Godhead and the latter to the three persons. Accordingly, the haecceity of the Godhead would be a primitive actuality irreducible to any set of properties while the individual essences of three persons would be that set of properties essential to each of them. The reverse application of haecceity and individual essence might also be possible. The danger in all of these strategies is that they risk implying that the Godhead is a fourth individual different from the Father, Son and Holy Spirit.

However it is done, we must maintain that the Godhead possesses a unique type of oneness and unity that can never obtain between separate individuals who merely exemplify the same natural kind essence. This is already implicit in the fact that Christians refer to God as well as the individual divine persons as "he" and speak of God in three persons with the singular term *God*. The three persons are divine, they are all God; but no Christian would refer to them as individual Gods.

Christian trinitarian language has other unusual features. For instance, "God" functions as a quasi-singular proper name—like a "rigid designator," to use Saul Kripke's term—and as an adjectival, descriptive term with certain implicit connotations. Thus it is informative to say, "The LORD *(Yahweh)* is God." At the same time, "God" is clearly more than an adjective. For example, to say that the Father, Son and Holy Spirit are all divine does not quite capture the complete content of saying that the Father, Son and Holy Spirit are all God. The word *God* implies a unique singularity shared by the three divine persons, whereas "divine" could be interpreted to mean that Father, Son and Spirit merely share a generic essence of divinity. Christian essentialism should preserve the former implication and avoid the latter.

The essentialist can affirm God's unity in a number of other ways. For instance, since there is no possibility of an unexemplified divine essence or of another instantiation of the divine essence by some other divine person, one might say that the Trinity is no less personal and no more abstract than the three divine persons individually. No merely abstract divine essence stands behind the three divine persons. Moreover, the divine persons share an existence, will, agency and subjectivity more unified than the most intimate of human relationships. The New Testament is replete with references to this intertrinitarian life. The Father can create all things in the Son and reconcile all things through him (Col 1:15-16). The Father sends the Holy Spirit to the church, and the Son speaks through the Holy Spirit (Acts 1:2). The Holy Spirit fills the Son (Lk 4:1) and descends upon him (Mk 1:10). The Son can baptize the repentant sinner with the Holy Spirit (Mk 1:8). No term for human community or society can capture such intimacy and unity.

Similarly, the modal relations of the divine persons are unique and without creaturely parallel. The three persons, unlike most individuals who instantiate a natural kind essence, are all essentially and necessarily related to each other. They cannot fail to be related and to be related in the very ways they are related, that is, with respect to their essential relations. The Father, Son and Spirit exist in every possible world and are related to each other in every possible world as they are related in the actual world. Their relations in various possible worlds differ only with respect to their accidents or contingent properties. Also, since God is immaterial (that is, apart from the incarnation) the divine persons are not separated from one another by space or physical bodies, but they coexist and interpenetrate one another as eternal persons of the one Godhead.

Although much more could be said, this should be adequate to suggest that essentialism has the basic resources for articulating an orthodox doctrine of the Trinity. Expressing the unique oneness and threeness of the Godhead in human language is never easy. But these difficulties attend trinitarian doctrine in general, not essentialism in particular. If anything, essentialism makes the task a bit easier.

Divine incommunicable attributes. Now that we have considered the divine perfections, the doctrine of the Trinity and divine accidents, we are ready to ponder the incommunicable attributes, such as simplicity, immutability, eternity, immensity, infinity and aseity. For the classical theist, if God has any essential properties, it is these. As Heppe notes, these attributes are God's "essential properties"; they are "God's essential properties of the first order . . . predicated as it were *a priori,* as He is; i.e., they declare the essence of God as it is in Himself absolutely" (p. 63). Moreover, these attributes, which seem to have their basis primarily in the *via negativa,* hang together very tightly. For instance, since immutability is classically taken to require the absence of all change in God, eternity is interpreted not only as everlastingness or necessary existence but also as timelessness. Why? If God were not timeless, then God would have temporal properties, so that, say, *now listening to Augustine's prayers* would be a divine property at, say, A.D. 400 but would not be one at A.D. 2000. In such a case, God would change as time passes.[38]

Classical theists also infer a doctrine of simplicity from the doctrine of divine aseity. In its various forms, simplicity can mean that God has no parts and composition, that God possesses no more than one property, that his existence is identical to his essence, and that he has no accidents or contingent properties. Moreover, some defenders of divine simplicity argue that God, God's properties, existence and essence are somehow identical.[39] Clearly certain formulations of these incommunicable attributes will not be compatible with essentialism. To succeed, therefore, the essentialist must block the inference from divine aseity and perfection to some forms of simplicity and immutability but certainly not to all. I will attempt this in chapters eight and nine.

While essentialism as described here emerges naturally from some basic Christian convictions, that large part of Christian tradition I have called classical theism has steadfastly avoided this strategy. Even Karl Barth and Charles Hartshorne, who were both deeply critical of the classical theistic doctrine of God, did not pursue this approach. If my argument is successful, I hope it will become clear how others, with other philosophical viewpoints, might have rightly avoided the distinctions I have recommended with respect to God, and, nevertheless, why it can still be appropriate for a contemporary doctrine of God, within a different philosophical framework.

---

[38] I will qualify this claim in chapter eight when I treat immutability directly.

[39] Although, as we will see in chapter nine, philosophers and theologians intensely dispute the meaning of these claims.

4

KARL BARTH'S
ACTUALISTIC DOCTRINE OF GOD

W e come now to the magisterial theology of Swiss theologian Karl Barth, especially his understanding of God as Being in Act. Barth defended his perspective, and in some ways defined it over against, Protestant liberalism or neo-Protestantism on the one hand and Roman Catholicism on the other. While he retained a sort of love/hate relationship with Protestant Scholasticism, he was deeply critical of the so-called *analogia entis* (analogy of being), which he understood as the fundamental conceptual motif of Roman Catholicism. He was generally critical of Protestant Scholasticism when it betrayed the influence of the *analogia entis*. Barth did not frequently criticize "classical theism" by name,[1] although much of his critique against the "general" or "abstract" concept of being employed by Catholics and Protestant Scholastics is a relevant critique of classical theism.

In the next two chapters I seek a creative interaction between Barth's proposal and my own, rather than a simple analysis of his views. In order to treat his thought fairly, I first introduce his theological method in general, isolating his doctrine of God and his so-called actualism, in which he thinks of God not as Being or a being, but as "being-in-act." I then discuss his understanding of analogy, which illustrates the role of actualism in his theological perspective.

---

[1]However, he does refer to Thomas's thought in at least one place as "classical theism." See "Fate and Idea in Theology," in *The Way of Theology in Karl Barth*, ed. H. Martin Rumscheidt (Allison Park, Penn.: Pickwick, 1986), p. 33.

THE PRIORITY OF THE WORD IN
BARTH'S THEOLOGICAL PROGRAM

Barth earnestly sought to ground his theological reflection in the revealed Word of God and not in any prior philosophical or anthropological program. Although he does not identify the Word with the text of Scripture as such, Barth's declarations of this priority reflect the traditional Reformed emphasis on the Word of God expressed in the dictum *sola Scriptura.* While he often showed great respect to nineteenth-century Protestant liberalism, Barth's decision to ground Christian dogmatics, or what we might call systematic theology, in the revealed Word of God is in part a polemic against the liberal turn toward the human subject as the primary object of theological reflection.[2] His break with his liberal mentors is obvious in the fiery and dialectical *Epistle to the Romans,* but he first announces his discovery of a different basis for doing theology in his work *Anselm: Fides Quaerens Intellectum.*[3]

While some interpreters may mistake Anselm's ontological argument for the existence of God as a rationalist enterprise par excellence, Barth argues that Anselm has taken his stand on the reality of God as he is revealed in the incarnation. Contrary to reputation, Anselm is expositing the implications of the faith that have been delivered to him. As Barth puts it, "Anselm always has the solution of his problems already behind him (through faith in the impartial good sense of the decisions of ecclesiastical authority), while, as it were, they are still ahead."[4] Because theology has a proper object of consideration, it is rational, and so for Barth theology is a science.

In the introduction to his *Church Dogmatics,* Barth defends the rational and scientific status of theology for similar reasons.[5] He also insists that the proper

---

[2] He expresses both these attitudes in *Die Protestantische Theologie im 19. Jahrhundert,* translated by Brian Cozens as *Protestant Thought: From Rousseau to Ritschl* (New York: Harper & Row, 1959). Chapter one, "Man in the Eighteenth Century," tells the story of the absolute man whose enlightenment and progress seemed inevitable. In *The Theology of Schleiermacher,* ed. Dietrich Ritschl (Grand Rapids, Mich.: Eerdmans, 1982), he exhibits the same general conviction.

[3] Karl Barth, *Anselm: Fides Quaerens Intellectum* (London: SCM Press, 1960).

[4] Ibid., p. 25.

[5] Karl Barth, *Church Dogmatics* 1/1, 2nd ed., trans. G. T. Thomson (Edinburgh: T & T Clark, 1975), pp. 3-17 (hereafter cited as *CD*). He argues that theology is a science for three reasons: (1) it is a human concern with a definite object of knowledge, (2) it has a definite and self-consistent path of knowledge and (3) "it must give an account of this path to itself and to all others who are capable of concern for this object and therefore of treading this path" (p. 8). He gives three practical reasons as

object of theology be grounded in faith in the reality of divine revelation and should not be encumbered by an a priori construct culled from philosophy[6] or metaphysics apart from revelation.[7]

The sole legitimate criterion for dogmatics is the Word of God.[8] At the same time, the theologian's access to the Word is indirect, because the Word of God proclaimed in the church is his or her direct object of concern:

> The datum from which dogmatics begins is neither God nor revelation nor faith. This is the datum from which proclamation starts . . . its datum is different, namely, the questionable fact that in proclamation God, revelation and faith are talked about by men in human terms. . . . It deals with God, revelation and faith only in respect of their reflection in proclamation. . . . We have it as it gives itself to us if we have it. In this way, in contrast to all the objects of metaphysics or psychology, it is the object of proclamation.[9]

We should attend to the precise meaning Barth gives to the phrase "Word of God." On the one hand, he does not strictly identify it with the biblical text; on the other hand, he is loath to separate the Word from the words of Scripture. In Barth's understanding, the Word has a threefold form like the Trinity. He speaks of the Word as preached, written and revealed (see below), which we might define as the definitive and particular divine act of and in Jesus Christ, who speaks uniquely through the witness of Scripture.

At times, Barth's dialectical language of what he calls God's veiling and

---

well: (1) it is a search for truth, (2) the theologian should not surrender the term *science* to pagans and (3) theology refuses to take heathenism seriously (p. 11). At the same time, he repudiates the verificationist criteria (pp. 8-9). Theology is also an enquiry: "Dogmatics as an enquiry presupposes that the true content of Christian talk about God must be known by men" (p. 13). But this true content is defined as divine act and not as a deposit of truths (p. 15).

[6]Barth speaks of "philosophy" variously. When he contrasts it with the proper basis or criterion for knowledge of God, he uses "philosophy" to refer to any human-inspired attempt to acquire theological knowledge apart from divine self-revelation. He does not, however, oppose philosophy as such any more than any other field of inquiry.

[7]"Dogmatics is quite impossible except as an act of faith, in the determination of human action by listening to Jesus Christ and as obedience to Him. Without faith it would be irrelevant and meaningless" (*CD* 1/1, p. 17).

[8]*CD* 1/1, pp. 47ff.

[9]*CD* 1/1, pp. 82, 91-92.

unveiling in the revelatory act is paradoxical: "Revelation in the Bible means the self-unveiling, imparted to men, of the God who by nature cannot be unveiled to men."[10] However, his motivation for this dialectical "rhetoric of grandeur" appears to be his desire to preserve God's freedom, rather than a mere penchant for confusing speech. The Word is unveiled in this revelatory act, according to Barth, but since we have it only in earthly form, it is also veiled.[11]

Reflecting his conviction that dogmatics is a rational enterprise, Barth's *Church Dogmatics* takes on a systematized form similar to Thomas's *Summa Theologica* and the works of the later Protestant Scholastics. While the Word is preeminent, the task of the theologian is not simply to summarize or repeat the claims of Scripture but to test "the coherence of present-day proclamation with the originally and prevailing essence of the Church."[12]

While Barth takes the traditional dogmatic enterprise very seriously, he does not hesitate to depart from a traditional form where he perceives a lack of congruence between it and the revealed Word. Consequently he switches the order of the traditional medieval and Protestant scholastic dogmatic *loci*, placing the doctrine of the Trinity at the beginning of the *Church Dogmatics* rather than after his discussion of God's essence and attributes.[13] In addition, he places discussion of the Trinity in what functions as his prolegomena, 1/1, *The Doctrine of the Word of God,* when he contemplates and defends the priority of God's self-revelation.[14] Most Barth scholars interpret this or-

---

[10] *CD* 1/1, p. 315.

[11] *CD* 1/1, p. 188. This paradoxical, even contradictory, way of speaking is common when Barth describes the dialectic of God's veiling and unveiling. For example: "A fully restrained and fully alive doctrine of God's attributes will take as its fundamental point of departure the truth that God is for us fully revealed and fully concealed in His self-disclosure" (*CD* 2/1, trans. T. H. L. Parker, W. B. Johnson, H. Knight and J. L. M. Haire [Edinburgh: T & T Clark, 1957], p. 341). This looks like a bald contradiction. However, given a principle of charity, we should probably interpret Barth as being provocative when he speaks in this way. If we take such statements too literally, we would have to conclude that Barth had no scruples about contradicting himself, which is unlikely, given the value he placed on the rational content of theology.

[12] *CD* 1/1, p. 56.

[13] The only medievals who reverse this order as Barth does were Peter Lombard in his *Sentences* and Bonaventura in his *Breviloquium*. See *CD* 1/1, p. 300.

[14] *CD* 1/1, p. 303. He criticizes Friedrich Schleiermacher for making the Trinity a mere appendix to his *Glaubenslehre* and states his own motivation clearly: "In giving this doctrine a place of prominence our concern cannot be merely that it have this place externally but rather that its content be decisive and controlling for the whole of dogmatics."

der as reflecting his intention that the Trinity be decisive for the content of his dogmatics.[15]

While the placement of the Trinity signals its importance for Barth's theology, it also underscores the proximity between Barth's understanding of the Trinity and his concept of revelation. Like the Trinity, the Word of God as revelation has a threefold, "triune" form: the Word of God preached, written and revealed.[16] The Trinity is its only analogy: "This is the doctrine of the triunity of God . . . we can substitute for revelation, Scripture and proclamation the names of the divine persons Father, Son and Holy Spirit and *vice versa*."[17] This Word is God's speech to human beings as God's act and is wholly the result of divine initiative. Since this revelation is actual, there is no sense in inquiring into the mere possibility of a revelation. Questions about the possibility or nature of revelation are "philosophical rather than theological questions."[18] From an analysis of revelation, we may infer that God is a personal, purposive and free subject.[19] The "speech-act" of revelation, however, is a mysterious divine decision and is not subject to human control.

Immediately following his introduction in 1/1 of his *Church Dogmatics*, Barth declares, "[T]he Christian concept of revelation already includes within it the problem of the doctrine of the Trinity."[20] Like a variation on a common theme, he repeats over and over: God "reveals Himself *through* Himself,"[21] beginning chapter 2 of 1/1 on "The Revelation of God" thus: "God's Word is God Himself in His revelation. For God reveals Himself as the Lord and according to Scripture this signifies for the concept of revelation that God Himself in unimpaired unity yet also in unimpaired distinction is Revealer, Revelation, and Revealedness."[22] God is subject, object and predicate in the act of revelation.

---

[15]The ordering is important to followers of Barth as well. For instance, Eberhard Jüngel deems it "a hermeneutical decision of the greatest relevance" in *Gottes Sein Ist im Werden* (Tübingen: J. C. B. Mohr, 1966); English translation by Horton Harris, *The Doctrine of the Trinity: God's Being Is in Becoming* (Edinburgh: Scottish Academic Press, 1976), p. 5.

[16]*CD* 1/1, pp. 88-120.

[17]Ibid., p. 121.

[18]Ibid., p. 125.

[19]Ibid., pp. 136-39.

[20]Ibid., p. 304.

[21]Ibid., p. 296.

[22]Ibid., p. 295.

In fact, the doctrine of the Trinity is simply an explication of the claim that "God reveals himself as the Lord." This statement is analytic and is not susceptible to a distinction between form and content.[23] Lordship expresses God's freedom and ability to reveal himself and is equivalent to God's deity, his *"[ousia], essentia, natura,* or *substantia."*[24]

THE TRINITY

To discuss Barth on revelation and the basis of dogmatics, then, is to unpack his concept of the Trinity. According to Barth, God reveals himself through a free act ("Godhead in the Bible means freedom, ontic and noetic autonomy") in these three ways, such revelation being God's self-interpretation: "It is proper to Him to distinguish Himself from Himself, i.e., to be God in Himself and in concealment, and yet at the same time to be God a second time in a very different way, namely, in manifestation, i.e., in the form of something He Himself is not." Without ceasing to be the veiled God, he becomes the unveiled in revelation. The hidden God *(Deus absconditus)* is the revealed God *(Deus revelatus)*. God can become his own alter ego.[25] Since revelation is God's self-interpretation, one can rightly say, "God corresponds to himself."[26] This dark saying is so central to Barth's understanding of the Trinity that Eberhard Jüngel contends, "In actuality Barth's Dogmatics is basically a detailed exegesis of this proposition. . . . The Church Dogmatics is the ingenious and diligent attempt to think the proposition 'God corresponds to himself' through to the end."[27]

The *Church Dogmatics* 1/1, §9, "The Triunity of God," begins, "The God who reveals himself according to Scripture is One in three distinctive modes of being, subsisting in their mutual relations: Father, Son, and Holy Spirit. It is thus that He is the Lord, i.e., the Thou who meets man's I and unites

---

[23]Ibid., p. 306. Colin Gunton softens the implications of this claim by noting that for Barth, the statement is analytic but is still grounded in the specifics of divine self-revelation. For this reason, Barth's claim is not a philosophical claim of an a priori analytic but is rather an analytic a posteriori statement. See Gunton's *Becoming and Being: The Doctrine of God in Charles Hartshorne and Karl Barth* (Oxford: Oxford University Press, 1976), p. 130.

[24]*CD* 1/1, p. 349.

[25]Ibid., pp. 316, 330.

[26]*CD* 2/1, pp. 657-60.

[27]Jüngel, *Doctrine of the Trinity*, p. 24, n.15.

Himself to this I as the indissoluble Subject[28] and thereby and therein reveals Himself to him as his God."[29] Barth settles on the term *triunity* as a dialectical outworking of the Trinity as a "unity in Trinity" and a "Trinity in unity."

He avoids the use of the term *person* as a translation of *hypostasis, prosopon* and *persona* because he fears that this might imply, in contemporary parlance, "that there are three personalities in God. This would be the worst and most extreme expression of tritheism against which we must be on guard at this stage."[30] On the contrary, "personality" in contemporary terms "belongs to the one unique essence of God which the doctrine of the Trinity does not seek to triple but rather to recognise in its simplicity."[31] God reveals himself, not just as power but as person, "i.e., as an I existing in and for itself with its own thought and will."[32] So the Godhead is irreducibly personal. Barth's motivation for applying categories of personality to the one God, and not to the three divine persons in distinction, is clear. In the nineteenth century, self-consciousness was added to (as Barth sees it) the already inadequate Boethian definition of person as an individual rational essence, making the connotations of the term inappropriate for trinitarian explanation.[33]

For Barth, "the doctrine of the triunity of God . . . does not entail . . . any abrogation or even questioning but rather the final and decisive confirmation of the insight that God is One."[34] Nevertheless, we should not think of God as a mere isolated singularity as in Hellenistic monotheism. Neither should we think that God is reciprocally related to the world in the sense that he needs the world, which would obviously violate God's freedom and aseity. Rather, we should recognize that the revealed unity of God includes a distinction in the essence of God of three modes of being (*Sein-*

---

[28]For more on this, see James Brown, *Subject and Object in Theology* (New York: Macmillan, 1955), chap. 6.

[29]*CD* 2/1, p. 348.

[30]Ibid., p. 351.

[31]Ibid., p. 350.

[32]*CD* 1/1, pp. 358-59.

[33]*CD* 2/1, pp. 356-58.

[34]*CD* 2/1, p. 348.

weisen). This expresses an incomprehensible mystery for which there is no analogy.[35]

The relation between God's acts and essence is central in Barth's doctrine of God. On the one hand, he says that God's acts are God's essence, even though God is not reducible to his acts.[36] On the other hand, he says we should distinguish between God's essence and his acts, although we know him only by his acts. What is clear is that Barth seeks to maintain a unity between the immanent and economic Trinity—between the Trinity as it is from eternity and the Trinity as revealed in history—so that the way God reveals himself in history discloses the way God is antecedently in himself.[37] Otherwise, revelation would not be real revelation but mere appearance, an example not of God's being but of his mere becoming. Barth wants to avoid a Platonic division of two worlds—one in which God exists in and unto himself (*in se*) and another in which he exists *ad extra* or "for us"—with its resultant skepticism concerning our knowledge of God.[38]

Barth does allow hesitantly the doctrine of appropriations, whereby specific works can be "appropriated" to one of the three divine modes of being. This emphasizes the concreteness of God's being. He balances this dialectically,

---

[35]Ibid., pp. 354-56. Some of his language leads critics to accuse Barth of modalism: "The name of Father, Son and Spirit means that God is the one God in threefold repetition, . . . the three persons being the *repetitio aeternitatis in aeternitate*" (ibid., pp. 351-53). At the same time, he is explicit that God's triunity is not merely part of the divine economy, as it was for ancient modalists such as the Sabellians, but is part of God's eternal essence: "God's modes of being are not to be exchanged or confounded. In all three modes of being God is the one God both in Himself and in relation to the world and man. But this one God is God three times in different ways, so different that it is only in this threefold difference that He is God, so different that in this difference, this being in these three modes of being, is absolutely essential to Him, so different, then, that this difference is irremovable" (ibid., p. 360).

The three are not simply masks, behind which hides the one hidden God. These three moments are not alien to God's being. Such ontological separation of the three "modes of being" from the divine essence is the core proposition by which he defines modalism (ibid., p. 382). In this way, he distinguishes his position from modalism. For Barth, there is a threefoldness in the way God "authenticates his reality," and from this we infer that there is such a threefoldness in God's being (Gunton, *Becoming and Being*, p. 128). This is a crucial methodological move for Barth, since it allows him to speak of God as a Trinity while avoiding the appearance of untoward "speculation," which for him was anathema.

[36]*CD* 2/1, p. 271. Cf. *CD* 1/1, p. 371. Just what this means requires careful deliberation. We return to it below.

[37]*CD* 1/1, pp. 479-80.

[38]*CD* 2/1, p. 371. See Jüngel, *The Doctrine of the Trinity*, p. 33.

however, with the doctrine of the *unum principium,* according to which God's total being is present in every divine act.[39]

Barth sees the *perichoresis* or *circumincessio* (indwelling) of the divine persons as a form of dialectical outworking, in which "the divine modes of being mutually condition and permeate one another so completely that one is always in the other two and the other two in the one."[40] *Perichoresis* has a dual function. On the one hand, Barth uses it to distinguish the divine persons: "God already negates in Himself, from eternity, in His absolute simplicity, all loneliness, self-containment, or self-isolation. Also and precisely in himself, from eternity, in His absolute simplicity, God is orientated to the Other, does not will to be without the Other, will have Himself only as He has Himself with the Other and indeed in the Other."[41]

On the other hand, the concept relativizes the distinction among the three since none of the three exists as a "special individual." Rather, "all three 'in-exist' or exist only in concert as modes of being of the one God and Lord who posits Himself from eternity to eternity."[42]

Barth's treatment of the Trinity appropriates a great deal from the tradition, including medieval and Reformed Scholasticism, which he often calls the "older theology." Unless one understands his so-called actualistic ontology, however, one will miss his proposal's peculiarity and originality.

BARTH'S ACTUALISTIC DOCTRINE OF GOD

The intended basis for dogmatic statements in Barth's *Church Dogmatics* is summarized nicely by Herbert Hartwell in his introductory text *The Theology of Karl Barth:* "The Church Dogmatics is concerned with the exposition and interpretation of a *story,* the story of God's gracious dealings with mankind in Jesus Christ from eternity."[43] This aspect of his thought, which Barth scholar George Hunsinger calls actualism, is most relevant to essentialism. Barth tries to avoid speaking of God as Being in the abstract but rather to always speak of him as being-in-act, specifically,

---

[39]Ibid., pp. 373-35.

[40]Ibid., p. 370; cf. p. 485.

[41]Ibid., p. 483.

[42]Ibid., p. 370. The expression that the Lord "posits himself" is peculiar to Barth and hints at the idealist concepts he exploits to explicate trinitarian doctrine.

[43]Herbert Hartwell, *The Theology of Karl Barth: An Introduction* (Philadelphia: Westminster Press, 1964), p. 17.

the "act" of Jesus Christ. But since Hunsinger's interpretation is itself so illuminating, it is worth summarizing before considering actualism in detail.

George Hunsinger's typology. Many Barth expositors have faltered by trying to subsume Barth's approach under a single interpretive scheme. In doing so, they have failed to capture the complexity of his theology. The virtue of Hunsinger's interpretation[44] is that it combines the various recurring themes isolated by other interpreters. Hunsinger does not seek to summarize Barth with these themes. He sees them rather as a result of "pattern recognition" and "motif research." He intends them to facilitate Barth interpretation but not to predict Barth's arguments or substitute for reading Barth.[45] Moreover, Hunsinger does not imply that these are systematic or philosophical principles in Barth: "The motifs are adjectival in force, not substantive." He surmises that Barth employs these themes "because he thinks they help to illuminate certain peculiar modes of thought implicit in the witness of scripture."[46]

The summary above already implies most of the six motifs Hunsinger isolates. They are "particularism,"[47] "objectivism,"[48] "personalism," "realism,"

---

[44]George Hunsinger, *How to Read Karl Barth: The Shape of His Theology* (New York: Oxford University Press, 1991).

[45]Ibid., pp. vii-viii.

[46]Ibid., p. 31. Hunsinger's approach has one implication certain scholars might find suspicious, namely, that Barth's views are generally consistent throughout the *Church Dogmatics*. There is no doubt some development in the *Dogmatics*. After all, Barth wrote them over a period of more than thirty years. Nevertheless, the *Church Dogmatics* manifest a remarkable thematic unity. Thus, I find Hunsinger's reading of Barth quite convincing overall.

The development of Barth's theology is a point of contention in Barth scholarship. Hans Urs von Balthasar argued early that Barth underwent a conversion in his thought. He claimed that, whereas Barth showed a strong dialectical emphasis in *The Epistle to the Romans* and the early parts of his *Church Dogmatics,* by the time he came to the christological sections of the *Dogmatics,* he had undergone a conversion to a method of analogy. *Karl Barth: Darstellung und Deutung Seiner Theologie* (Köln: Verlag Jakob Hegner, 1951), translated into English by Edward T. Oakes, *The Theology of Karl Barth* (San Francisco: Ignatius Press, 1992). More recently, Bruce L. McCormack has argued that far more continuity exists between Barth's earlier and later thought, in *Karl Barth's Critically Realistic Dialectical Theology: Its Genesis and Development 1909-1936* (Oxford: Clarendon, 1995). I will not enter this debate here, except to submit that the theme of actualism continues throughout the *Church Dogmatics,* even if an emphasis on analogy does appear more frequently in the later volumes.

[47]Robert Jenson emphasizes this theme in *God After God: The God of the Past and the Future as Seen in the Work of Karl Barth* (Indianapolis: Bobbs-Merrill, 1969).

[48]Thomas Torrance, in *Karl Barth: An Introduction to His Early Theology, 1910-1931* (London: SCM Press, 1962), emphasizes the objectivism of Barth's view of revelation. Hunsinger notes (correctly in my opinion) that Torrance so emphasizes this theme in Barth that the other themes are given short shrift. And with respect to particularism and especially actualism, Torrance's reading weakens the uniqueness of Barth's proposal. See Hunsinger, *How to Read Karl Barth,* pp. 10-11.

"rationalism"[49] and, most relevant to our concerns, "actualism."[50]

Barth's particularism is his emphasis on the event of Jesus for our knowledge of God and for our theological understanding. It names his intention to move in dogmatic theology from the particular acts of God to our understanding of God and not to pursue that knowledge through some general extrinsic metaphysical or philosophical procedure. Objectivism relates to Barth's understanding of revelation and salvation. Contrary to theological liberalism, Barth believes our knowledge of God as well as our salvation lies outside ourselves. Personalism is reflected in the intimate language of I-Thou, which Barth uses to describe our encounter with God. God's self-revelation "comes to the creature in the form of personal address."[51] God remains "indissolubly subject" in his revelation, a subject we cannot "get behind."[52] Realism describes Barth's understanding of reference in theological language. He believes such language can rightly refer analogically to its object, although he insists that this reference is a miracle implying no intrinsic capacity of language. So, while different from Thomas's account of analogical reference, Barth's position, according to Hunsinger, lies between the literal reference of univocity on the one hand and mere expressivism on the other. (Barth's understanding of analogical theological language puts Barth in the company of Thomas, unbeknownst to Barth. See below.)

Finally, rationalism points to Barth's conviction that, since the theologian uses reason in theological reflection, theology is rational. While theology is not reducible to a posit of truths, it has cognitive and assertive implications. Of course, Barth is not a rationalist in the sense that he seeks to ground dogmatics in a neutral and universal reason. On the contrary, he takes his stand with Anselm that theology is an expression of "faith seeking understanding."

I mention these other themes to avoid implying that actualism is the only important theme in Barth's theology. That said, I will limit consideration to ac-

---

[49]This motif and this term come from Hartwell's *Theology of Karl Barth,* pp. 32-37, which Hunsinger credits, *How to Read Karl Barth,* p. 20. While not naming them as Hunsinger does, he also recognizes objectivism and realism.

[50]While Barth and the possible worlds actualist intend to grant priority to the actual over the merely possible, Barth's actualism is not the same as the actualism described in chapter two. Actualism in Barth might be summarized by the proposition that God as the preeminent Subject has his being in his act.

[51]Hunsinger, *How to Read Karl Barth,* p. 5.

[52]*CD* 1/1, p. 382.

tualism because it has the most significant implications for Barth's criticism of the Thomistic, medieval and Protestant Scholastic doctrine of God. It is also the most germane point of contact with Christian essentialism.

This theme is easily confused with Barth's particularism, which indicates the epistemic importance he places on God's self-revelation in his Word. The actuality of God's revelation trumps all abstract questions about the nature or possibility of a divine revelation. This theme is related to actualism but does not come to the same thing.[53] For this reason, the Barth interpreter should avoid conflating particularism with actualism. Particularism *simpliciter* does not entail actualism any more than empiricism entails phenomenalism.

Actualism in particular. Generally, Barth's actualism is his insistence always to think of God not simply as being but as being-in-act. Thus Barth conceives of being as an event, or as an act when an agent is involved. Language of event, decision, occurrence and act permeates the *Church Dogmatics,* from the treatment of revelation and the Trinity to the divine attributes, election, reconciliation, ecclesiology and eschatology. No doctrine lacks its influence. This insistence on viewing God as being-in-act has different facets. When Barth contemplates the status of creation and human beings, he stresses their dependence on the free act of God in sustaining them.[54] When he ponders election, he speaks of God's choosing his people "in and with Himself."[55] In his doctrine of God, actualism is manifest in his refusal to separate God from his acts: "God is who He is in the act of His revelation."[56] Out of context, such a claim is ambiguous. Usually, however, Barth qualifies such statements to prevent one from interpreting "is" in his statement as a simple identity claim. His concern is clear: he wants to avoid the traditional error he perceives of positing a God *a se* "behind" the concrete revelation of God *ad extra.* He seeks to avoid a dualism of an unknown God, derived from a general concept of being, lurking behind "God" as he is known in revelation.[57] To posit such a dualism is for

---

[53]One interpreter who makes too little of the difference between these themes is John Colwell in *Actuality and Provisionality: Eternity and Election in the Theology of Karl Barth* (Edinburgh: Rutherford House Books, 1989), pp. 183-95.

[54]*CD* 2/1, pp. 257-321.

[55]*CD* 2/2, p. 76.

[56]*CD* 2/1, p. 257; cf. p. 272.

[57]"The reality of God in His revelation cannot be bracketed by an 'only,' as though somewhere behind His revelation there stood another reality of God" (*CD* 1/1, p. 479).

Barth tantamount to denying that in Jesus Christ God truly is revealed. He shuns any bifurcation between God's acts in revelation and his being or between his saving activity and his eternal attributes. To do otherwise is to eschew the very basis by which we come to know God. Our access to God's essence is in revelation and nowhere else: "What God is as God, the divine individuality and characteristics, the *essentia* or 'essence' of God, is something which we shall encounter either at the place where God deals with us as Lord and Saviour, or not at all."[58]

Actualism also appears in Barth's refusal to separate God's will and being: "To say 'God' is to say 'God's will.'" "It is as He wills that He is God, and as He is God that he wills." God is the "One who wills Himself,"[59] and "His being is decision."[60] Unlike all other realities, God "exists absolutely" in his act. "No other being is absolutely its own, conscious, willed and executed decision."[61] Moreover, God is self-moved and self-determined.[62] When developing the doctrine of election, Barth even says that God in some sense "wills" to be God:

> We maintain of God that in Himself, in the primal and basic decision in which He wills to be and actually is God, in the mystery of what takes place from and to all eternity within Himself, within His triune being, God is none other than the one who in His Son or Word elects Himself, and in and with Himself elects His people. . . . There is no height or depth in which God can be God in any other way.[63]

Understandably, some interpreters say that, in Barth's view, God is "event"[64] and is "something that happens."[65] The *Church Dogmatics* offers some textual support for this interpretation: "God is in Himself free event, free act and free life." Despite the startling nature of such claims, Barth insists that their mean-

---

[58]*CD* 2/1, p. 261.

[59]*CD* 2/1, pp. 548, 550.

[60]*CD* 2/2, p. 175; cf. p. 271. Similar ways of speaking may also evince a commitment to divine simplicity. See below.

[61]Ibid., p. 271.

[62]Ibid., p. 269.

[63]Ibid., pp. 76-77.

[64]Jüngel, *Doctrine of the Trinity*.

[65]Colin Gunton, "Karl Barth's Doctrine of Election as Part of His Doctrine of God," *Journal of Theological Studies* 31 (1980): 387.

ing comes from revelation, and not from any abstract definitions of event, act and life.[66]

Robert Jenson interprets this aspect of Barth's thought in this way: "Here is Barth's final ontological classification of God's being. God is the free event, independent even of his own nature yet nonetheless having a nature, because he decides to be and to be what he is."[67] Jenson seems to read Barth as claiming that God's essence is subject to his choice, that God is in some way "independent" of his essence. Since this interpretation of Barth's actualism is obscure and difficult to interpret, it merits detailed analysis below.

Person as being-in-act. More than a simple argument, actualism seems to function as an overarching presupposition that informs Barth's entire *Church Dogmatics.*[68] Clearly Barth's actualism expresses his conviction that God is a Subject, in fact, the indissoluble Subject. And he assumes that the sine qua non of a subject is that it is a being in act. While it is similar terminologically, we should not identify this claim with the classical notion of God as *Actus Purus.* While there is some similarity, classical theists meant that God is Pure Act in the sense that he has no mere potency. This Aristotelian potency-act distinction is different from Barth's meaning.[69]

So actualism seems to emerge from a definition of what it is to be a person. It comprises a sort of "macro-argument" in the *Church Dogmatics,* which David Kelsey describes this way. Barth infers from the premise of freedom and love in Jesus, that is, God *ad extra,* to God's being *in se.* The "warrant" for the inference is the assumption that a person is a being-in-act.[70]

In a way similar to Thomas's application of perfections *via* the *analogia attributionis,* Barth asserts that only God is truly a person in this way:

No other being exists absolutely in its act. No other being is absolutely its own,

---

[66]*CD* 2/1, p. 264.

[67]Jenson, *God After God,* p. 127.

[68]I owe this point to a conversation with Bruce L. McCormack.

[69]Thomas's view may be less distant from Barth than Barth realized, since Thomas understood existence as itself an act. So Thomas frequently claimed, *"agere sequitur esse."* See W. Norris Clarke, *Explorations in Metaphysics* (Notre Dame, Ind.: University of Notre Dame Press, 1994), pp. 5-12.

[70] See David Kelsey, *The Uses of Scripture in Recent Theology* (Philadelphia: Fortress, 1975), pp. 133-34, for a diagram of Barth's "macro-argument" for the divine perfections. Nancey Murphy simplifies the argument somewhat in *Reasoning and Rhetoric in Theology* (Valley Forge, Penn.: Trinity Press International, 1994), p. 187.

conscious, willed and executed decision. . . . Now, if the being of a person is a being in act, and if, in the strict and proper sense, being in act can be ascribed only to God, then it follows that by the concept of the being of a person, in the strict and proper sense, we can understand only the being of God. Being in its own, conscious, willed and executed decision, and therefore personal being, is the being of God in the nature of the Father and the Son and the Holy Spirit. . . . We cannot speak of "personalising" in reference to God's being, but only in reference to ours. The real person is not man but God. It is not God who is a person by extension, but we. God exists in His act. God is His own decision. God lives from and by Himself.[71]

This analysis rests on the assumption that a person is a being-in-act and that God is the exemplary person. Barth is able to derive the divine attributes from the premise that God is the paradigmatic personal agent, which is a being-in-act.[72]

So, although this notion may be generally consistent with the biblical witness, it is not the product of exegesis alone but also of a particular philosophical analysis of "person."[73] Barth apparently sees the notion of a person as being in act to be a philosophical concept which, when rightly appropriated, illuminates and is congruent with the revealed Word. On this analysis Barth builds his searching treatment of the divine attributes.

ACTUALISM AND *ANALOGIA ENTIS*
Comprehending Barth's actualism requires understanding his polemic against what he calls the *analogia entis* (analogy of being). This is for him, as Hans Urs von Balthasar puts it, "the guiding and all-determining formal principle" in Roman Catholic theology.[74] Barth probably acquired this interpretation from

---

[71]*CD* 2/1, pp. 271-72. This reasoning is common if usually implicit: "In the light of the definition of His being as a being in act we described God as a person." "Man finds what a person is when he finds it in the person of God and his own being as a person in the gift of fellowship afforded him by God in person" (p. 284).

[72]Incidentally, if this use of *analogia attributionis* is legitimate in principle with respect to the concept of person, then it is legitimate for Thomas to pursue the same strategy with respect to the concept of being. And this is precisely what Thomas does. So Barth's criticism of Thomas's actual procedure appears wide of the mark.

[73]Kelsey calls Barth's analysis in §§28-29 "a rudimentary ontology of personal agency" (*Uses of Scripture in Recent Theology,* p. 134).

[74]Von Balthasar, *Theology of Karl Barth,* p. 35, n. 47.

Erich Przywara.[75] Barth's polemic against the *analogia entis* permeates the *Dogmatics* and constitutes his harshest criticism of Roman Catholicism.[76] His relentless animadversion toward natural theology stems from this polemic.

His depiction of the *analogia entis* is the foil over against which he developed his *Church Dogmatics*. In his view, the theologian who uses the *analogia entis* commits the disastrous error of interpreting divine revelation according to a general and abstract concept of being, which we use to understand creatures in the finite realm. By doing so, the theologian restricts God by circumscribing God and creatures under a general concept.[77] Not only does this put both "really within a system of being superior to both," it also leaves open the possibility of inverting the place of Creator and creature.[78] Such a theologian thinks in terms of a "God-creature system," which is really ontology and not theology.[79]

In its place Barth puts the *analogia fidei* (analogy of faith), whereby he grounds what we know and say about God squarely in what God reveals to us by his free decision. Our access to God is always personal and is never susceptible to our control. The theologian must "think and teach about the relation between God and the creature only in the way prescribed by the fact of the assumption of the flesh by the divine Word in the person of Jesus Christ and the consequent assumption of sinful man to be the child of God."[80] Knowledge of God as Reconciler and Creator comes only through this miraculous revelation. No possibility of a true interpretation of theological language exists for Barth outside revelation.[81] All

---

[75]In Erich Przywara, *Analogia Entis* (Munich: Kosel & Pustet, 1932; reprint, Einsiedeln: Johannes Verlag, 1962).

[76]"I regard the *analogia entis* as the invention of Antichrist, and I believe that because of it, it is impossible ever to become a Roman Catholic, all other reasons for not doing so being to my mind shortsighted and trivial" (*CD* 1/1, p. xiii).

[77]For more, see Gottlieb Söhngen, "Analogia Entis in Analogia Fidei," pp. 266-71, and Walter Kreck, "Analogia Fidei oder Analogia Entis?" pp. 272-86, in *Antwort,* ed. Ernst Wolf, Ch. von Kirschbaum and Rudolf Frey (Zollikon-Zürich: Evangelischer Verlag, 1956).

[78]*CD* 2/1, p. 581.

[79]*CD* 2/1, p. 583. Barth is not saying here that theology has no ontological concerns. Rather, he is criticizing the theologian who imposes an abstract ontology on the self-revealing God that is incongruent with how God has revealed himself.

[80]Ibid.

[81]Battista Mondin, *The Principle of Analogy in Protestant and Catholic Theology* (The Hague: Martinus Nijhoff, 1963), p. 153.

theological knowledge is the pure expression of God's free grace,[82] not an intrinsic human capacity.[83]

Barth does allow another use of analogy, namely, the *analogia attributionis*.[84] This type of analogy designates "a similarity of two objects which consists in the fact that what is common to them exists first and properly in the one, and then, because a second is dependent upon it, in the second."[85] So with respect to God and creatures, there may be some proper analogical predication of both. But such analogical similarity exists not because God and the creature share some third thing, such as being, wisdom, goodness or knowledge. Rather, these properties reside preeminently in God and only partially and derivatively in creatures. Their application to the divine nature determines their use in the creaturely realm, and not vice versa. Whether or not there is a Platonic dependence to this type of analogy, it is structurally similar to the Platonic conviction that only the Forms have complete reality, while particular exemplifications in the material realm are mere reflections of the reality of the Forms. Ironically, this understanding of *analogia attributionis* is precisely that of Thomas Aquinas.[86] It seems, therefore, that Barth has misinterpreted the Thomistic doctrine of *analogia entis*, even if he has in his sights another "textbook" version of the doctrine.[87]

In a long treatment of the Scholastic A. Quenstedt's adoption of *analogia attributionis*, Barth contrasts his use of *analogia attributionis*, judging Quenstedt's to be unacceptably akin to the Thomistic view.[88] Quenstedt affirmed *analogia attributionis intrinseca*, which implies for Barth that the analogy

---

[82]*CD* 2/1, p. 275.

[83]Ibid., p. 270. See also G. C. Berkouwer, *The Triumph of Grace in the Theology of Karl Barth* (Grand Rapids, Mich.: Eerdmans, 1956), pp. 179-95, for defense of the thesis that Barth's polemic against natural theology and the *analogia entis* is a function of his commitment to grace.

[84]He also has a developed view of *analogia relationis*, but this type of analogy is less relevant to our discussion.

[85]*CD* 2/1, p. 238.

[86]See John McIntyre, "Analogy," *Scottish Journal of Theology* 12 (1959): 11-12.

[87]This is a fruitful way of expressing the dependence of valuable attributes on God. See Roger White, "Notes on Analogical Predication and Speaking About God," in *The Philosophical Frontiers of Christian Theology,* ed. B. Hebblethwaite and S. Sutherland (Cambridge: Cambridge University Press, 1982), pp. 197-226. White contends that Barth misunderstood some of the traditional vocabulary of analogy (p. 198).

[88]*CD* 2/1, pp. 237-43.

might be intrinsic to the creature itself, apart from "God's gracious action."[89] Therefore he prefers *analogia attributionis extrinseca* in order to emphasize that even the derivative analogy that might exist between some divine reality and a creaturely one is wholly dependent on God making it so in his revelation. He accuses Quenstedt of abandoning the Reformation conviction of justification by grace alone.[90] Still, Barth does accept a highly qualified use of the term *analogy,* even though he fears its lingering connotations of natural theology.[91] Under Barth's interpretations, the *analogia fidei* and *analogia attributionis extrinseca* are forms of "analogy" that are compatible with his actualism.[92]

Thomist scholars have vociferously denied that theirs is a view of God and creation commonly participating in a third reality, being.[93] An investigation of Thomas's *Summa Theologica* justifies their complaint. Thomas's view is essentially that of Quenstedt's, whereby all things that have being derive it from the primary being of God. God is the basis of all being.[94] Similarly, for Thomas all perfections exist preeminently in God; creatures only participate in those perfections. Thomas argues that there are not independent perfections in which both God and creatures participate.[95] Barth defends the propriety of using the

---

[89]Berkouwer, *Triumph of Grace,* p. 189. It is evidence of Barth's actualism that he does not consider a third possibility: that there might be an analogy intrinsic to the creature precisely because of God's gracious action.

[90]*CD* 2/1, p. 239. Barth has here transplanted the doctrine of justification from soteriology to epistemology and semantics.

[91]This section follows the text of Jay W. Richards, "Barth on the Divine 'Conscription' of Language," *The Heythrop Journal* 38, no. 3 (1997): 251-52.

[92]Given his extensive qualification of analogy, it is unlikely that Barth sought a rapprochement between his analogy of faith and the analogy of being, as von Balthasar suggests (*Theology of Karl Barth,* p. 163, n. 47). Given Barth's definition of *analogia entis,* however, his view may be closer to Thomas's view than he realized. He may even draw unwittingly on resources also available to the actual Thomistic doctrine. Nevertheless, Barth's view of *analogia attributionis* is more strongly actualistic than is Thomas's. Moreover, his proposal is negatively shaped by the fact that he defines the *analogia fidei* over against his understanding of the *analogia entis.* For these reasons, even if a rapprochement of the type von Balthasar imagines is possible, it will not be Barth's position.

[93]See Berkouwer, *Triumph of Grace,* p. 190, especially his references. See the excellent description of Thomas Aquinas's actual position in Mondin, *The Principle of Analogy,* pp. 169-73, and comparison in Henry Chavannes, *L'Analogie entre Dieu et le Monde Selon Saint Thomas d'Aquin et Selon Karl Barth* (Paris: Les Editions du Cerf, 1969). Cf. Grover Foley, "The Catholic Critics of Karl Barth: In Outline and Analysis," *Scottish Journal of Theology* 14 (1961): 136-55.

[94]*Summa Theologica* 1.35.

[95]*Summa Theologica* 1.4.2.

concept of person for God in precisely the same way.[96] Apparently Barth's polemic against *analogia entis* led him to misstate things.

Of course, he would still have disagreed with Thomas and the many Catholic theologians who share the Thomistic view, but his disagreement would have taken the same form as his disagreement with Quenstedt. Barth would have rejected an intrinsic *analogia attributionis* because it implies an objective ontological state of affairs, apart from divine revelatory action. So Barth's polemic against *analogia entis* is a function of his actualism.

Still, even if some of the arrows Barth fired at the Thomistic *analogia* fall wide of the target, might he nonetheless have sensed a problem in the Thomistic and Protestant Scholastic concept of God (that is, classical theism)? Perhaps he could have reformulated his complaint to account for the criticisms above. For instance, he might have argued, "You may be right. Thomas Aquinas and the Protestant Scholastics may have affirmed that God is the source of all being and denied that he participates in some extrinsic being that he shares with creatures. Nevertheless, in their actual theorizing, they clearly adopted a general, that is, Aristotelian or Neo-Platonic concept of being, which was fundamentally inadequate for accommodating what God has revealed of himself." In his treatment of the divine attributes, Barth gives many examples of how so-called Aristotelian convictions deeply shaped the traditional understanding of God, not all of which are congenial to claims that seem to emerge from the biblical witness. His criticism of the overweening influence of the doctrine of simplicity is one example. Another is his complaint that the traditional use of the *via negativa* is inadequate because it merely negates finite and relative being. For Barth, such an exercise is still telling evidence that the theologian has adopted a concept of being in abstraction from the trinitarian God who has revealed himself in Jesus Christ.[97]

This way of construing the problem has some textual support in Barth. It also has more bite, since it is fairer to the Thomistic view, thus allowing one to apply his critique to classical theism in general. He insists that while we speak of being, it is not with a neutral concept of being as such.[98] We are concerned,

---

[96]*CD* 2/1, p. 272.

[97]Ibid., pp. 347-49.

[98]"We have already had to resist the threatened absorption of the doctrine of God into a doctrine of being. . . . Yet we must not yield to a revulsion against the idea of being as such, which for some time had a part in modern Protestant theology" (*CD* 2/1, p. 260).

rather, with God's being in its concrete revelation—never in abstraction from the Trinity—even if we do "define" God as *a se et per se.*[99] We encounter God's essence in revelation and nowhere else.[100] These claims at least suggest that Barth would have continued to criticize classical theism, even if he had not misconstrued the *analogia entis.* We will return to this below, after discussing Barth's account of the divine perfections.

BARTH'S TREATMENT OF THE DIVINE PERFECTIONS

Barth's bountiful discussion of the divine attributes in *Church Dogmatics* 2/1 is a breviary of the extended conversation that constitutes the history of Christian reflection on God. Rather than attempting to consider his treatment in detail here, we will restrict our focus to the ways in which Barth's actualism affects his treatment of God's perfections.

Barth is always in dialogue with the traditional approach to the subject and usually appreciates the Scholastic arguments, even when he departs from them dramatically. The most obvious such departure is the way he derives and distributes the divine attributes. As we noted in chapters one and three, the order of treatment in classical theism was usually dictated by the methods employed, namely, the *via triplex.* Barth does concede that the *via negationis* and *via eminentiae* may "perform their specific though limited services in the formation of concepts to describe the divine perfection."[101] Nevertheless, he insists that we not confuse them with the proper method of grounding theological reflection in revelation particularly. This difference in method gives him a somewhat critical posture toward the traditional procedure, which he

---

[99]He admits that God's existence does have one thing in common with all other beings, namely, objective reality. Of course, God's reality, unlike that of creatures, cannot be imagined away (Barth, *Anselm: Fides Quaerens Intellectum,* pp. 178-80; see von Balthasar, *Theology of Karl Barth,* pp. 164-65). Also, since God is a self-positing Subject, and creatures are other-posited, this implies a contrariety between the two that militates against the *analogia entis* as Barth defines it. See also Berkouwer, *Triumph of Grace,* p. 162, n. 51.

[100]CD 2/1, pp. 260-61. Jüngel claims that for Barth "the concept of being must be measured by the revelation of God. God's revelation is the criterion of all ontological statements in theology. In the face of this criterion ontological statements in theology are not only legitimate but indispensable" (*God's Being Is in Becoming,* pp. 62-63). Notice that Barth's claim makes it clear that he does not oppose speaking of God's essence as such but opposes discussion not grounded in God's revelation.

[101]CD 2/1, p. 348.

calls "the whole earlier doctrine of God."[102] In chapter six, *The Reality of God,* his master concept is of God as Being in Act, as the One who loves in freedom.[103] So he orders the perfections according to either love or freedom. While he believes his actualistic and particularistic emphasis implies this procedure, he concedes that Holy Scripture does not require a certain order of the divine perfections.[104]

Barth elucidates aspects of divine love and freedom, and then he treats *The Divine Perfections* together in the next subsection (§29).[105] In §30 he clusters certain perfections under *The Perfections of the Divine Loving.* In himself and his works, he argues, "God is gracious, merciful and patient, and at the same time holy, righteous and wise."[106] By treating love before freedom, Barth seeks to counterbalance a traditional error of seeing divine freedom as more properly concerned with God *in se* than love, which is consigned to God *ad extra,* that is, with his relation to creation. By beginning with love, Barth emphasizes that love is essential to God apart from creation.[107] It is not merely a relation or something we project onto God.

In addition, he treats the perfections in dialectical pairs, under the two groupings of love and freedom. While he admits this ordering is not a dogmatic requirement, it serves to underscore the unity of God's being. In discussing a particular perfection, we may be focusing on a certain aspect of God's being; nevertheless, we are always speaking of "the one God integrally." The dialectical pairing shows that there is a reciprocity in which each can describe the one divine Subject. So he treats God's grace and holiness together, reminding the reader that God's grace does not conflict with his holiness.[108] For a similar reason, he treats together mercy and righteousness as well as patience and

---

[102]Ibid.

[103]Ibid., p. 257.

[104]Ibid., p. 352.

[105]By speaking of "perfections" instead of "attributes," Barth hopes to avoid the semi-nominalism in much of the tradition, which to him may imply that while we "attribute" these things to God, they have more to do with how we conceive of God or relate ourselves to him than with how God actually is. He also strives to distinguish his procedure from the traditional or classical one. He specifies that God is the perfect being "in the fact that He is the One who loves in freedom" (*CD* 2/1, p. 322).

[106]Ibid., p. 351.

[107]Ibid., pp. 344-45, 348-50.

[108]Ibid., pp. 351-68.

wisdom.[109] This ordering suggests a more organic divine unity than does, say, Thomas Aquinas's treatment of the incommunicable attributes prior to and even in priority over those attributes revealed in history. In Barth's treatment there is no appearance that the incommunicable attributes, derived from the *via negativa*, might overshadow the attributes derived from God's acts in history. How God has acted in revelation has a clear priority in Barth's reflection on how God is from eternity.

In §31, *The Perfections of the Divine Freedom*, he pairs unity and omnipresence, constancy and omnipotence[110] and eternity and glory.[111] He rejects those "nominalistic" aspects of the doctrine of simplicity that demote the perfections from God's essence to his appearance to us *ad extra*.[112] He also criticizes the Neo-Platonic and Aristotelian "general conception of God," which in simplicity became an "all-controlling principle, the idol."[113] In contrast, he insists that the multiplicity of perfections has a basis in God's being or essence.[114]

Nevertheless, Barth does retain language tinged with simplicity doctrine. So he says that while God "lives His perfect life in the abundance of many individual and distinct perfections," still each perfection is "nothing else but God Himself, His one, simple, distinctive being."[115] He also conscripts simplicity language to deny that God participates in other beings or notions[116] and to defend God's unity. Indeed, he virtually equates simplicity with aseity: "The simplicity of God means that within the Godhead there is no additional or subsequent being." Finally, he uses it to defend God's unique individuality.[117] So he affirms both multiplicity and simplicity in the divine essence.[118]

---

[109]Ibid., pp. 368-439.

[110]I consider Barth's treatment of divine omnipotence in more detail below.

[111]*CD* 2/1, pp. 440-677. Notice that Barth chooses the word *constancy* instead of "immutability." This word choice presages his critical stance toward much traditional theological speculation on divine immutability, which he deems uncongenial to the radically personal divine self-revelation.

[112]Ibid., p. 349.

[113]Ibid., p. 329.

[114]Ibid., pp. 327, 333-34.

[115]Ibid., p. 322.

[116]Ibid., p. 333.

[117]Ibid., pp. 445, 447.

[118]Ibid., p. 331.

For Barth, by rooting the perfections in revelation we concretely and realistically describe God's being. For the perfections,[119] like the trinitarian modes of being, exist essentially in God and are not merely ways of relating God to us or to creation.[120]

While brief, this exposition should make clear that Barth's concept of God as the preeminent Being in Act, as the One who loves in freedom, allows him to develop a doctrine of God that, while maintaining continuity with the tradition, is not constrained by the classical theistic method. As such, it promises to overcome some of the problems of that procedure. Now we should consider its relevance to essentialism.

---

[119]Important in this regard is Barth's denial that God has accidents. This might foretell a serious conflict with my proposal. However, his claim has to do less with a denial of contingency in God than with his desire to avoid making the perfections accidents: "The maxim opposed to the realistic understanding of these perfections: in Deum non cadit accidens, is therefore correct in itself" (ibid., p. 330). While I contend that God has some accidents owing to his freedom, I do not say that God's perfections are accidents. So on this point, I agree with Barth.

[120]Ibid., p. 323.

5

DEALING WITH
BARTH'S DOCTRINE OF GOD

Having summarized Barth's doctrine of God, I am now in the position to analyze it. I will first seek to identify the role of the "three themes" in his method, and then consider possible interpretations of his actualism, as well as the virtues and problems that attend them. Finally, I will mention some ways that Barth's proposal either harmonizes or conflicts with essentialism, and suggest how his view might serve as a warning for the essentialist.

THE THREE THEMES IN BARTH'S THEOLOGY

It is not difficult to identify the three themes of Christian theology in Barth's methodology. The priority of Scripture and divine self-revelation (biblical normativity) is obvious. He restructures and reorders the divine attributes in light of our knowledge of God through his self-revelation, doing so to "correct" the philosophical apriorism he detects in much of the tradition. In George Hunsinger's terms, this is the Barthian motif of particularism.[1]

---

[1]Some critics dispute whether Barth applied this commitment consistently (consider Moltmann in his critique of Barth on the Trinity). Since the influence of philosophical thought forms is pervasive throughout the *Church Dogmatics,* these critics suspect that such forms hold more sway over his thought than he would have admitted. However, the presence of such philosophical forms is not itself a denial of biblical normativity as I have construed it. No one denies that Barth intended to give the Word marginal control over his systematic theology, even if he did not always succeed in doing so. Even some generally sympathetic to Barth recognize a philosophical influence in his theology more pervasive than he was likely to admit. George Hendry notes that Barth does not merely "use" philosophical concepts—a procedure Barth allows—he has "laid his theological eggs in philosophical nests." Philosophy is for Barth "something more than a handmaid who hands him his tools, it is a mis-

The Principle of Perfection (PP) is easy to detect as well. With most of the Reformed tradition, he seems to assume that it arises from God's revelation in Scripture.[2] He insists that God is the perfect being, the standard of perfection, but chastises those who apply a priori criteria of perfection to God. Rather, by listening to God we come to realize what perfection is.[3] So while Barth displays a commitment to PP, he also insists that revelation rather than intuitions of perfection provides the content of what it means to say God is perfect.

The Sovereignty-Aseity Conviction (SAC) is as obvious in Barth as it is in any theologian. For Barth, God is self-sufficient and lacks nothing in himself. He is radically free from external constraint. He does not participate in or depend on any created reality or anything outside himself, not even on conditions of possibility or necessity. God defines what is genuinely possible.[4] His aseity knows no bounds. He is able to move himself, however, and so cannot be described as aloof, inert, or uncompassionate.[5] In some sense God's freedom and will are not constrained even by his own essence. What this means I consider below.

So we can detect the presence of all three themes in Barth's theology. Insofar as this is the case, his project has much in common with the essentialism I have defended, even if there are important differences.

INTERPRETING BARTH'S ACTUALISM

Although Barth denounces certain uses of general or abstract concepts,[6] he clearly recognizes the need to appropriate philosophical concepts.[7] He did so

---

tress with whom he goes to bed." See George Hendry, "On Barth, the Philosopher," in *Faith and the Philosophers,* ed. John Hick (New York: St. Martin's Press, 1964), p. 211. Still, this judgment is different from a glib dismissal of Barth because philosophy influences his thought.

Moreover, Barth admits the inevitability of using philosophy in theology. His overall burden is not to eschew the theological use of philosophy but to assure that theology's use of philosophy is *Schriftgemass,* that is, consistent with the biblical witness.

[2]*CD* 2/1, p. 376.

[3]Ibid.

[4]Ibid., pp. 532-38.

[5]Ibid., p. 370.

[6]H. R. Mackintosh puts it nicely: "[Barth's] writing, so often, is temperamental. He states this or that absolutely, when what he really means is that it is an indispensable part of the truth." *Types of Modern Theology: Schleiermacher to Barth* (1937; reprint, Digswell Place, U.K.: Nisbet, 1962), pp. 313-14.

[7]See quote in James Brown, *Subject and Object in Theology* (New York: Macmillan, 1955), pp. 16-17.

in his exposition of the doctrine of the Trinity and especially his understanding of the concept of person. The fact that he draws heavily on his philosophical milieu in his use of expressions and conceptions has provoked much criticism.[8] It seems unfair to dismiss Barth, however, because he is "dependent on philosophy" in his doctrine of God. One could criticize Barth for some specific use he makes of philosophical concepts in, say, his trinitarian doctrine, without faulting him for using philosophical concepts as such. After all, Barth argues that this procedure is inevitable, or as he says, "If we open our mouths, we find ourselves in the province of philosophy."[9] He seems to recognize that general concepts and particular revelation are dialectically related, even if revelation should always have marginal control over general concepts.[10] If this is correct, then we can understand Barth arguing simply that the particularity of God's self-revelation must have priority over general concepts such as being. On this interpretation, the distance between Barth and Christian essentialism narrows further.

---

[8]For example, Wolfhart Pannenberg and Jürgen Moltmann contend that the threefoldness Barth speaks of has less to do with the actual economy of salvation to which Scripture testifies than with a formal concept of revelation. Jürgen Moltmann, *The Trinity and the Kingdom* (San Francisco: HarperSanFrancisco, 1991), pp. 139-44; Wolfhart Pannenberg, *Systematic Theology,* 3 vols. (Grand Rapids, Mich.: Eerdmans, 1991), 1:303-4. It is difficult to deny that Barth's exposition of the Trinity adopts ways of speaking from Continental Idealism in general and Hegelianism in particular. When Barth speaks of God as "positing" himself (e.g., *CD* 1/1, p. 370), he has appropriated Hegelian images. In Hegel, "The subject posits itself as an Other, knows itself in that Other, and then negates the otherness of that Other, in a return to itself" (Lisabeth During, "Hegel, Barth and the Rationality of the Trinity," *Kings Theological Review* 2, no. 2 [1979], p. 80). Likewise, his explication of the doctrine of creation owes much to Hegelian imagery (*CD* 2/1, pp. 67, 266, 267). See Barth's admission to "doing a bit of Hegeling" in Eberhard Busch, *Karl Barth* (London: SCM Press, 1976), p. 387. Cf. George Hendry, "The Freedom of God in the Theology of Karl Bart," *Scottish Journal of Theology* 31 (1978): 239-44. He tempers his use of Hegelianism, again by means of philosophy—in this case existentialist I-Thou imagery. Again, with Fichtean "reflection logic" he conceives of a subject as an "I existing in and for itself with its own thought and will." All these judgments seem accurate. However, since Barth judged that theological use of philosophical concepts was unavoidable, the mere fact that he does so is hardly an indictment. So the strength of these critiques is not in the claim that he merely makes use of a philosophical concept but rather that the concept he uses is not fully consistent with the requirements of revelation. Appropriately, such a critique is compatible with Barth's deepest commitment.

[9]See Karl Barth, *Credo, A Presentation of the Chief Problems of Dogmatics with Reference to the Apostles' Creed* (London: Hodder, 1936), p. 183. For an explicit statement of Barth's understanding of the status of philosophy relative to theology, see his "Fate and Idea in Theology," in *The Way of Theology in Karl Barth,* ed. H. Martin Rumscheidt (Allison Park, Penn.: Pickwick, 1986).

[10]Other interpreters of Barth have made this point by speaking of Barth's use of Scripture as "theological exegesis." See Mary Kathleen Cunningham, *What Is Theological Exegesis? Interpretation and Use of Scripture in Barth's Doctrine of Election* (Valley Forge, Penn.: Trinity Press International, 1995), and Hans Frei, *The Eclipse of Biblical Narrative* (New Haven, Conn.: Yale University Press, 1984).

Barth's actualism in particular is a philosophical form he considered congruent with the revealed Word. Still, it is not entailed by revelatory particularism concerning our knowledge of God. Arguing from actuality to corresponding possibility, that is, does not entail actualism.[11] The biblical witness to God's special actions in history underdetermines Barth's actualism. There is considerable slack between the biblical witness and actualism per se. Therefore, other conceptions may be equally compatible with the biblical witness. This in itself is no reason to reject Barth's actualism. But just because we share Barth's commitment to biblical normativity does not require us to accept all its details if we find that it conflicts with other important claims or leads to conceptual difficulties. As we will see, essentialism is able to accommodate many of the concerns Barth expresses by way of actualism.

Barth's primary motivation for actualism in his doctrine of God seems to be his desire to protect the unity of God's being and act: "God is who He is in His works." As Barth explains:

> He is the same even in Himself, even before and after and over His works, and without them. They are bound to Him, but He is not bound to them. They are nothing without Him. But He is who He is without them. He is not, therefore, who He is only in His works. Yet in Himself He is not another than He is in His works.[12]

Barth seeks to preserve the possibility of knowing God's essence by knowledge of his works without committing himself to a reductionist theological behaviorism in which God is his acts without remainder.[13]

This may be the fundamental intention behind Barth's actualism. Some Barth interpreters extend his actualism, however, with some textual support, to the claim that God's essence is somehow subject to his will, that God, in a primal decision, chooses to be who and what he is—to be God. To distinguish this stronger thesis from actualism per se, let us call it strong actualism. It is unclear whether Barth would have advocated strong actualism once it was

---

[11]As Barth describes his method in *CD* 2/1, p. 5.

[12]*CD* 2/1, p. 260.

[13]Barth's fear of bifurcating divine essence and acts is well-founded. If these are too sharply separated, deriving knowledge of God from his acts becomes well-nigh impossible, as Maurice Wiles shows in "Some Reflections on the Origins of the Doctrine of the Trinity," *Journal of Theological Studies* 8 (1957): 92-106.

framed explicitly; however, some respected Barth interpreters such as Robert Jenson[14] and Bruce McCormack[15] interpret his doctrine of God in this way. Evaluating their interpretation is difficult because Barth speaks of God's freedom in several different senses, without always saying what sense he means. In an insightful article, George Hendry has delineated five meanings or senses of the freedom of God in Barth's *Church Dogmatics:*[16]

(1)   Freedom as gratuity.[17]

(2)   Freedom as option, or choice between alternatives.[18]

(3)   Freedom as self-determination.[19]

(4)   Freedom as initiative.[20]

(5)   Freedom as energy.[21]

As Hendry puts it, these senses are compatible, but they are not "mutually implicatory."[22] For example, in a given instance God could be free in senses (1), (3) and (5) but not in senses (2) or (4). Actualism in the doctrine of God is not problematic in sense (3). God could be "free" or "choose" to be triune, to be merciful, to be omnipotent, in that no external force constrains him. There is no force or compulsion outside him that requires that he be these things. God's essence does not restrict him in any inimical way.

By speaking of God as choosing or deciding to be God, however, Barth risks connoting a freedom in sense (2), as a choice among alternatives. This may seem implausible, but since he speaks of God's freedom in several senses, it is a possible interpretation. So we have two related but distinct questions. First, does Barth endorse strong actualism? Second, what makes strong actualism problematic? I am unsure how to answer the first question, though I would

---

[14]See n. 58, p. 118.

[15]See Bruce McCormack, "Grace and Being: The Role of God's Gracious Election in Karl Barth's Theological Anthropology" and "Christ and the Decree: An Unsettled Question for the Reformed Churches Today," currently unpublished.

[16]Hendry, "The Freedom of God," pp. 233-37.

[17]*CD* 4/1, p. 39.

[18]*CD* 2/2, pp. 28-32.

[19]*CD* 2/1, p. 301; *CD* 1/1, p. 323; *CD* 2/1, p. 302.

[20]*CD* 2/2, p. 168.

[21]Ibid.

[22]Hendry, "The Freedom of God," p. 235.

incline to answer no. First, however, let us consider strong actualism, if only to preempt it as a viable solution.

Take strong actualism to be the following claim:

(SA) For any essential property P, God has P if and only if God has chosen P from a set of alternatives.[23]

(SA) generates the following dilemma: If God chose P, could God have willed otherwise? That is, is there a possible world in which God lacks P? If so, then in what sense is P an essential property, since God could have existed as God without it? If the strong actualist responds that God could not have willed otherwise, then in what sense does he mean that God chooses P? This is surely among the stickiest of problems.

Apart from the logical vortex produced by this dilemma, strong actualism creates some theologically unsavory questions. If God can choose his essence or essential properties among alternatives, then, presumably, God could have chosen to be, say, essentially evil or ignorant or unjust. And there would be no recourse to the traditional argument that God is essentially good, all-knowing or just. To be sure, the strong actualist would insist that God is all these things essentially, but only because God willed to be so. He could have willed otherwise.

Given these problems, why would a theologian want to affirm (SA)? Presumably, one might seek to defend strong actualism out of commitment to divine sovereignty, aseity (SAC) and freedom. We might understand strong actualism as a sort of theological existentialism or radical voluntarism, akin to the French philosopher Jean Paul Sartre's axiom that existence precedes essence. Unlike Sartre's concept, however, strong actualism is a theological principle. God—not human beings—is truly the one who "chooses" his essence. Christopher Stead explains this aspect of existentialism:

---

[23](SA) should not be confused with a similar claim, namely (O)

   If God willed to be four eternal persons in one essence, then he would be a quaternity.

   If God is essentially triune, then clearly enough, he could never be other than triune. Being omniscient, he would know this, and so would never will to be other than triune. There is no possible world in which God wills nontriunity for himself. Nevertheless, (O) might be true, even necessarily true, just in case God is omnipotent and necessarily triune. For in such a case, the antecedent of (O) would never obtain in any possible world, actual or counterfactual. And so (O) would be true in the sense that any conditional with a necessarily false antecedent is true, namely, trivially true.

Idealist philosophers have held that the fundamentally important truth about any *x* is that which declares what kind of being *x* is, and so assigns it to its proper place in the 'scale of being.' Statements about existence, on this view, play a relatively subordinate role; their function is to indicate whether some type of being actually occurs or crops up among the phenomena of our world. Modern existentialism can well be understood as a reaction against this type of thought; by laying its stress on existence, it tries to persuade us to see things in the actual context in which they occur, to give full recognition to their individuality and to refrain if possible from classifying them and so losing our grasp of their authentic character in the interests of a spurious demand for order and comprehensibility. For this school, then, that *x* exists, is, roughly, that *x* makes its own unique impact on the world.[24]

Actualism with respect to God's choice of his own being appears to be quite similar to existentialism as described by Stead.[25] To be sure, the strong actualist need not refer to some time in the distant past at which God chose, say, to be triune. This is the import of the adjective *primal* in "primal decision." However difficult to imagine, it would be a decision taken in eternity. So even if one opted for the strong actualist reading of Barth, it would be incorrect to conclude that he is saying there was a time when the Son was not. While Barth does not conceive of eternity as Boethian timelessness, his notion of God's primal act includes the transcendence of time. Some may mistake this claim as dangerously close to Arianism, but actualism distinguishes it from this ancient heresy.

Nevertheless, even if God's primal decision to choose his essence takes place in eternity, strong actualism still gives rise to a question of conceptual priority. Such a question is reminiscent of the debate between infralapsarians and supralapsarians in Reformed Scholasticism. In those debates all Reformed Scholastics agreed that God did not first decide to create the world at time *t* and then choose the elect at *t* + 1, or vice versa. All agreed that God's choices were in eternity rather than time. Still, they argued about the "priority," conceptually or ontologically, of election to God's choosing to create. Analogous questions emerge in response to strong actualism. Placing God's primal deci-

---

[24]Christopher Stead, *Divine Substance* (Oxford: Clarendon, 1977), p. 8.

[25]In general, existentialists also reject the application of substance to human beings. See William Shearson, "The Common Assumptions of Existentialist Philosophy," *International Philosophical Quarterly* 15 (1975): 131-47.

sion concerning his being or essence in eternity does not make such a decision any less perplexing.

Probably the most serious difficulty with strong actualism is that to speak of God as choosing anything in sense (2) is to presuppose that God is such that he can so choose. In order to choose, clearly enough, God would have to have the property of *being able to choose*. Did he choose to have that property? Well, then he has another property . . . and off goes an infinite regress. Appealing to divine eternity to avoid these problems would look suspiciously like explaining an absurdity with a mystery. While it may seem like an exalted expression of divine freedom and aseity to speak in this way, choice in the sense of choosing among alternatives is an exceedingly unhelpful way of speaking of the relation of God's will to his essence. Choosing to be a being who is able to choose one's being looks incoherent and so impossible.[26] Of course, if our commitment to the biblical witness or divine sovereignty required that we ascribe this ability to God, perhaps we could search relentlessly for a plausible rendering of it. But as it is, this choice looks about as chimerical as the ability to square a circle. It is a logical absurdity. There just is no such ability, so lacking it does not insult God's freedom, aseity, majesty or omnipotence.

Not only is strong actualism in general highly problematic, but attributing it to Barth also generates conflicts with other central themes in his thought. We can see this most easily in the terms introduced in chapters two and three. If some property M, say, *being perfect in mercy,* is one of God's essential properties, then God will exemplify M in every possible world. In order for it to be sensible to say God could choose among alternatives with respect to exemplifying M, there would need to be some possible world $w_{\sim m}$ in which God does not exemplify M. But if there is a possible world $w_{\sim m,}$ then M is not one of God's essential properties, since he would not exemplify M in every possible world. So if God could choose his essential properties in sense (2), then God would have no essential properties.[27]

---

[26]Some analogous arguments appear in Horst Georg Pöhlmann, *Analogia Entis Oder Analogia Fidei?* (Göttingen: Vandenhoeck & Ruprecht, 1965), pp. 20-28, 120-26. While there is general agreement between my criticisms and his, Pöhlmann's way of putting things is somewhat different from mine.

[27]To reiterate a point from chapter three, if the strong actualist denies that there are any counterfactual possibilities for God, then she will undercut the libertarian sense of her own claim that God *chooses* certain things.

Alternatively, perhaps he would have only one essential property, the property of being able to choose every other one of his properties—call it *A*. But he would enjoy *A* at the cost of lacking any other essential properties. And he would not be able to choose *A* itself. This position looks like a commitment to divine freedom and sovereignty so extravagant that it drifts into incoherence. More to the point, it contradicts Barth's claim that the perfections are essential divine properties and results in a nominalism more severe than any Barth rejects.[28] Perhaps most troubling, it posits a counterfactual God "behind" the "chosen" God who could presumably have been different from how he has revealed himself to be. This image is dramatically contrary to Barth's emphasis on the reality of revelation.[29] So, on the assumption that Barth is not contradicting himself, we should opt out of the strong actualist interpretation.

Moreover, there is evidence that Barth would have denied strong actualism if he had carefully delineated the different senses of divine freedom. While Barth can say that God "wills" to be God, he never says that God "chooses" his being as a choice among alternatives. In addition, Barth says early on in his doctrine of God in *Church Dogmatics* 2/1:

> If . . . we say that God is *a se*, we do not say that God creates, produces or originates Himself. On the contrary, we say that (as manifest and eternally actual in the relationship of Father, Son and Holy Ghost) He is the One who already has and is in Himself everything which would have to be the object of His creation and causation if He were not He, God. . . . He cannot 'need' His own being because He affirms it in being who He is. It is not, of course, that His being needs this affirmation. But He does actually affirm it in this way.[30]

Here Barth denies that God creates himself and implies that God's choice of his being is one of self-affirmation rather than a libertarian choice among alter-

---

[28]*CD* 2/1, p. 323.

[29]This dislike for a hidden God behind the God revealed in Jesus Christ leads him to criticize the Reformed doctrine of a *decretum absolutum* when it led to a positing of a secret decree independent of Christ (*CD* 2/2, pp. 60-76). Strong actualism seems to reintroduce such a notion, as a counterfactual *way-God-could-have-been-if-he-had-so-willed,* even if the strong actualist insists that God never actually *is* that way.

[30]*CD* 2/1, p. 306.

natives, such as the choice either to exist or not to exist.[31] From this we may infer
that Barth would not extend the libertarian choice God enjoys in his act of creation to God's choice of his own being. Hence, we may conclude that Barth, at
least on this reading, avoids the dilemmas that attend strong actualism.

If this is correct, then it appears that the actualism Barth endorses is generally compatible with the essentialism I endorse. In fact, to say that God
"chooses" to be God in the sense that God affirms his essence, that there is no
tension between God's essence and his will, is helpful. We can speak of God
as self-moving, as free with respect to his essence in that he continually affirms
his being and is not externally constrained by it. This language counters the
image that God's essence, particularity and concreteness imprison him. Quite
the contrary, God is supremely free in being what he essentially is. He does not
first find himself to have a certain essence and then concede that he is stuck
with it. On the contrary, unlike creatures, he always wills to be what he actually and essentially is.

SIMPLICITY

A more likely point of conflict with essentialism is Barth's way of describing
God's simplicity. Despite his harsh criticisms of the traditional doctrine,[32] in
the end he employs language reminiscent of it. For instance, he does not only
say that God's essential properties and perfections are not isolated from each
other and that God is not composed of them. He goes further and affirms
their equivalence. He may do this indirectly, as when he identifies two different divine properties with God's total essence: "We must affirm that with the

---

[31]Bruce L. McCormack, a chief proponent of the view that Barth claimed that God chooses his essence,
has argued (in private conversation) that Barth would certainly have to deny the inference that God
could "choose" his essence as a choice among alternatives. That is, upon hearing the argument presented here, Barth would deny this. McCormack argues that Barth would still say that God chooses
his essence in the same way that he chooses to create the world. Since both are primal decisions taken
in eternity, however, neither can meaningfully be described as a choice between alternatives. Only
temporal choices, on this interpretation, can be free in the libertarian sense. This saves the strong
actualist interpretation of Barth, but at a stiff price. It requires denying that God has libertarian freedom even with respect to contingent choices such as creation. Surely this is at best a Pyrrhic victory,
since the only reason for affirming strong actualism in the first place would be to preserve God's freedom and sovereignty. And, if human beings have libertarian choice over any decisions, it would also
imply that humans exercise more freedom in such instances than God had when choosing to create
the world. This is a disturbing implication.

[32]CD 2/1, pp. 327ff.

two statements 'God knows' and 'God wills' we are describing the one total essence of God. God's knowledge is God himself, and again God's will is God Himself."[33] And he may claim with Augustine and others that with respect to omnipotence, being, real power and genuine possibility, "God not only has these things, but is these things."[34] This is a traditional way of expressing God's simplicity.

Though common enough in the tradition, Barth's affirmation of simplicity is difficult to analyze and seems, at least on first blush, to conflict with essentialism. This is most apparent when he identifies God's will and his being or essence.[35] He clearly does not want to reduce one to the other or by affirming simplicity to deny that God really has these multiplicities.[36] Still, with or without qualification, it is not clear that Barth can maintain all he wishes to maintain.[37]

The problem is that identifying God's will with his essence, without some qualification, makes it difficult if not impossible to see how God's will to create this world, with its constituents, could be contingent. If God's will to create this world, for instance, is equal to his freedom or his mercy or his omnipotence, then all these properties must have the same modal status—since a contingent property cannot be equivalent to an essential one. So, if God is essentially merciful, as Barth affirms, then God's having created this world (an act based on God's will) is one of his essential properties. In the language of possible worlds, we might say that in every world in which God is omnipotent, he creates the actual world w_a. Since he is omnipotent in every world, he creates w_a in every possible world. So w_a exists necessarily. And this surely contradicts the claim that God created this world freely—in all but a very re-

---

[33]Ibid., p. 549.

[34]Ibid., p. 542.

[35]E.g., *CD* 2/1, pp. 550-51.

[36]"The equation cannot mean that God's will is to be reduced to His knowledge if the thinker's taste is intellectualistic, or His knowledge to His will if it is voluntaristic. . . . We have to treat His knowledge seriously as knowledge and His will as will, and God Himself in the unity and also in the particular characteristics of both as spirit, as a divine person" (*CD* 2/1, p. 551). It seems to me that the first thing to do in taking knowledge and will seriously in God is not to equate them.

[37]Over against Polanus's view of simplicity, Barth complains: "It suggests that the *multiplicitas* in which the will of God confronts us does not belong to the real essence of God, but is only an appearance assumed by God to help our human weakness. If, however, we are to take seriously the will of God which confronts us in the divine reconciliation as itself the true and real will of God, we must see in it and therefore in its multiplicity the simple essence of God Himself" (*CD* 2/1, pp. 550-51).

stricted sense of the word *free*. Indeed, this contradicts one of Barth's most
stable convictions, namely, that God is radically free in creating and interacting
in the world.

So simply identifying God's will and essence, without further explanation,
could suggest an internal conflict in Barth's doctrine of God. But this problem is not unique to Barth's theology. Rather, as I will argue in chapter nine,
the problem attends all attempts to reconcile certain versions of the doctrine
of divine simplicity (but not all) with a robust doctrine of divine freedom.
Overtures to troublesome forms of simplicity are relatively rare in Barth's
overall view. So criticizing it on this point is not terribly disruptive of his
doctrine of God.

At most, Barth could say that God's freedom is essential to his being, that
he is essentially free or that freedom is one of his essential properties. Perhaps
this is all he intends. Saying that each of God's properties is identical with his
total essence, however, muddles the distinction between the essentiality of
God's freedom and the contingency of God's free choices. For example, if God's
choice to create the world w_a is contingent, then it is not identical with God's
freedom per se or with God's essence. Since the commitment to God's freedom
in creating the world is more fundamental to Christian as well as Barthian convictions than commitment to strong simplicity, the reasonable course would
be to excise those versions or aspects of simplicity that create the conflict.

Perhaps it is Barth's endorsement of simplicity that prevents him from pur-
suing the essentialist strategy, which is to attribute to God essential and accidental properties,[38] while carefully qualifying what we mean by "property." Interestingly, once we define simplicity carefully, we can find resources in Barth
for this procedure. For Barth is willing to defend the presence of contingency
in God. So he says that if we begin by affirming that "every possible object is
bound first and foremost to [God's] will," then

> it becomes clear that it is not a question of ascribing only necessity to the being
> and essence of God and excluding contingency. There is in God supreme neces-

---

[38]On the contrary, Barth endorses the classical maxim, *In Deum non cadit accidens* (CD 2/1, p. 331).
One should not make too much of this, however, since his motivation seems to be to avoid a sort of
skepticism which posits an unknown God behind the extrinsic attributes which we can know or to
divide the divine being. The modern essentialist affirmation of divine accidents entails neither of
these unfortunate consequences.

sity and supreme contingency. This supreme contingency in the essence of God which is not limited by any necessity, the inscrutable concrete element in His essence, inscrutable because it never ceases or is exhausted—is His will.[39]

This striking passage marks a bold departure from much of the tradition, at least rhetorically. For Barth, contingency in God is possible because God possesses free will. I will postpone discussing the conjunction of necessity and contingency in God until discussion of Charles Hartshorne in chapters six and seven. We should note, however, that Barth, despite the significant differences between his thought and Hartshorne's, recognizes the importance of relating God to contingent reality. So essentialism provides a way to express one of Barth's convictions better than Barth did.

On this point essentialism clarifies Barth's view. Barth's apparent identification of God's essence and will has the unfortunate implication (contrary to his intentions) of either making all of God's properties contingent or all of them necessary. Or it makes God's essential properties equivalent to his contingent properties. So shackled, Barth is unable to preserve the essentiality of God's nature and the contingency of God's choice to create. By distinguishing those contingent properties or accidents that are the product of God's free will from his essence and his will itself, we can more clearly preserve both these claims. A casualty of this strategy is some manifestations of the doctrine of divine simplicity. I will discuss this in more detail in chapter nine.

SOME INSIGHTS
God's choices as self-implicating. Essentialism can accommodate much of Barth's actualistic language—separated from the strong actualist interpretation—and much of his motivation. For Barth makes it clear that some of God's choices, such as his choice to create this world and its constituents, were self-implicating. That is, for God to choose to create this world is simultaneously to choose to be Creator of this world, to be the one on whom all else depends. To put it baldly, God could not choose to create the universe or elect humanity while still having no real relation to the creation. This is not to say that God's omnipotence is impugned by his choice to create. Rather, it is that God's choice is itself a relational matter, which he could not pursue without impli-

---

[39]*CD* 2/1, pp. 547-48.

cating himself. For God to choose to create the world was for him to choose to be related to a creation, to be God with creation, to be a Creator.

This is not to say that God chooses his essence or an essential property. There is nothing about being God that requires that our world exist. This does not mean that God's relation to the world is not a real property or that it is not real to God but only to the world. The relation is real, and it is a property God does exemplify; it is just not one of his essential properties.[40] *Choosing to create* w_a—where w_a is the actual world—is one of God's contingent properties. *Being created by God* is an essential property of w_a, the actual world. So the relation is radically asymmetrical between God and the world. Some of God's properties, some ways in which God is, are the contingent product of his will.

Subject and essence. Both Barth's defenders and detractors report his intention to replace the traditional static ontological category of being, essence or substance with the dynamic notion of being in act.[41] Barth's reorientation of our understanding of God by means of the notion of a subject is a helpful corrective to the classical theistic emphasis on substance. As noted in chapter one, however, there are different concepts of essence or substance, some doctrinally objectionable, some not so. To reject every use of substance or essence in theology risks misinterpreting individual uses. For instance, it is unfair to accuse the Thomistic concept of substance of being inert or inactive,[42] as some Barth interpreters do. At the same time, Barth rightly perceives a lack of balance in the tradition, which his emphasis can help to correct. Barth reminds us to

---

[40]I discuss internal, external and real relations in the chapters that follow.

[41]E.g., Hendry, "The Freedom of God," pp. 231, 235; George Hunsinger, *How to Read Karl Barth: The Shape of His Theology* (New York: Oxford University Press, 1991), pp. 30, 67; Moltmann, *Trinity and the Kingdom,* pp. 10-16, 139; Eberhard Jüngel, *Gottes Sein Ist in Werden* (Tübingen: J. C. B. Mohr, 1966), translated into English by Horton Harris, *The Doctrine of the Trinity: God's Being Is in Becoming* (Edinburgh: Scottish Academic Press, 1976), p. 107; Colin Gunton, *Becoming and Being: The Doctrine of God in Charles Hartshorne and Karl Barth* (Oxford: Oxford University Press, 1976) p. 143.

[42]See W. Norris Clarke, "To Be Is to Be Substance-in-Relation," in *Explorations in Metaphysics,* pp. 102-22, for a "retrieval" of the Thomistic concept of substance, which he argues is different from the Cartesian and Lockean concepts. The latter might be characterized as inert, but not the former. He regrets that these other notions of substance replaced the Thomistic one: "The three successive phases of this distortion can be summed up as (1) the Cartesian self-enclosed substance; (2) the Lockean inert substance as unknowable substratum; and (3) the Humean separable substance, rejected as unintelligible—which it indeed is as so understood" (p. 102). While this is a common contemporary criticism of Thomas, Barth does not criticize Thomas for this reason.

guard against the danger of distorting our theological terminology through impersonal connotations.[43]

In fact, the apparent restriction of personal categories in classical theism does not seem to stem from the terms *substance* and *essence* but rather from certain forms of the notions of simplicity and immutability. If we can distinguish the language of substance and essence from certain forms of simplicity and impersonal immutability, then, we might resolve the dilemma.

Still, there is no need to understand the notion of subject as an alternative to "essence." Even if aspects of the classical notion of substance or essence prove inadequate, there is nothing intrinsic to the notion of essence that contradicts the truth that God is radically personal.[44] Barth, while emphasizing personalism, nevertheless speaks of God's essence. Allowing will and subjectivity to have overweening priority over essence leads to difficulties. On strong actualism, the act and will of the divine Subject conceptually precede essence in a way that seems impossible. Barth does not argue for the priority of subject over essence in God. Rather, he encourages us to view them as existing in perfect simultaneity and harmony.[45] Unlike strong actualism, this is not problematic. If God is eternal without creation[46] or at least not dependent on temporal succession for his essence or existence, then surely the relation between his decision, will and being is less asymmetrical than it is with finite beings such as humans. With Barth, we can affirm such simultaneity of God's will and essence, which prevents the appearance that God's essence constrains God's freedom.

Being and act. In defending Barth's actualism, some scholars, among them Colin Gunton, warn that using essentialist language will encourage "a conception of a being of God that lies behind and apart from his revelation, and thus

---

[43]Barth's personalist emphasis is a valuable corrective; this does not mean one must accept all the details of his analysis of "subject" or its application to God.

[44]"Subject" does a great deal of the work in Barth that "substance" did in Thomistic thought. Barth follows Hegel among others in using subject as the primary category. Perhaps Hegel substituted "subject" for "substance" because the notion of substance he encountered was that of an inert substratum (as Clarke argues in "To Be Is to Be Substance-in-Relation," p. 111). If this is so, the separation of substance and subject is an unfortunate historical accident and does not entail that they are contradictory concepts.

[45]*CD* 2/1, p. 550. Something like simultaneity of will and essential properties might be an appropriate image for understanding God's relation to his world-indexed properties.

[46]Whether God freely enters into temporal relations upon creating a universe distinct from himself is another matter.

. . . overturn what is most original and interesting in Barth's theology."[47] And in some instances, this is no doubt correct. Gunton's fear is unwarranted, however, with respect to essentialism as articulated in this book. Use of essence in this sense does not imply that there is some hidden God who really exists but always hovers behind his acts or properties that are manifest in revelation. Some types of substantialism, such as that of John Locke, which depicts a substratum that underlies all properties, may pose such a danger, but that danger is not inherent in essentialism per se.[48]

Nevertheless, Gunton's worry seems to capture a Barthian intuition. For surely one motivation for Barth's actualism—with its emphasis on the unity of God's being and acts—was his desire to preserve the possibility of knowledge of God's essence via his revelatory acts. By making contingent divine acts in history accidental properties of God, might Barth complain that essentialism provides at best a tenuous connection between God in himself and God as revealed?

Clearly the unity of divine being and act that Barth defends, if correct, does provide warrant for inferring how God is from what he does. It also fortifies the claim that in Jesus, God reveals himself. But essentialism enables us to articulate this more precisely. Simply to say that God's being is in his acts does not distinguish between essential and contingent properties clearly enough, although, depending on how we interpret the claim, it may be compatible with essentialism. By blurring this distinction, Barth risks implying that God's acts in history are essential to him. Instead of risking the dangers in identifying God's being and acts (or his being with his contingent acts), why can we not simply maintain that if God is truthful, he will not reveal himself in a way that contradicts how he actually is? His acts will never be alien to or contradict his being or essence. Yes, his being is in those acts, because it is really God who so acts. *Being incarnate in A.D. 10* may be one of God's contingent properties (or more precisely, one of God the Son's contingent properties), but it is one of *his*

---

[47]Colin Gunton, *Becoming and Being*, p. 170. Gunton is criticizing Pöhlmann's suggestion that the Aristotelian concept of substance is in fact a congenial middle ground between "Parmenidean substantialism" and "Heracleitean actualism." Gunton's way of putting things does not allow for the sort of essence I propose.

[48]It may be that the theologian could call on the doctrine of simplicity at this point, but it is less hazardous simply to deny that God's essential properties and his essence are separable. However, the theologian will want to avoid connoting that God is just a cluster of essential attributes.

properties nonetheless. This assumption appeals to a belief—divine truthfulness and faithfulness—which is basic to a Christian understanding of God. Also, it is less susceptible to the interpretation that God's acts in history are part of God's essence, that is, are essential divine properties.

A simple bifurcation between God's being and acts could call into question any claims to knowledge or justified assertions of God based on his acts. If we construed God's "essence" as analogous to a Lockean "substance," as a substratum detachable from all properties essential and accidental, this might be a problem.[49] But essentialism demands no such bifurcation. For instance, to preserve the commitment to divine freedom in creating the world, I said that

(I_a) becomes incarnate as the man Jesus

is a contingent divine property.[50] It does not follow from the contingency of I_a, however, that the trinitarian distinction between Father and Son is itself contingent. For, given the actuality of the incarnation, we can infer that however God is, he is able to become incarnate while remaining divine. In other words, God's contingent act of becoming incarnate entails his essential property of being able to become incarnate while remaining divine. This type of inference plus some other premises—such as the trinitarian identity statements mentioned in chapter one and the claim that there is only one God—are some of the things that give rise to trinitarian doctrine. Essentialism plus the plausible assumption that God is truthful to himself in his revelation can still ground claims about God's essence. Essentialism encourages a distinction and a relation but not a bifurcation between God's historical acts and his essence. Those acts still lead to knowledge of or at least grounded claims about the divine essence.[51] The path is less direct than perhaps Barth would prefer, but it still grounds our knowledge of God's essence in God's acts. In this respect, it accomplishes what Barth sought by way of actualism.

---

[49]As W. Norris Clarke describes Locke's concept in *Explorations in Metaphysics,* p. 16.

[50]Notice that this property is the same as the property *becomes incarnate as Jesus in the actual world.* But it is different from the world indexed property *becomes incarnate as Jesus in w_a,* where w_a specifies the actual world that exists contingently.

[51]That is, divine acts may provide knowledge to aspects of the divine essence. At best, however, such knowledge would be an apprehension of a reality that to finite minds is incomprehensible. So there would still be no question of our comprehending God's essence. Unfortunately, the word *to know* in English is inadequate for negotiating such distinctions.

To say that God acts does suggest a more direct claim about God's essence than the essentialist inference alone implies. As Barth realized, if God "acts" in history, then clearly God is an Actor, an agent, a person. He is one who is able to act.[52] And if anyone who is a person is essentially a person, then being a person or—more carefully—being personal would be an essential divine property.[53] So there is some warrant, if we grant priority to God's acts for our knowledge of him, for considering the notion of personality to be particularly important in our understanding of God.

We should distinguish, though, between two related actualistic inferences. The inference (A_1) *if x is a person, then x acts* has a certain necessitarian ring that is uncongenial to God's freedom and to the essentialist distinction between essential and contingent properties. In contrast, the inference (A_2) *if x acts, then x is a person* lacks these weaknesses.[54] (A_2) is not necessitarian and avoids the connotation that some or another act is essential to God's being. Moreover, with (A_2) we can still infer God's personality from his acts, without implying that if God is a person, he must act in some particular way or at all.[55]

Necessity and divine sovereignty. Barth's treatment of necessity and possibility in his discussion of divine omnipotence is a potential corrective, or at least a warning, for the essentialist. Consistent with his commitment to divine aseity, when he treats omnipotence he insists that we not impose an extrinsic

---

[52]E.g., *CD* I/1, p. 139.

[53]There are all sorts of complexities to using language of personality here, since God is triune. Concluding that God is triune requires more than the mere observation that God acts in history. After all, the Jews believed the latter but not the former. Trinitarian doctrine also requires additional claims about Jesus' and the Spirit's divinity.

[54]I am using "acts" with its modern connotation, and not as the medievals understood it, according to which existence is itself an act. In the sense I mean here, action implies the existence of an intentional agent who does the acting. So we do not say that a rock acts, even though a rock exists.

[55]The essentialist also commends some inferences closer to Barth's than to classical theism. For instance, we are unlikely to infer from any divine act in time that eternity entails timelessness. That concept of eternity, if it is to be defended, likely would derive from either a certain interpretation of divine perfection or the Sovereignty-Aseity-Conviction (SAC) distilled through the *via negativa*. A focus on God's historical acts, especially the incarnation, also encourages modification (or qualification) of the strongest forms of the doctrines of divine immutability and simplicity. These modifications seem to be departures from classical theism. So the modern Christian essentialist can hardly be accused of encouraging a simple separation between God *in se* and God *pro nobis*.

concept of necessity and possibility on God.[56] At the same time, Barth contends—contra Schleiermacher—that we must not dissolve this perfection into omnicausality. On the contrary, the theologian must say that God's power extends beyond the merely actual to the genuinely possible but nonactual. So with the essentialist, Barth admits a distinction between what God can do and what he does do.[57] This follows from the claims that God is perfect in power as well as supremely free.

At the same time, Barth insists that God's perfect power is not a general or abstract omnipotence but is the concrete power of the all-defining God. Accordingly, he takes issue with the traditional formula, found in Thomas Aquinas, Quenstedt, and others, that we should restrict the omnipotence of God to what is logically possible or free of contradiction. This procedure, he protests, "introduces a general concept of what is possible, which is independent of the concept of God, and must be stoutly resisted."[58] Taken out of context, the reader might suspect that Barth is ready to affirm a sort of "universal possibilism" such as Descartes'. For Descartes, God's omnipotence extends even to the logically impossible, or more precisely, God's omnipotence entails that nothing is logically impossible.[59] Despite some extreme voluntaristic ways of speaking, however, Barth avoids this path,[60] as when he qualifies his disapproval of Thomas and others:

> There is no more question of asserting the opposite here than there is in the case of the possibilities or impossibilities which compromise God. We do not argue that the possibilities of God are of such a kind that, for example, He can make two and two five. But the *prius* must certainly be rejected. We cannot accept the idea of an absolutely possible or impossible by which even God's omnipotence

---

[56]*CD* 2/1, pp. 534-38.

[57]Ibid., pp. 530-31.

[58]Ibid., pp. 534, 537-38.

[59]See Harry Frankfurt, "Descartes on the Creation of the Eternal Truths," *Philosophical Review* 86 (1977): 36-57, and Alvin Plantinga, *Does God Have A Nature?* (Milwaukee: Marquette University Press, 1980), pp. 95-126.

[60]We should admit that there are troublesome passages, such as, "The law of contradiction, as the limit of the possible imposed by the creature itself, is so far from being tenable in all circumstances that sooner or later it will inevitably be directed against itself and without the slightest doubt will render impossible all certainty and every certain advance in the realm of creation" (*CD* 2/1, p. 537). However, such statements seem to be rhetorical devices to emphasize the preeminence of "the order of the divine grace," and not attempts to deny the legitimacy of the law of contradiction.

is to be measured. On the contrary, we have to recognise that God's omnipotence is the substance of what is possible.[61]

Thus Barth's objection is not to the concept of necessity and possibility as such but to the suggestion that these are standards that stand over God in some way, like the Forms in Plato's *Timaeus,* which the Demiurge consults in creating the world.[62] Plato's image plainly violates God's aseity, and so Barth rightly rejects it, as well as any interpretation of necessity that he thinks implies it.[63]

I share his motivation and discomfort. There is something inappropriate and impious about imposing our a priori modal intuitions on God. Moreover, such a procedure is likely to generate difficulties in the practice of Christian theology. For example, if one were to evaluate in the abstract the claim that the infinite and invisible God could become incarnate as a human being, one might judge this to be logically impossible, as some contemporary skeptics have done.[64] If one takes the incarnation as an actuality (and a fortiori a possibility), however, it will shape one's intuitions about what is possible. The light cast from the actuality of the incarnation will then illuminate one's understanding of human and divine nature. The Christian should studiously avoid imposing a concept of necessity or possibility that contradicts the Christian witness. So as a call to priority, I think Barth's emphasis is well motivated.

But Barth's treatment of this point does have its problems. For instance, he

---

[61]Ibid., p. 534.

[62]His discussion is complicated by traces of simplicity doctrine. Insofar as this is the case, it conflicts with essentialism. However, as already mentioned, I strongly think simplicity could be excised from his proposal without damaging its overall integrity.

[63]For an extensive but somewhat contentious treatment of Barth's understanding of divine omnipotence, see Sheila Greeve Davaney, *Divine Power: A Study of Karl Barth and Charles Hartshorne* (Philadelphia: Fortress, 1986), pp. 27-99.

[64]See, for example, John Hick, ed., *The Myth of God Incarnate* (1977; reprint, Philadelphia: Westminster Press, 1993), p. 178: "For to say, without explanation, that the historical Jesus of Nazareth was also God is as devoid of meaning as to say that this circle drawn with a pencil on paper is also a square." Clearly Hick is following what he thinks is possible on a priori definitions of "human" and "divine" to determine his evaluation of the truth of the incarnation. Such intuitions and definitions have more force for him than the actuality of the incarnation. Barth would balk at such a priority, as would I. I have discussed this in more detail in "Is the Doctrine of the Incarnation Incoherent?" in *Unapologetic Apologetics: Meeting the Challenges of Theological Studies,* ed. William Dembski and Jay Richards (Downers Grove, Ill.: InterVarsity Press, 2001) pp. 131-143.

asks, "If the fact that two and two make four is not based completely on God's will, and therefore on His omnipotence, and in virtue of it on His work of creation, what real basis could it have?"[65] One answer might be: God's eternal knowledge. But this does not commend itself to Barth because it would require a stronger distinction (but not bifurcation or separation) between God's will and knowledge than he was willing to make. Such a distinction would violate his understanding of God's simplicity. He also might judge it to be a demotion of the priority of God's will.

The degree of voluntarism in Barth's discussion of omnipotence is hard to discern. He does vie for the priority of God's will and choice, but does not specify the sense of "will" that he intends. So he says that mathematical truths have their basis in God's will. Since God's will is for him the most stable basis for anything, however, this claim does not lead him to a mere voluntarism or nominalism. Therefore, he can say "that it is only wantonly and irrationally that we can aspire to the statement that two and two are five."[66] His motivation is noble: he wants to preserve mathematical and necessary truths without compromising divine sovereignty. Grounding mathematical truths in God's will is for Barth as firm a foundation as any one could want.

But again, does God will mathematical truths in the sense that he chooses them from among alternatives? Barth is not altogether clear on the matter. Strictly speaking, the issue is not whether two and two are five (which Barth denies), but whether two and two could have been other than five if God had so willed. If not, then God's choice of such things is certainly different from, say, his choice to create the heavens and the earth. Perhaps Barth intends only to claim that God freely affirms logical and mathematical truths. But this view gives rise to another problem, which looms for essentialism as well: If God did not choose these truths among alternatives, does this entail that some order of mathematical and modal truths exists separately from and simultaneously with God?

I think not. There are ways to block this inference. The first strategy is to explain God's power over necessity and possibility *via* the *analogia attributionis,*

---

[65] *CD* 2/1, p. 538. Elsewhere he says that God "controls and decides what is possible and impossible for Himself and therefore at all" (*CD* 2/1, p. 535). This seems to suggest something like strong actualism, although, as we have mentioned, he may not mean by "controls" and "decides" a choice among alternatives.

[66] *CD* 2/1, p. 538.

so that we understand all modalities as existing preeminently in God and only derivatively in creation. This is in keeping with the spirit of Barth's project, if not fully with the letter. The second strategy is the doctrine of divine ideas. I will develop these subjects in the conclusion.

CONCLUSION

While initial appearances may indicate otherwise, there is significant agreement between Barth's proposal and my own. He is determined to allow the particularity of divine revelation to control his understanding of the divine attributes and is willing to depart from the tradition where he perceives the influence of sources contrary to that revelation. He shows this not only in his derivation and distribution of the divine attributes but also in his use of the notion of God as Subject to correct the traditional language of substance, although he still speaks of God's essence. There is nothing in particularism in itself that is incompatible with essentialism.

Differences do exist between his actualism and my essentialism. Besides his misinterpretation of the Thomistic use of *analogia entis* and the polemic around it, the most likely conflict occurs if we interpret Barth as endorsing strong actualism. Since Barth uses the notion of divine freedom and choice in different senses, however, it is possible not to interpret Barth in this way. Therefore the substantive disagreements between the two proposals—at least on the matters considered here—are relatively minor. Barth is emphatic about preserving the free contingency of God's choice to create. Essentialism provides categories for expressing this conviction more clearly than does the notion of God as being-in-act. Also, some aspects of simplicity may generate unnecessary internal conflicts in his doctrine of God, as they do in any proposal that seeks to preserve the necessity of the God's essence and the contingency of God's choices.

Without these types of simplicity, the category of a free subject helps correct the traditional emphasis on substance.[67] At the same time, theologians should

---

[67]Or at least it is generally helpful. The specifics of Barth's use and definition of "subject" and "person" are other matters, which go beyond this discussion. I am not endorsing Barth's application of the idealist subject of "an I existing in and for itself with its own thought and will" to the one Godhead, as opposed to the three divine persons. I agree that applying this definition of person to the divine persons would produce tritheism. For me, however, this reveals the inadequacy of this definition of person for application to the divine persons. It says nothing about the viability of some other definition of "person," such as a relational one, for such application.

not treat these categories as alternatives. The Christian doctrine of God needs the concept of person or subject and the concept of essence,[68] both properly chastised of course. Barth reminds us to define essence in a way that is compatible with the fact that God is supremely and irreducibly personal.

---

[68]The word *essence* may seem less laden with antique baggage than "substance," although they often do much the same work.

6

CHARLES HARTSHORNE'S
SURRELATIVIST DOCTRINE OF GOD

If we were to draw a spectrum of twentieth-century theologians, on almost any topic, Charles Hartshorne would end up on one side and Karl Barth on the other. These two thinkers differ dramatically. Nevertheless, they were both concerned with the same cluster of theological problems, even if they usually offered different solutions to them. Hartshorne accurately diagnoses some problems that attend classical theism, such as its failure to attribute necessity and contingency (in some sense) to God. Nevertheless, much of his metaphysic is problematic for Christians, in particular his radical modification of the concepts of divine sovereignty and aseity. We may accept some of his critique and agree that God exemplifies necessary and contingent properties, without accepting a panentheistic model of the God-world relation, in which the world is construed as part of God.

Hartshorne was neither a biblical theologian nor the son of one. So, to put his views in the light he intends, let us briefly consider his philosophical method and some of its central themes.

HARTSHORNE'S METAPHYSICAL METHOD

In an intellectual world in which few treat metaphysics as de rigueur, Hartshorne is a metaphysician par excellence. He calls his metaphysics "neo-classical," which expresses his conviction that contemporary philosophy must supersede the classical metaphysics (of being or substance) and that metaphysics as such is not obsolete.[1] Like most metaphysicians, he believes reason properly

---

[1]Charles Hartshorne, *The Logic of Perfection and Other Essays in Neo-Classical Metaphysics* (LaSalle, Ill.: Open Court, 1962), pp. ix-x (hereafter *LP*).

exercised can acquire universal truths.[2] Just as Kant attempted to discern the conditions of possible experience, Hartshorne seeks to abstract the fundamental components of all experience. The metaphysician asks, How do we distinguish between the essential and contingent aspects of experience? Hartshorne is concerned with objective modality—which for him is temporality—and with an "unrestricted or completely general theory of concreteness." That is, as metaphysician he seeks abstractions, but only via their "location" in concrete particulars.[3]

He defines metaphysics as an a priori theory of value, creativity and cosmology and a "rational or secular approach to theology."[4] The metaphysician seeks variables in experience with a universal range of applicability, including logical, moral, theological and aesthetic fields. He searches for truths implicit in all experience, truths that no experience could falsify, or more correctly, that every possible experience confirms.[5] In this sense, the metaphysician seeks a priori and necessary truths, not in Kant's sense of being nonempirical, but in Karl Popper's sense of contradicting no possible experience. So his method is still broadly empirical and inductive, even if it seeks the a priori and necessary variables in experience.[6] In this way he procures several related necessary existential truths, such as "something exists," "experience occurs" or "creative synthesis occurs" (see below).[7] These are, as he puts it, "non-restrictive existential statements," confirmed by every experience and falsified by none. They

---

[2]So he recounts his early decision: "About the age of seventeen, after reading Emerson's *Essays,* I made up my mind (doubtless with a somewhat hazy notion of what I was doing) to trust reason to the end" (*LP,* p. viii).

[3]Charles Hartshorne in *A Reply to My Critics,* "Frankenberry on Method in Metaphysics," in *The Philosophy of Charles Hartshorne,* ed. Lewis Hahn (LaSalle, Ill.: Open Court, 1991), pp. 634-35 (hereafter *PCH*).

[4]See Hartshorne's list of eleven definitions of metaphysics in *Creative Synthesis and Philosophical Method* (LaSalle, Ill.: Open Court, 1970), p. 24 (hereafter *CSPM*).

[5]"Metaphysical truths may be described as such that no experience can contradict them, but also such that any experience must illustrate them" (*LP,* p. 285).

[6]Nancy Frankenberry, "Hartshorne's Method in Metaphysics," in *The Philosophy of Charles Hartshorne,* ed. Lewis Hahn (LaSalle, Ill.: Open Court, 1991), pp. 296-97. So Hartshorne says of the metaphysical role of deduction that it "is not to bring out the content of the initially certain, but to bring out the meaning of tentative descriptions of the metaphysically ultimate in experience so that we shall be better able to judge if they do genuinely describe this ultimate" (*Reality as Social Process* [Boston: Bacon, 1953], p. 175).

[7]*CSPM,* p. 172. For Hartshorne, the production of these truths also demonstrates that metaphysics is possible.

rule out no contingent experience or its logical complement. This method also leads to the conclusion that the concept of utter nothingness is nonsense, since it could never be experienced.[8] While he repudiates all strong forms of positivism, this grounding of meaning in verification betrays his acceptance of a verificationist criterion of meaning in metaphysics,[9] as well as his adoption of the idealist thesis that to be is to be perceived or experienced.[10] (Verificationists attempted—unsuccessfully—to restrict meaningful statements to those statements that could be empirically verified. The central problem, of course, was that no statement of verificationism could itself be empirically verified, meaning verificationism, according to its own criterion, would be meaningless. But this is another discussion.) In any case, these assumptions—verificationism and idealism—allow him to criticize certain metaphysical views such as materialism, determinism and atheism, since they are pure denials, which are incapable of being known or experienced.[11]

Metaphysical truths are confirmed by every fact; but strictly speaking, they are not facts themselves. Hartshorne confines "facts" to contingent states.[12] Metaphysical truths are rather universal correlates of facts.[13] Since they restrict no fact, they are necessarily positive, being exemplified and entailed by every fact, whereas any contingent fact has an alternative or so-called negativity. That is, a fact, since it is contingent, rules out its alternative. This alternative is a possibility that is not actual but excluded by an incompatible actuality.[14]

---

[8]*CSPM*, pp. 159-72; *LP*, p. 283.

[9]*CSPM*, pp. 21-22.

[10]Hartshorne counts this judgment among his metaphysical convictions, although he insists it is compatible with epistemological realism, according to which "subjects . . . are dependent on objects." "Response to Peters," in *Existence and Actuality*, ed. John B. Cobb Jr. and Franklin Gamwell (Chicago: University of Chicago Press, 1984), pp. 12-13. (See his formalization of his intuition that produces theistic idealism, *CSPM*, p. 286.) There are other senses in which Hartshorne is an idealist. He cannot conceive of two internally coherent, clear systems that contradict each other. They would be at most specializations of a broader metaphysical system. "Metaphysical statements are not opposed to anything except wrong ways of talking. Metaphysical error is exclusively a matter of confusion, inconsistency, or lack of definite meaning, rather than factual mistakes." This common claim exhibits an inability to see any real alternative to "classical theism" than his own. So his understanding of metaphysics collapses if an internally coherent metaphysical alternative exists.

[11]Eugene Peters, "Methodology in the Metaphysics of Charles Hartshorne," in *Existence and Actuality*, ed. John B. Cobb Jr. and Franklin Gamwell (Chicago: University of Chicago Press, 1984), p. 6.

[12]E.g., *LP*, p. 295; *CSPM*, pp. 157-58.

[13]*LP*, p. 296.

[14]Peters, "Methodology," pp. 2-3.

Metaphysical necessities, by contrast, are exemplified by any conceivable actuality. In this sense, while not factual in the sense of being contingent, metaphysical truths are nevertheless existential,[15] since they have to do with all actual (concrete) entities. In this way, he confers ontological priority on actuality, as opposed to the merely possible.[16]

Metaphysics for Hartshorne requires a healthy dose of logic and intuition.[17] He uses logic to "exhaust possible solutions to a problem and arrive at the best or truest by elimination of those that are unsatisfactory."[18] Frequently he employs "position matrices" using the categories of quantification—all, some or none—which then derive their content by analyzing concepts and the history of philosophy.[19] This procedure protects the metaphysician from overlooking real options, and it is an important element in his critique of classical theism, as we will see below.[20]

SOME CENTRAL THEMES

Hartshorne's metaphysic has a striking unity, emphasizing temporal becoming or process, relativity and creativity.[21] He is a panpsychist, seeing all concrete entities as experiencing minds. In addition, he emphasizes so-called event occasions over individual entities or substances. These core commitments inform and even determine his theological conclusions.

Relativity. Fundamental to Hartshorne's thought is the notion of relativity. Grounding metaphysics in experience requires "close attention to the temporal structure of experience,"[22] which he extrapolates as the fundamental struc-

---

[15]*CSPM,* pp. 159-72.

[16]Peters, "Methodology," pp. 4-5.

[17]*CSPM,* p. xviii.

[18]Ibid., p. 84.

[19]Ibid., pp. 86-88; Frankenberry, "Hartshorne's Method in Metaphysics," pp. 300-301.

[20]While Hartshorne employs numerous methodological principles throughout his substantial literary corpus, in *CSPM* he cites four. (A) The principle of least paradox (pp. 88-89); (B) The principle of inclusive contrast (p. 90). (See Hartshorne's list of "metaphysical contraries," pp. 100-101. Cf. *PSG,* p. 2); (C) The principle of generality (pp. 90-92); and (D) The principle of balanced definiteness (pp. 92-98).

[21]"Causality, substance, memory, perception, temporal succession, modality, are all but modulations of one principle of creative synthetic experiencing, feeding entirely upon its own prior products" (*CSPM,* p. 107). "The social theory, then, is pan-psychistic, pan-indeterministic (or pan-creationistic), pan-relativistic, and pan-temporalistic, in the sense that every concrete being has psychic, free or creative, relative, and temporal aspects" (*RSP,* p. 135).

[22]*CSPM,* p. xxi.

ture of reality. An emphasis on becoming is inevitable. Relativity for Hartshorne is what *could not not be*. "Relativity is the absolute principle!" There is
no experience that does not include relation as a constituent. We cannot abstract from all relationships but at most "from relationships to particular contingent things."[23] Therefore the category of relation becomes a central theological category. For God and everything else, to be is to be in relation.[24] In
distinction from the classical metaphysical emphasis on being, he emphasizes
becoming. He does not reject the category of being, however, but subsumes it
under becoming. Since becoming includes being and becoming, he surmises,
it is the more general category.[25] Thus he calls his proposal a metaphysics of
creativity or process.[26] The successive accumulation of experiences in which
there is a continual creation of "novel wholes with non-novel elements" he
calls "creative synthesis."[27] If one were to reduce his proposal to a single ultimate principle, it would likely be indeterminate creativity.[28] "*To be is to create,*"
he declares. As long as there are individuals, there is creativity.[29]

Closely related to relativity and becoming is Hartshorne's axiomatic intuition that time is objective. It is the "givenness" and irreducibility of "time's ar-
row" that allows for real possibility, which is a prerequisite for true creativity.[30]
In general, then, he understands the logical modalities of possibility and necessity as temporal concepts. Time for him is objective modality; it is quantal,
atomic and discrete rather than continuous and dense. It is asymmetric and
the basis of freedom and possibility.[31]

Related to his understanding of time is his distinction between internal and
external relations. Hartshorne sees in the history of philosophy a false di-

---

[23]Charles Hartshorne, *The Divine Relativity: A Social Conception of God* (New Haven, Conn.: Yale University Press, 1948), p. 73 (hereafter *DR*).

[24]*CSPM*, pp. 47, 114.

[25]Frankenberry, "Hartshorne's Method in Metaphysics," p. 293.

[26]*LP*, pp. ix-x.

[27]*CSPM*, p. 89.

[28]Eugene Peters, *Hartshorne and Neoclassical Metaphysics* (Lincoln: University of Nebraska Press, 1970),
p. 80.

[29]*CSPM*, p. 1.

[30]Charles Hartshorne, "A Revision of Peirce's Categories," *Monist* 63, no. 3 (1980): 285-86.

[31]See James P. Devlin, "Hartshorne's Metaphysical Asymmetry," in *The Philosophy of Charles Hartshorne*,
ed. Lewis Hahn (LaSalle, Ill.: Open Court, 1991), pp. 281-87. We treat Hartshorne's concept of time
in more detail below.

lemma between viewing all relations as internal or all relations as external to their terms. According to philosopher G. E. Moore, a term A is external to a term B just in case A could be essentially the same without B.[32] While Hartshorne seems to agree with Moore in his definition of external relation, it is not clear that he understands an internal relation as "essential" to its term, and an external relation as "accidental" to its term, as does Moore. Rather, he tends to describe the distinction in terms of dependence and independence. If a relation is internal to an entity, it "makes a difference" to that entity in some way. For a relation to be "internal" to a term, the term must in some sense "depend" on the related term. If a relation is "external" to a term, then that term is "independent" of the term to which it relates.[33] Monists such as Bradley, Spinoza, Royce and Blanshard saw all dependent relations as symmetrical (the same on both ends of the relation) and internal (although Bradley finally argued that these are illusory). On the other hand, pluralists such as Ockham, Hume, Russell, G. E. Moore and Carnap saw every independent relation as symmetrical and external, and required a third entity, namely, the relation itself, to explain the total situation. Many have argued that this strategy fails because it leads to an infinite regress.[34]

Hartshorne splits the difference, arguing against both of these "symmetrical" views of relations as a false dilemma. Not only are there external and internal relations, but also there are asymmetrical relations, in which a relation is internal to one term (or relatum) and external to another. In fact, he sees asymmetrical relations as primary and symmetrical ones as derivative.[35] So he calls "*symmetry within an overall asymmetry* . . . a paradigm for metaphysics."[36]

His favorite examples of asymmetrical relations are the relation of knowledge and the relation of past states and events to present and future ones.[37] As

---

[32]G. E. Moore, "External and Internal Relations," *Philosophical Studies* (London: Routledge & Kegan Paul, 1922) n.p. Interestingly, Moore also claims that the idealists argue that all relations are internal and so essential to their terms (p. 276).

[33]His use of "internal" and "external" relations is tied up with his temporal understanding of modality. We consider this in more detail below.

[34]Frankenberry, "Hartshorne's Method of Metaphysics," pp. 304-5; *DR*, pp. 60-67; *CSPM*, pp. 211-18.

[35]*CSPM*, p. 226.

[36]Ibid., p. 210.

[37]Other examples include logical implication, the relation between the abstract and the concrete, and the relation between part and whole. See, for example, *CSPM*, pp. 205-11.

a relation my knowledge of the number two is internal to me, since to know 2 is to be dependent on 2 in some requisite sense. The relation is external to the number two, however, since it is not dependent on my knowledge of it in any way. My knowledge relation does not "enter into the term." This also proves for Hartshorne another crucial point about the meaning of "absolute": "That the abstract is absolute or independent in relation to the concrete, and that the known is, or at least may be, absolute in relation to the knower."[38] So for Hartshorne the subject is always "dependent on" the object for knowledge of it.[39] This epistemic use of the internal/external distinction in relations is important in his concept of God, which we will consider shortly.

But what if the object of knowledge is concrete? This question leads to another important example of an asymmetrical relation: the temporal one. For Hartshorne past events are internal to present events; future events, in contrast, are not internal to present or past ones. A future event is not "given" without remainder in present or past events. The past is fixed with respect to the present and the future, whereas the future, while shaped by the actualities of its past, is not determined or fixed by them. The present event has a restrained self-creation, conditioned by the past events that partially constitute but do not determine it. The future is partly indeterminate and indistinct,[40] the unspecified and not yet actual realm of potentiality. The future is an undifferentiated continuum rather than an infinite set of discrete possibilities. To deny this is to deny what we all take for granted concerning the reality of time and to make nonsense of the decisions and actions we take. In this way, Hartshorne hopes to preserve the cause-effect relation without making it deterministic.

Panpsychism. Hartshorne's generalization from experience also leads to

---

[38]*DR*, p. 67. He says:

> Look deeply enough into anything and you will, it may be, find its ancestors and its history inscribed upon its nature. But will you equally find its posterity and its destiny? This is the question of indeterminism, in one of its forms. There is a purely logical reason both for asserting that effects are related to causes and for denying that there is in a cause any relation whatever to ("its") *particular* future effects. Temporal relations must be somewhere, properties of something, and if particulars are not related prospectively to particulars, then they must be related retrospectively to particulars—else there would be no temporal order of particulars. But particulars cannot be related prospectively to particulars. (p. 68)

> To say otherwise is to reduce "the idea of time to an absurdity" (p. 69).

[39]Note that Hartshorne holds both this "realist" thesis as well as the "idealist" thesis that "any entity must be (or at least destined to become) object for some subject or other" (*RSP*, pp. 69-84).

[40]*DR*, pp. 67-69.

panpsychism or psychicalism, according to which all individual constituents of the universe are "experiencing," internally related minds or subjects.[41] Every concrete actuality has a type of experience, and reality as a whole is experiencing reality.[42] Appropriately, David Ray Griffin calls this view "panexperientialism."[43] Hartshorne can argue that, since all individuals have experiences, "sentient individual" is redundant.[44] He thinks it is anthropocentric to conclude that experience *simpliciter* is restricted only to us. As it would be solipsistic to restrict subjective experience only to oneself, so it would be solipsistic to restrict experience only to human beings or complex organic life forms.[45] At the same time, he does not say that all concrete individuals are necessarily sentient as we are.

Since this theory attributes experience to entities lacking sense organs, it requires that feeling and perception not be reducible to mere sensory perception. For help in this regard, Hartshorne turns to Alfred North Whitehead's notion of immediate nonsensory perception or "prehension," which all events exemplify. One's access to one's body and memory are examples of such direct prehension.[46] Prehension is an immediate "intuition of the antecedently real," and as such is common to both memory and sense perception.[47] It is "feeling

---

[41]*RSP*, pp. 78-84.

[42]Reiner Wiehl, "Hartshorne's Panpsychism," in *The Philosophy of Charles Hartshorne*, ed. Lewis Hahn (LaSalle, Ill.: Open Court, 1991), p. 450.

[43]David Ray Griffin, "Hartshorne's Postmodern Philosophy," in *Hartshorne, Process Philosophy and Theology*, ed. Robert Kane and Stephen H. Phillips (Albany: SUNY Press, 1989), p. 5.

[44]*CSPM*, p. 143. This entails that strict "inanimateness" is "a natural illusion of commonsense and primitive science" (*CSPM*, p. 51).

[45]Establishing this doctrine is probably an unattainable goal and, strictly speaking, it is unfalsifiable, given its metaphysical generality (*LP*, p. 128). Hartshorne argues, however, that panpsychism has advantages over the other live options, namely, monistic idealism, dualism and materialism. Hartshorne's arguments usually appeal to the explanatory power of panpsychism and its immunity from problems that beset the alternatives. Among his arguments are the following. Monistic idealism makes short shrift of the reality of our experience of plurality and personal freedom. For dualism and materialism, the objectivity of temporality and natural law without determinism is unintelligible (Charles Hartshorne, *Beyond Humanism: Essays in the New Philosophy of Nature* [Chicago: Willet, Clark, 1937], pp. 138-49, hereafter *BH*). Panpsychism does not leave matter wholly mysterious and alien. It is not plagued with the dualistic obscurity of relating the mind and the body, as well as the implausibility of the theory that mind emerged from brute matter. The panpsychist can also appeal to quantum physics, in particular to the discovery that fundamental particles are active and indeterministic, rather than inert (*LP*, pp. 183-84, 211, 216-33; *CSPM*, p. 9; Griffin, "Hartshorne's Postmodern Philosophy," pp. 6-7).

[46]Griffin, "Hartshorne's Postmodern Philosophy," p. 12.

[47]*CSPM*, p. 91.

of feeling," that is, "the manner in which one subject feels the feelings of one or more other subjects."[48] Past prehensions are repeated in present experience by way of sympathetic feeling, the preeminent example being God's prehension of all reality and retention of all past events. In fact, feeling or direct acquaintance is the fundamental metaphor for God's knowledge.[49] Prehension appropriates the "realist" insight that all experience is dependent upon the thing experienced. By defining love as "the relation of sympathy," Hartshorne is able to unify reality via divine love.[50]

Hartshorne does not suppose that, say, rocks and trees are sentient. Such things lack particular experience, not because they are brute matter but rather because they are really aggregrates of concrete individuals such as atoms or organic cells.[51] Aggregates might still be determined as physical objects while allowing for indeterminacy (and hence freedom) of the concrete individuals that constitute them. These individual constituents are the experiencing subjects.[52]

A human person, unlike either an aggregate or a fully concrete entity, is a compound individual in which there is a unity of feeling and experience. He or she has a dominant center that gives it a self-determination lacking in an aggregate such as a rock, whose various individual constituents (the fundamental particles) cancel each other out statistically in their movements.[53] Compound individuals like human beings are really hierarchies of compound individuals, since they are made up of atoms and individual organic cells. Once we understand hierarchies of compound individuals, from atoms to cells to animals to the entire universe, we can infer from the freedom and indeterminacy at the subatomic levels to a freedom and indeterminacy of the universe as a whole.[54]

---

[48]Charles Hartshorne, *Omnipotence and Other Theological Mistakes* (Albany: SUNY Press, 1984), p. 27 (hereafter *OOTM*).

[49]Donald Wayne Viney, "God Only Knows? Hartshorne and the Mechanics of Omniscience," in *Hartshorne, Process Philosophy and Theology*, ed. Robert Kane and Stephen H. Phillips (Albany: SUNY Press, 1989), p. 83.

[50]*BH*, p. 26; *LP*, pp. 129-32; Griffin, "Hartshorne's Postmodern Philosophy," p. 17.

[51]*BH*, pp. 111-12.

[52]Similarly, groups of persons such as a nation of citizens are aggregates and not concrete individuals (*CSPM*, p. 141).

[53]Griffin, "Hartshorne's Postmodern Philosophy," p. 9; Charles Hartshorne, *Man's Vision of God* (LaSalle, Ill.: Open Court, 1941), p. xvi (hereafter *MVG*).

[54]*BH*, p. 112.

Complexity increases as one goes up the hierarchy,[55] with God as the highest level. God is the all-inclusive compound individual, which Hartshorne illustrates with Plato's World Soul. As "Soul" God is the total series of personally ordered experiences. The world as God's body is "certain other and subordinate subjects on a lower level of conscious or nonconscious feeling.[56] So panpsychism provides Hartshorne with an understanding of God's relation to the universe as a whole; in fact, it allows him to argue that panpsychism is implicit in theism.[57]

The concrete actual event as fundamental. It would be inaccurate to identify Hartshorne's panpsychism with Leibniz's, in which the universe consists of an immense number of individual monads or substances that endure through time.[58] Unlike Leibniz, Hartshorne combines panpsychism with the conviction that the fundamental concrete reality is the occasion or event, not an enduring individual or substance. The most concrete particular is not an "individual" per se, but an actual event.[59] "Individuals are neither wholly actual and concrete nor merely potential and abstract, but both. Only actualities, particulars, are wholly concrete and definite."[60] This leads to his important distinction between existence and actuality (we will discuss this below). Individuals and species exist; singular actualities occur and are self-actualized.[61] This does not entail a radical individualism or pluralism, however, because "individuals" such as human persons, according to Hartshorne, are streams of actual experiences. A human person, an atom and a cell are all abstractions from particular sets of temporalized quanta of event-experiences; they are "low-level universals"[62] and as such are best understood as societies or social processes. They

---

[55]Ibid., pp. 115ff.

[56]Hartshorne, *A Reply to My Critics,* in "Ford on Whitehead's and My Philosophy," *PCH,* p. 642.

[57]*CSPM,* p. 143.

[58]See Hartshorne, *A Reply to My Critics,* in "Frankenberry on Method in Metaphysics," *PCH,* p. 638.

[59]"Events, Individuals and Predication: A Defense of Event Pluralism," *CSPM,* pp. 173-204. Event speaking is "the most analytically complete way of speaking"; substance speaking "is a simplification or shorthand" (p. 175). But even an event sequence is "fully determinate only retrospectively" (p. 177) since only the past is actual. Not surprisingly, this ontological privilege bestowed on event is most explicit in Buddhism. So Hartshorne chastises Western philosophers for long ignoring Buddhism (pp. 177, 191, 269). The priority of event leads him to conclude that "the genuinely concrete or inclusive unity, the determinate subject, is a new creation each moment" (p. 180).

[60]Hartshorne, *A Reply to My Critics,* in *PCH,* p. 660; also *CSPM,* p. 92.

[61]Hartshorne, *A Reply to My Critics,* in *PCH,* p. 643.

[62]*CSPM,* p. 73.

are "stabilities" which are in the events.[63] Events are not things that happen to enduring individual substances. Rather, endurance is an abstraction or construction from the relation of certain event-states through remembering, loving and feeling.[64] This is reminiscent of Whitehead's conception of reality as a "social integration of occasions."[65] Emphasizing the fundamental concreteness not of enduring substances or individuals but of event-experiences is crucial for Hartshorne's thought in general and for his concept of God in particular.

HARTSHORNE'S SURRELATIVE CONCEPTION OF GOD AS A CRITIQUE OF CLASSICAL THEISM

Hartshorne's concept of God so permeates his thought that it cannot be separated from his philosophy as a whole. He offers his theological view as a coherent alternative to a classical conception he believes is beset with internal contradictions. Hartshorne levels many arguments against what he calls classical theism. For instance, like contemporary "open theists," he alleges that if God exhaustively knew the future, it would destroy human freedom and implicate God in evil. He also argues that creation ex nihilo is contradictory because it requires a beginning of time. While these arguments are important, they are less worrisome than his case for the incoherence of classical theism, in which he contends that an immutable and impassible God could not know a temporally ordered, contingent creation.[66] Similarly, he argued for decades that the notions of a greatest possible value and of a being exemplifying all actuality are incoherent.[67]

Consider first his argument against the possibility of an absolutely perfect, completely actual God. Most simply, he maintains that it is impossible that God could contain all possibilities, since not all possibilities are compossible—they cannot all obtain. To put it directly, God cannot actualize all possibilities. To choose to create this world, for instance, God had to choose not to create worlds that were not compatible with it. By creating a world in which

---

[63]*LP*, p. 219.

[64]Ibid., pp. 66, 121.

[65]Charles Hartshorne, "Whitehead's Idea of God," in *The Philosophy of Alfred North Whitehead* (Evanston, Ill.: Northwestern University Press, 1941), p. 540.

[66]Such arguments are a common theme in Hartshorne's writings. See his brief treatment in *OOTM*, pp. 10-50. Griffin lists six central arguments against classical theism (p. 17).

[67]*CSPM*, p. 229.

Augustine lives during the fourth and fifth centuries A.D., he had to forego creating a world in which Augustine never exists. So there are potential states of affairs that God chose not to make actual.[68] In order to avoid this incoherence, Hartshorne rejects the classical idea of God as pure actuality, opting instead for a view of God as actual and potential. To say otherwise is to deny that God truly creates. God is actual with respect to what is actual and potential with respect to what is potential. God cannot be actual to what is not actual. So it makes no sense to say God is pure actuality.

Similarly, to deny that there are any unactualized possibilities is to deny divine and creaturely freedom and to deny that the world is contingent. Finally, to conceive of God as *ens realissimum* or a greatest possible being is to understand concrete value as fixed. This is as inconceivable as a highest even number. So the classical theistic understanding of divine perfection is incoherent.

At the same time, Hartshorne does not abandon the conviction that God is perfect. Rather, he seeks a consistent definition of perfection that is compatible with his metaphysic.[69] He agrees fully with the classical theist that a being that might not exist is not as exalted as one that must exist. In other words, any being perfect in any plausible sense, and one worthy of unreserved devotion, will exist necessarily rather than contingently.

He reinforces this conviction with his vigorous defense and restatement of the ontological argument for the existence of God, which, in modalized form, claims that if God is conceivable, then he exists, since necessary existence is part of the concept of God. If God's necessary existence is conceivable, then God exists.[70] Reflecting this conviction, Hartshorne spent much of his career seeking and defending a coherent concept of God. According to Hartshorne, however, to establish a consistent meaning for God is only to establish his bare abstract existence[71] but not his concrete, contingent actuality.[72]

---

[68]Because of Hartshorne's emphasis on the partial self-creation of all individuals, it is not quite correct to say that God unilaterally chooses any state of affairs which includes other free agents.

[69]*MVG*, p. 6.

[70]His fullest treatment of the ontological argument is *Anselm's Discovery: A Re-examination of the Ontological Argument* (LaSalle, Ill.: Open Court, 1965).

[71]J. Van der Veken, "From Modal Language to Model Language: Charles Hartshorne and Linguistic Analysis," in *Hartshorne, Process Philosophy and Theology*, ed. Robert Kane and Stephen H. Phillips (Albany: SUNY Press, 1989), p. 33.

[72]*RSP*, p. 172.

Moreover, to say God exists necessarily is different from saying, as in classical theism, that God is Pure Act (*Actus Purus*). To say with Anselm that God is "such that none greater is conceivable" certainly "excludes merely contingent existence, though not all contingent properties."[73] God's perfection requires some types of necessity, such as necessary existence. To say God exists necessarily is to say that he is necessarily in some or another concrete actuality. But perfection does not require that God be necessary in every respect. Quite the contrary, for Hartshorne God's actuality is always contingent, since it always includes some contingent state.[74] God exists necessarily, but God's concrete actuality is contingent.

To locate a coherent definition of perfection, Hartshorne develops a "position matrix" that expresses the possible ways an entity might be absolute, relative or imperfect. With such a position matrix, Hartshorne hopes to exhaust the conceptual options for theistic belief. He argues that classical theism has often dealt with a restricted set of options, assuming that only static absolute perfection suffices for an appropriate concept of deity. Hartshorne's matrix, in contrast, expresses all the possible types of divine perfection, its options falling into three groups, corresponding to the three types of quantification: (1) absolute perfection in all respects, (2) in some respects and (3) in no respects. While there are various ways in which one may construe groups (2) and (3), it is necessarily true that there is a being described by one of these three options.[75] To be absolutely perfect (with no potentiality) in all respects is the classical theistic understanding of divine perfection, according to which God is pure actuality; however, Hartshorne judges that idea to be incoherent, not least because any actuality will rule out other incompatible options. So, as an alternative, he defends the second type of perfection, namely, perfection in some respects—or more precisely, absolute perfection in some, relative perfection in other respects. Anything falling under the third type would not be a proper object of worship and obviously would not constitute a perfect being. So, if position (1) is incoherent, and position (3) does not allow perfection in any sense, then divine perfection must fall somewhere under position (2).

---

[73]*LP*, p. 35.

[74]*CSPM*, p. 84.

[75]*MVG*, pp. 8-12, 72, 230; also *RSP*, pp. 110-25.

Besides his argument against pure actuality, Hartshorne attempts to demonstrate the incoherence of classical theism with what we might call the argument from unsurpassability (AU). It concludes that in order for God to be unsurpassable by another, God must include the totality of all things. Consider the possibility that God does not include this totality. In such a case God plus the world would have a greater value than God alone. To deny this is to deny that the world has any value.[76] So then God without the world, defined as a being unsurpassable by another, would be surpassed by another, namely, God plus the world, which is a contradiction. To avoid this contradiction, we must define God as the totality of God plus all things "distinct" from God. Then there is nothing outside God that can surpass him.

Moreover, since the total value of reality as a whole is constantly increasing, we cannot define God's perfection as unsurpassability *simpliciter*. Rather, God is the "self-surpassing surpasser of all," "the integrated sum of existence" and "the self-identical individuality of the world."[77] This constitutes his perfection, wherein he "enjoys" the values of the totality of things (akin to the aesthetic enjoyment of variety and the distinction between the actual and the potential).[78] By having all actual value, nothing outside God surpasses him in value[79]: "For any increase anywhere is a fortiori increase in him." Rightly conceived then, God's perfection is dynamic rather than static.[80]

Even if God cannot be unsurpassable absolutely, it is important to understand God as unsurpassable by another. For if God could be surpassed by another, he would not be ultimately worthy of worship, since worship of anything less than the preeminent reality would be an idolatrous contradiction of the religious spirit.[81] For Hartshorne, God's perfection is his "modal complete-

---

[76]This is a common argument in Hartshorne's works. See, for example, *DR*, pp. 90-91.

[77]*MVG*, p. 20; also *CSPM*, p. 277.

[78]Aesthetic value is for Hartshorne more intrinsic and immediate even than moral value. See his "The Aesthetic Dimensions of Religious Experience," in *Logic, God and Metaphysics*, ed. James F. Harris (Dordrecht: Kluwer Academic, 1992), p. 9. Hartshorne wonders what possible reason God could have for creating a world if it does not add any value to him. See Charles Hartshorne, "Clarke's Thomistic Critique," in *Charles Hartshorne's Concept of God* (Dordrecht: Kluwer Academic, 1990), p. 271.

[79]*MVG*, p. 21.

[80]Charles Hartshorne, *A Natural Theology for Our Time* (LaSalle, Ill.: Open Court, 1967), p. 72 (hereafter *NTT*).

[81]*NTT*, pp. 3-7; Alan Gragg, *Charles Hartshorne* (Waco, Tex.: Word, 1973), p. 88.

ness"[82] or "modal coincidence,"[83] since he includes everything actual as actual and everything possible or potential as possible or potential. So Hartshorne can claim that at any time t, God is perfect. Even God's value can and does increase (but it can never decrease), however, so that what constitutes divine perfection at a time t will be less than what constitutes divine perfection at $t + 1$. Because of the reality of creativity and relativity, "there will always be a net increment of value accruing to God at each moment."[84]

But God is not simply an entity constantly increasing in every respect as a world-process. Such a position would be indistinguishable from evolutionary pantheism.[85] Rather, God is "the self-identical individuality of the world somewhat as a man is the self-identical individuality of his ever changing system of atoms."[86] God is not merely an individual; he is *the* individual.[87] As the all-inclusive individual, God supervenes over the world-process rather than being reducible to it.

But what about all those claims to divine absoluteness so central in Western theistic religions? Surely Hartshorne's proposal would be inadequate if he simply rejected such claims. He hopes to accommodate many of the classical claims to divine immutability, necessity, absoluteness, eternity and simplicity by distinguishing between two aspects or "poles" of God. That aspect of God capable of increase is God's relative aspect. That aspect which is always maximum is God's absolute aspect. The convergence of the absolute and relative in God is that unique type of perfection called surrelativity.[88]

Hartshorne identifies God's absolute aspect with what Whitehead desig-

---

[82]Hartshorne, *Anselm's Discovery*, p. 123.

[83]*LP*, pp. 34-40.

[84]*DR*, p. 46.

[85]He does say that it is time "that leads us to God as the self identity of process" (*MVG*, p. 269).

[86]Ibid., pp. 230-31.

[87]Charles Hartshorne, "Cloots and Van der Veken on Panentheism," in *Charles Hartshorne's Concept of God* (Dordrecht: Kluwer Academic, 1990), p. 281.

[88]Besides being coherent, Hartshorne believes his theological conception does greater justice to the religious spirit than does the absolutely absolute deity of classical theism. And while the classical conception is clearly the majority view in Western history, a stream of loyal opposition has signaled agreement with Hartshorne's dipolar intuition. Moreover, the religious view of God embodied in the Western Scriptures (the Old and New Testaments and the Qur'an) seems more attuned to his understanding than to the classical view of God as absolute in every respect. See "The Two Strands in Historical Theology," *MVG*, pp. 85-141.

nated God's primordial nature and God's relative aspect, with what Whitehead called God's consequent nature.[89] So for Hartshorne there are two divine aspects or poles, which is why his doctrine of God is often called dipolar, in contrast to classical theism, which is monopolar. With this distinction, Hartshorne can attribute to God categorical contraries (not contradictories), while arguing that classical theism erred in attributing to God only one side of such contraries. So, for example, God as absolute, independent, externally related, atemporal, potential, necessary, infinite, simple and generic refers to God in his primordial nature. But this is only God in the abstract. In God's consequent nature, he is relative (has relations), experiencing, affected, becoming, temporal, actual, contingent, finite, complex and individual.[90] He is concrete and particular in his consequent nature. And since God is the total reality of both natures, God as a concrete actuality is always contingent[91] because a conjunction of a necessary and a contingent proposition is always contingent. Analogously, if God is a totality of necessary and contingent aspects, then his total concrete reality is contingent, although his existence abstracted from all contingent relations is necessary. God necessarily exists, but always in some or another contingent state of actuality. That God exists in some or another actual state is necessary; nevertheless, every actual state in which God exists is contingent. God's contingent actuality includes his absolute abstract aspect, as any concrete entity "includes" its abstract essence. To deny this is, for Hartshorne, to deny that God is a concrete individual and to relegate him to the merely abstract.[92]

So while perfection does require necessary existence, it does not require exclusively necessary properties. If perfection required all necessary properties, then for Hartshorne, God would be purely abstract, which would be utterly inadequate religiously and metaphysically. In fact, it would be a defect, not perfection.[93] While God in his total actuality is always contingent, his contingency is preeminent, because, unlike all other individuals, the class of God's

---

[89]This is not to say that Hartshorne agreed with Whitehead on every detail of his doctrine of God. In fact, he disagreed with Whitehead's understanding of eternal objects, among other things.

[90]See the complete list of "metaphysical contraries" in *CSPM*, pp. 100-101.

[91]*RSP*, p. 204. Also Hartshorne, "Response to Martin," in *Existence and Actuality*, p. 75.

[92]*CSPM*, p. 254.

[93]Hartshorne, *Anselm's Discovery*, p. 143.

possible states could not be empty.[94] There is no time or event in which God does not exist. So, Hartshorne can say that God as the totality is the most dependent as well as the preeminent reality. In God's actual concrete state, he is dependent on every other entity, not for his abstract essence or existence but for the particularity of his actuality. His contingent states "contain" as it were his necessary aspect.[95] For this reason, Hartshorne can claim that relativity is itself the basic principle of contrary theological attributions. It is the one "absolute."[96] So God in his concrete states is "forever incomplete"[97] but also forever increasing in value. Herein lies true divine perfection.

Hartshorne argues that the classical theist inappropriately discriminates by ascribing to God the preeminence of only some of these terms. While the theologian can consistently use the *via eminentiae* if he considers all the categories, with the *via negativa* he "plays favorites among the categories" by restricting the ways in which God can be preeminent.[98] Hartshorne's strategy allows them all to apply to God without contradiction. In this way he can say that God is perfect while preserving divine and creaturely freedom and maintaining a real relation between God and creatures.

Hartshorne suspects that the different forms of theism primarily differ in how they understand God's independence from things other than himself, and in what sense they understand that God is perfect.[99] While differing from the classical understanding of God as independent in every respect, surrelativism still includes a notion of God's independence. God as the self-surpassing surpasser is understood as independent of any particular world, such as this one. The existence of this world is contingent, while God's existence is necessary. However, God is not independent of "world-as-such." Since God is supreme cause, "the class 'possible worlds' has some actual member."[100] Therefore surrelativism differs from classical theism, which sees God as independent of this or any creation, and from pantheism, which sees God as identical with nature or creation. For

---

[94]*CSPM*, p. 144.

[95]Ibid., p. 145.

[96]Ibid., p. 104. "Relation is a positive idea," in "Logic of Panentheism," *PSG*, p. 510.

[97]Hartshorne, *Anselm's Discovery*, p. 235.

[98]*DR*, p. 78. See also *MVG*, p. 124.

[99]Hartshorne, "Logic of Panentheism," *PSG*, pp. 499-500.

[100]Ibid., p. 501.

Hartshorne, all reality is in God, but God is not simply identical with nature. So he has dubbed his view panentheism, which suggests a mediating position between theism and pantheism. Such attempts at mediation are characteristic of Hartshorne's method.[101] Put in terms of relativity, panentheism is the "view that deity is in some real aspect distinguishable from and independent of any and all relative items, and yet, taken as an actual whole, includes all relative items."[102] It is here that his understanding of relations intersects his concept of God and leads to another important argument against classical theism.

Hartshorne observes that God cannot be necessary in every sense if creation is contingent and if God's choice to create this world is free.[103] While obviously related to his argument about divine unsurpassability, this claim has important differences.[104] Classical theists maintain the strongest contrast between God and the world, conceiving of God as necessary in every respect and the world as contingent in every respect. The most metaphysically adequate and coherent is the view in which there are aspects of both God and the world that are necessary and contingent, although in different ways. Hartshorne's process philosophy is an instance of this option: "God is, in uniquely excellent ways, both necessary and contingent, both infinite and finite, independent and dependent, eternal and temporal." This constitutes God's perfection, which he calls the principle of dual transcendence.[105] For Hartshorne, to identify God with only the absolute categories is to have a merely abstract God. In contrast, a God who has dual transcendence can be the preeminent eternal individual, not merely being or a being, but *the* being.[106] God is reality itself. As Hartshorne puts it, God is "all the categorial features of reality."[107]

---

[101]This is betrayed in the title of one of his more recent books, *Wisdom as Moderation: A Philosophy of the Middle Way* (Albany: SUNY Press, 1987).

[102]*DR,* p. 89.

[103]Ibid., p. 116.

[104]This point can be expressed by another position matrix, depicting the God-world relation and construed in terms of the modalities of the various options. This matrix contains nine possibilities. A more recent version of this matrix has sixteen possibilities. See "God, Necessary and Contingent; World, Contingent and Necessary," in *Metaphysics as Foundation,* ed. Paul Bogaard and Gordon Treash (Albany: SUNY Press, 1993), p. 298.

[105]See Charles Hartshorne, *Aquinas to Whitehead: Seven Centuries of Metaphysics of Religion* (Milwaukee: Marquette University Press, 1976), pp. 15-24; *OOTM,* pp. 44-49.

[106]*OOTM,* pp. 44-47.

[107]*CSPM,* p. 149.

Hartshorne often frames this argument in terms of God's knowledge, which for him is an asymmetrical relation of the knower to thing known. If, according to the doctrine of simplicity, God's knowledge is his essence, then how can he know that some contingent thing is actual? For if the thing is contingent, then knowledge of it is contingent as well. But a contingent property cannot be equivalent to an essential one. So the claim that God's knowledge is equal to his essence means either that God knows no contingent things (which contradicts God's omniscience), or that there are no contingent things. With respect to immutability, if different things were actual at different times, then in order for God to have accurate knowledge, he would have to know different things as actual at different times. But such "change" violates his immutability.[108]

This argument is most effective against certain formulations of two divine attributes, simplicity and immutability, although Hartshorne seems to aim it at immutability primarily. It creates a trilemma:

> The argument proves, in my opinion, that one of these three must be true: (1) there is nothing whose existence is in any sense contingent; all things are necessary in the same sense; (2) God does not know the contingent as existent; or finally (3) there are contingent properties in God. This last is of course the solution accepted by surrelativism. It is the only way to combine, without contradiction, the assertions: God knows the truth, and, not all truths are necessary.[109]

While Spinoza opted for (1) and Aristotle opted for (2), neither seems appropriate for the Western religious concepts of God, which require divine omniscience and freedom. If this is correct, then (3) is our choice by default. Note that since Hartshorne thinks of knowledge as an internal relation, he could just as easily frame the argument in terms of God's relational properties to a contingent reality.

This argument for divine contingent properties is compelling; however, it does not establish the status of God's contingent properties but merely their reality. The essentialist also accepts that God has contingent properties, since God's freedom in creating a contingent universe entails it. However, Hartshorne seems to assume that this entails panentheism. He does so because he bundles this insight with the notion that God's perfection is dependent on the

---

[108]DR, pp. 116-17.
[109]Ibid., p. 117.

world process and that some creation distinct from God must exist. These two ideas, when joined, entail panentheism. Since this clearly violates the Sovereignty-Aseity Conviction (SAC), the question for Christians is whether we can affirm necessity and contingency in God without affirming panentheism. To answer that question, we need to spend some time analyzing Hartshorne's view of God.

7

DEALING WITH HARTSHORNE'S DOCTRINE OF GOD

Like any well-developed doctrine of God, Hartshorne's has wide-ranging implications. But since this is not just a book about Hartshorne, we will not explore all those implications. Instead, let us contemplate his views insofar as they are relevant to Christian essentialism.

HARTSHORNE'S DOCTRINE OF GOD AS A NATURAL THEOLOGY

Hartshorne's commitment to a metaphysic that abstracts from the general features of concrete experience is obviously different from the biblical commitment that is central both to the Christian tradition generally and to Karl Barth specifically. In fact, Hartshorne develops his entire doctrine of God without reference to the biblical texts.

Nevertheless, Hartshorne insists that many features of his process theism are more attuned to the actual beliefs of theists such as Christians than is the classical theism exemplified by Thomas Aquinas and many other Western theists. He even predicts that religious folk will increasingly realize this.[1] He appeals to the Christian claim that God is love as a "magnificent intellectual content" and thinks surrelativism accounts for this content better than classical theism.[2] Specifically, he claims to detect "two strands" in the history of theology, the "religious" one speaking of a God of love, the "secular" speaking of a

---

[1] MVG, p. viii.

[2] Ibid., p. xi. For a critique of process philosophy as an inadequate biblical hermeneutic, see Royce Gordon Gruenler, The Inexhaustible God: Biblical Faith and the Challenge of Process Theism (Grand Rapids, Mich.: Baker, 1983).

purely actual and immutable God. Strangely, the secular vision became the "philosophic rationale of the religious strand."[3] Process philosophy is in his view more attuned to this primary religious strand, which for so long has been shackled with the Procrustean categories of Hellenistic philosophy.[4]

Hartshorne has little use for the doctrine of the Trinity[5] and thinks the Chalcedonian conception of the incarnation is incoherent.[6] So Christians will not look to him for help in these areas. On the other hand, surrelativism does not explicitly contradict these doctrines.[7] Perhaps Hartshorne, despite his method, can provide some helpful considerations for Christians who seek to develop a theological view formed by God's special revelation in concrete acts in history. Hartshorne notes that his metaphysic does not provide information concerning the concrete aspects of divinity, even if it requires that God will have some or another concrete aspect.

For these reasons, one may appraise Hartshorne's doctrine of God as a proposal that seeks to accommodate certain aspects of theistic belief, such as divine perfection, freedom and creativity, and to do so better than classical theism. While Hartshorne thinks his proposal does far greater justice to the needs of the religious sensibility and experience, in general his is a natural as opposed to a revealed theology, grounded in his empirical rendering of pure reason.[8] Nonetheless, it might harmonize with certain aspects of Christian theology.[9]

---

[3]*MVG*, p. 128.

[4]Ibid., p. xiv.

[5]He does admit that there is a sense in which his metaphysic posits a number of persons in God, since God is a successive society that is in some sense a new person every moment. However, this idea entails that there are an infinite number of divine persons, not just three (*RSP*, p. 169). This sense of "divine persons" is too far removed from the trinitarian claim to help trinitarian formulation much.

[6]*RSP*, pp. 152-53.

[7]Moreover, Hartshorne believes a religion's practitioners should be allowed to assert what they take to be true without requiring that they pass before the bar of some or another philosophy (such as Aristotelianism or Neo-Platonism). The philosopher, by means of position matrices, can provide some guidance in what the logically conceivable theistic positions are. This can help religious theists in seeking a metaphysical formulation of their beliefs. But the philosopher does not dictate which position a particular religion should take (*MVG*, pp. x-xi).

[8]James P. Devlin, "Hartshorne's Metaphysical Asymmetry," in *The Philosophy of Charles Hartshorne*, ed. Lewis Hahn (LaSalle, Ill.: Open Court, 1991), p. 275. See also David A. Pailin, "Rigor, Reason and Moderation: Hartshorne's Contribution to the Philosophy of Religion and Philosophical Theology," in *Charles Hartshorne's Concept of God* (Dordrecht: Kluwer Academic, 1990), pp. 219-20, and *NTT*.

[9]I will not tarry on whether Hartshorne's proposal might prove or provide evidence for the existence of God. My concern with his project reaches only to its capacity to accommodate certain Christian claims.

THE THREE THEMES IN HARTSHORNE'S DOCTRINE OF GOD

The Principle of Perfection (PP) is the most obvious of the three themes in Hartshorne's doctrine of God. He argues that to claim that God is in no sense perfect is to misunderstand what "God" means. And on this point, the Christian tradition agrees.

As already noted, he also has a notion of divine independence and transcendence,[10] although, for Hartshorne, God is not free to choose whether he will create anything distinct from himself, even though the existence of any specific world is contingent. This significantly abridges the traditional view of divine freedom, aseity and sovereignty (SAC). So traditional Christians will regard his claim warily. Of course, he has arguments to support his view. So let us deal with them.

UNSURPASSABILITY, DIVINE INCLUSION AND THE PRIORITY OF EVENT-STATES

An obvious congruence between Hartshorne's concept of God and essentialism is his insistence that a consistent doctrine of God will admit necessary and contingent divine aspects. He says, with the essentialist, that God has contingent as well as necessary properties.[11] Contrary to traditional opinion, however, this claim does not violate the PP. Rather, divine perfection seems well served by this conjoining of the contingent and necessary in God. Hartshorne agrees with the tradition and classical theism that to lack certain necessary properties, such as necessary existence and omniscience (rightly defined), would indeed be a deficiency. Again contrary to classical theism, however, he contends that to have only necessary properties is less exalted than to have some contingent properties,[12] since creativity is preserved only with the latter.

A God who is free is surely greater than one who acts by sheer necessity. More importantly, the biblical portrayal of a radically free God should trump any intuition of perfection that precludes all contingency in God. So for one

---

[10]See DR, p. 72.

[11]LP, p. 27; DR, p. 32. Still, he usually avoids the language of properties, perhaps because of its essentialist connotations.

[12]Charles Harshorne, *Anselm's Discovery: A Re-examination of the Ontological Argument* (La Salle, Ill.: Open Court, 1965), p. 145.

committed to the PP and biblical normativity, a strong case can be made that God's freedom opens up a place for divine contingent properties.

Regrettably, Hartshorne's understanding of this point conflicts with SAC by making God's perfectibility dependent on the world process: "It is only creative, self-enriching process which can unite harmoniously within itself an abstract, necessary eternal aspect with concrete, contingent, ever partly-new actual states." And because he identifies God with all of reality, he infers that everything necessary and contingent must be "in" God.[13] This is a different matter entirely. Although Hartshorne insists that this world itself is contingent, it is inconceivable to him that God could have done without any creation. Some or another contingent creation is necessary for God's perfection. Thus in Hartshorne's proposal, divine necessity and contingency are part and parcel with panentheism.[14] God always has, and always will, be actualized in a succession of actual states that includes entities "distinct" from him. (This entails, as he admits, that God has already traversed an infinite succession of event states.[15]) In contrast, the Christian essentialist will seek to affirm necessity and contingency in God but deny panentheism as a flagrant violation of SAC. So we want to sever the inference that contingency in God entails panentheism. Can we do so?

I believe we can. Extricating points of agreement from points of disagreement is a complicated affair in Hartshorne's case, however, because there are several components of his thought that either independently or jointly lead to panentheism. For that reason, it is necessary to include critique and appropriation of insights together in what follows.

Boiled down to basics, there seem to be three main points of agreement between Hartshorne's perspective and essentialism. Arguably, these are three things that any Christian concept of God should contain: (1) God has necessary and contingent properties; (2) There are theologically relevant, internal, external and asymmetrical relations; and (3) Temporal actuality is significant and irreversible. These truths are buried in Hartshorne's metaphysic as a whole, and some might think they cannot be retrieved from that metaphysic. For instance,

---

[13]Ibid., p. 193.

[14]Hartshorne does not consider the possibility of affirming that God has necessary and contingent properties while denying panentheism: "I scarcely need to say that surrelativism and panentheism are logically the same doctrine with only a difference of emphasis" (*DR*, p. 90).

[15]*CSPM*, pp. 125-26, 235.

Hartshorne sometimes gives the impression that his is the only coherent option between positivism and classical theism.[16] I think he is mistaken.

It is not the mere postulate of bipolarity—that God has two aspects—or attributing necessity and contingency to God that entails panentheism. Panentheism follows from ideas more peculiar to Hartshorne's metaphysical perspective, including (1) the emphasis on the ontological priority of the event-state for God and the world, (2) the idealistic thesis that since God knows all things perfectly, everything must somehow be "included" in him[17] and (3) the assumption that God must be everything; otherwise, the principle of perfection or unsurpassability (in Hartshorne's case) is violated, since God plus the world would then be greater than God alone.[18] These assumptions are related. It seems that argument (3) requires (1) and (2) to come off. If we can block these three assumptions, or just (1) and (2), we can admit necessity and contingency in God without committing ourselves to panentheism. Moreover, we can then see that the distinction between God's primordial and consequent natures is unnecessary, at least for the essentialist. Probably the argument from unsurpassability is his most significant argument for panentheism, but it presupposes his emphasis on event-states and the idealistic assumption about knowledge.

Consider again the argument from unsurpassability (AU). With it Hartshorne hopes to establish that, if God is to be unsurpassable by any other reality, in some sense God must include the creation, or "that which is not God." Otherwise, the total reality of God-and-what-is-not-God would be greater than God. But then there would be something that surpasses the perfection of God in himself (*a se*).[19] Since God is already defined as unsurpassable by another, this is a contradiction. To avoid the contradiction, we must understand God as the total reality at any time. So the commitment to divine perfection,

---

[16]So he does not distinguish divine contingency from the rest of his metaphysical baggage. See Charles Hartshorne, *Aquinas to Whitehead: Seven Centuries of Metaphysics of Religion* (Milwaukee, Wis.: Marquette University Press, 1976), pp. 12ff. However, admitting divine contingency does not entail all the details of surrelativism.

[17]Hartshorne also says we are "in God" by being objects of his love and knowledge in "The Logic of Panentheism," in *Philosophers Speak of God*, ed. Charles Hartshorne and William L. Reese (Chicago: University of Chicago Press, 1953), p. 513.

[18]See, e.g., Hartshorne, *Anselm's Discovery*, pp. 109, 129; and "Logic of Panentheism," p. 505, for (2) and (3).

[19]DR, p. 19.

defined as "unsurpassable by another," plus a concept of time as an increase in value, appears to entail panentheism.

This claim has an initial plausibility that dissipates on closer inspection, for its strength derives from presuppositions that the theist can easily deny. Thus there are several viable responses to this claim. The first is that Hartshorne seems to presuppose that God's perfection is finite and quantitative and so is capable of addition and increase. In contrast, most theists have maintained that God's perfection is somehow infinite. So adding a world does not increase his perfection. This response seems correct but not very helpful, because it suffers the same malady as any argument that appeals to infinity: perhaps the term merely hides an absurdity. So it is not a persuasive argument.

In any event, it does not quite address Hartshorne's argument, which draws its strength more from the fact that certain actualities are incompatible than from an assumption about God's finitude. And on this narrow point, Hartshorne is correct. It seems clear that even if God has infinite value, he still does not "possess" all actuality.[20] For example, God does not possess the actuality of having created a world without Augustine. In fact, now that he has created a world with Augustine, he can never have that actuality.

There are several more promising responses to his argument. For instance, Thomists and others frequently point out, as the medievals did, that God plus creation equals *plura entia, sed non plus entis,* that is, many beings, but not more being. God, in creating, allows other entities to participate in the being of which he is the source, but this does not entail that more being or perfection exists or that God is perfected by the addition of creation.[21] By presupposing that God's relationship to the creation is one of inclusion rather than participation,[22] Hartshorne has already smuggled in the idea that God and creation can be thought of as one entity, even if an internally diverse one. For Hart-

---

[20]Moreover, although he presupposes that God in his total concrete actuality will always be finite and contingent, he also believes that God includes in himself an infinite set of past states in his actuality. I have serious misgivings about the possibility of an infinite past succession of events, but this is another matter.

[21]See W. Norris Clarke, "Charles Hartshorne's Philosophy of God: A Thomistic Critique," in *Charles Hartshorne's Concept of God* (Dordrecht: Kluwer Academic, 1990), pp. 108-9; and Robert Sokolowski, *God of Faith and Reason* (Washington, D.C.: Catholic University of America Press, 1982, 1995), pp. 8-9.

[22]Clarke, "Charles Hartshorne's Philosophy of God," p. 108.

shorne inclusion is yoked with idealism, which means that one must "include" something to know it. The more perfectly one knows something, the more one includes it.[23] This view of knowledge may have something to commend it, but it is hardly obligatory, especially if it conflicts with other important beliefs. If one wants to maintain a stronger distinction between God and the world than does Hartshorne, for instance, then one is likely to reject this view of knowledge, divine or otherwise.

Here we see a characteristic weakness in Hartshorne's argument: it relies crucially on his specific, and somewhat idiosyncratic, metaphysical assumptions. Notice what he compares. He says that God *a se* would be surpassable by God plus the created world. In what sense is he surpassable? Hartshorne seems to have in mind some greater total value, such as the aesthetic value of enjoyment and increase of experience, since however "valuable" God is, when the value of creation, whatever immense or paltry sum it is, is added to God, the total value will be greater. If God enjoys and experiences the beauty of his creation, then such enjoyment must increase, since a maximum of beauty is no more conceivable than a highest number.[24] An unchangeable value of this sort is nonsense. And this would contradict our initial assumption, which is that God is unsurpassable by another. Few will want to block the inference by denying that the world has any value, especially since, in Scripture, God calls his creation good and very good (Gen 1:4, 31 et al.).[25]

But once again, the force of the argument is more apparent than real, depending as it does on a subtle switch of concepts. An increase of aesthetic perfection via increasing variety (unity and diversity, the contrast between the possible and the actual) is not what theologians usually have in mind when they say God as perfect. By focusing on God's aesthetic experience, Hartshorne is speaking past the traditional claim that God is perfect. Surely there is an-

---

[23]See Hartshorne's quote in Andres Cloots and Jan Van der Veken, "Can the God of Process Thought Be 'Redeemed'?" in *Charles Hartshorne's Concept of God,* pp. 133-34.

[24]See, for example, *OOTM,* pp. 9-10.

[25]However, the sense in which God calls the creation *tov* in the Genesis creation narrative is probably juridical rather than aesthetic. See Scott N. Morshauser, "Created in the Image of God: The Ancient Near Eastern Background of the *Imago Dei,*" *Theology Matters* 3, no. 6 (1997): 3. "This biblical 'good' . . . is not to be derived from some neutral point, nor is it to be regarded primarily as an aesthetic quality; but, too, is legal in nature. 'Good/goodness' is '*that which is agreeable to the initiator and author of the covenant.*'"

other way to construe this scenario. For instance, God may be perfect in power, love, mercy, knowledge and justice, even perfect in appropriate sensitivity to his creatures. Perhaps God does enjoy things when they come into existence. Certainly he delights in his creation. Such enjoyment could be among God's contingent properties. But it does not follow, as Hartshorne implies, that such enjoyment constitutes or adds to God's perfection.

What is clear is that it follows for Hartshorne. On his terms, there does seem to be a problem, because he thinks of God and the world as an individual entity of some sort. This is possible because he presupposes the ontological priority of event states. It is this assumption that lends plausibility to his claim that God plus creation is somehow a single entity that can be compared with God sans creation.

As previously noted, for Hartshorne the event or occasion is more definite or concrete than the individual or substance.[26] Although arguments for this idea are possible, Hartshorne tends to take it for granted. It seems finally to rest on a fundamental metaphysical intuition. Formalized as a definition of identity, it would be something like the Procrustean form of Leibniz's law that we discussed earlier:

(LL)   **For any objects x and y, if x is identical with y, then for any property P, x has P if and only if y has P.**

In chapter two I argued that (LL) is far too stringent as an accurate or helpful analysis of identity and should have time and possible world indexes added to it:

(LL_{tw}) For any object, x, and any object, y, if x is identical with y, then for any property, P, any world, w, and any time, t, x has P in w at t if and only if y has P in w at t.[27]

---

[26] *CSPM*, p. 173. So he defines event: "Suppose by event we mean a minimal temporal unit, or cross section, so to speak, of some actual process, such as the process of experiencing in a certain human being." Neither Hartshorne nor Whitehead opposes all application of the notion of individual substance; rather, they make it a secondary abstraction from the more concrete reality of events or occasions. Selves or substances are more properly thought of as societies or sets of successive events or occasions, which have a type of self-transcending identity. Charles Hartshorne, "Whitehead's Idea of God," in *The Philosophy of Alfred North Whitehead*, ed. Paul Arthur Schilpp (Evanston, Ill.: Northwestern University Press, 1941), p. 547; *CSPM*, pp. 181-82. Ultimately "God" is the complete class of every actual experience and event, which is itself the member of no class (*DR*, p. 157)

[27] See Michael J. Loux, "Introduction," in *The Possible and the Actual*, ed. Michael J. Loux (Ithaca, N.Y.: Cornell University Press, 1979), p. 42.

Since he sees (LL) as the correct analysis of identity,[28] it is hardly surprising that Hartshorne sees event-states as more concrete than substances or persons.[29] In contrast, I defended (LL$_{tw}$) because (LL) failed to accommodate our intuitions, perhaps even our knowledge, that persons and objects often retain their identity through different moments and possible states of affairs.[30] From this perspective, event-states look like the abstractions, and obscure ones at that. In any case, if (LL$_{tw}$) is the correct analysis of identity, this undercuts his argument.

In addition, a specifically theological argument commends itself: Hartshorne's emphasis on event-states makes panentheism more likely. If we want to avoid this view, then we have a theological reason for demoting event-states from the status Hartshorne has given them. That is, if we wish to avoid panentheism, we should not exalt event-states as Hartshorne does.[31] By making the event-state most real or actual, it becomes difficult to resist Hartshorne's argument that God plus the world is greater or more perfect than God sans world is. If we speak of the greatness of beings or individual essences (as described in chapter two), however, the inference doesn't go through.

To see this, return to the claim that God is that being than which none greater is possible. That claim seems clear enough to apprehend if not to comprehend. But what is Hartshorne's entity, God plus the world? To me it looks like a gerrymandered concept, designed to appeal primarily to someone who assumes the priority of event-states and combines simultaneous micro-events into one ontological unity. We can affirm that God exists in different states of affairs without thinking that God plus the world is another being that could be compared with God alone. In fact, to do so seems already to presuppose an ontological unity between the two that is not given by the PP. "God and the created world co-existing" describes a state of affairs that may obtain. As a single entity, however, at best God and the world are a set (to speak for the sake

---

[28]As Hartshorne does, *OOTM*, p. 105.

[29]Hartshorne does think that persons have an identity of sorts through time and different states of affairs, but their identity is as a successive society of occasions. It is that succession that constitutes the identity of a person. It is not the identity of the person that is fundamental and retains self-identity through different states. The person strictly speaking is an abstraction that emerges from the prior reality of discrete occasions.

[30]Diogenes Allen points out that (LL) neglects the identity of agents as well.

[31]He often offers the notion of event as an alternative to substance, which he says, "taken seriously and literally, is an intellectual prison" (*CSPM*, p. 189).

of argument). Comparing a state of affairs or a set with a being in respect to greatness or unsurpassability does not make clear sense. Moreover, comparing God without the created world and God with the created world presupposes that God with the created world is a single entity, which itself presupposes the priority of event-states.[32] Apart from such an assumed priority, this comparison of states is neither logical nor relevant to the principle of perfection, which has to do with God as the greatest conceivable or possible being. Thus Hartshorne's argument from unsurpassability depends on his contentious assumptions about the ontological priority of occasions or events.

.However, if God is only actual as some or another event state, and God as individual essence is an abstraction from that, then God's existing in a state and his actual essence seem to converge. What is most actual is God's existing in a contingent state. It is that convergence that makes Hartshorne's argument plausible. God's existing in an actual contingent state is God's consequent nature or concrete actuality in Hartshorne's terms, and by definition it includes all contingent relations. God as actual is built up or composed, so to speak, from the succession of event-states, being constituted by temporal parts. God's finite consequent nature increases from moment to moment. So if we concede Hartshorne's privileging of event-states and the notion of consequent nature it informs, his argument has strength. Reject them, however, and his argument loses its appeal.

There is an essentialist alternative to Hartshorne's idea. Why not see God's essence as actual in any contingent state of affairs that might obtain and regard God's relations to other beings that obtain in those states of affairs as accidental properties of God's one essence? If we apply perfection to God's essence (that is, his essential properties), there is less danger of imagining that God's perfection increases from state to state. That contingent truths about God and his accidental properties vary from moment to moment does not entail that such variation affects his perfection. His freedom to exist in various contingent

---

[32]Since developing this argument, I have discovered a similar argument by Thomas V. Morris, in which he distinguishes between an individual entity on the one hand and a state of affairs on the other. With this distinction, he can preserve the claim that God is the greatest possible being while conceding that God with the world is a "greater" state of affairs than God without the world. While this resolves a logical difficulty, I doubt whether this concession is necessary. For if God is infinite in value, what sense is there in the claim that one state is greater than another? See Thomas V. Morris, "The Metaphysical Doctrine of Creation," *The Asbury Theological Journal* 46, no. 1 (spring 1991): 98.

states of affairs may be one aspect of his perfection, and essentially so, but the particular states of affairs themselves need not be.

DIVINE FREEDOM AND CREATIVITY

Besides the argument from unsurpassability, Hartshorne makes two less compelling arguments for panentheism, both concerning God's creative freedom. He seems to think it is conceivable that God chose not to create anything, but he thinks this does not evade panentheism since God's choice not to create would be a decision God created "in himself."[33] He concludes that God's creating is somehow a necessity. Moreover, on his understanding of creativity, creation is always "a responding to prior stimuli." To deny this in the case of God is to deny all analogy between creaturely creativity and divine creativity.[34]

In the first argument, Hartshorne seems to be stretching the notion of creation beyond its normal use. For if God is truly free, then presumably God could choose to create or not to create. The notion of creation presupposes that God could have different choices, so that the choice he takes is contingent. True enough. But does this mean that God's having a particular choice is the same as his creation of some world distinct from himself? Surely not. At most, what Hartshorne has shown here is that, owing to God's freedom, God will always have some or another contingent property. If God is essentially free, then we might say that one of his essential properties is that he possesses one or more contingent properties. Hartshorne has not shown that such a decision requires that some creation distinct from God exist. Arguing that God must have some or another contingent property does not by itself establish panentheism. God might have had the contingent property of not creating a world distinct from himself. This would be an implication of the fact that he is essentially free, not that there must be a created world to which he is necessarily related.

His second argument results from allowing an a priori definition of "creativity" to control what he means when he says that God is Creator. Cer-

---

[33]*CSPM*, p. 9.

[34]Ibid., p. 12. A doctrine of the Trinity could help Hartshorne here, for if God is eternally active in the triune life, then he needs no action *ad extra* to be active and responsive.

tainly if there is no common semantic sense between the human and divine acts of creating, then we should not use the word *create* in both cases. But it does not follow that "responding to prior stimuli" is one of those common senses. And if we think that the doctrines of divine aseity and creation ex nihilo should have priority over Hartshorne's general notion of creativity, then one can quite easily give them conceptual pride of place. In a sense, these ideas function as control beliefs when drawing out what we mean by affirming God as Creator. Hartshorne's control belief, in contrast, is his a priori concept of creativity, of which God's creativity is one instance. Here is an example where the particularity of what a Christian says about God may serve to correct a general concept, a procedure Barth so exuberantly encouraged. If defining creation as response to prior stimuli is not compatible with God's aseity and creation ex nihilo, then this means that creation as "response to prior stimuli" is not the sense in which a Christian means that God is Creator. On this point, there is a disanalogy between God as Creator of the universe and me as the creator of a book about God. So Hartshorne's argument from the meaning of creativity rests on his seemingly arbitrary preference for a nonbinding general concept over the requirements of a Christian concept of God. It is not compelling to those with different priorities.

Once we tease out these assumptions, it is clear that Hartshorne's arguments for panentheism are fairly weak. For even if God's having some contingent property is an aspect of his perfection, it does not follow that God needs a contingent relation with his creation in order to be perfected. God might just as well have enjoyed the contingent property of *not having created any world.* This contingent property would still have been the product of his will. If—contrary to fact—God had so chosen, he would have had at least this one contingent property. Since God is free to create or not to create this or any other world distinct from him, this is how it should be. There is the implication here that God is not free to have no contingent property whatsoever. However, this need be no more troubling than the claim that God, while omnipotent, is "incapable" of sinning. *Having one or more contingent properties* is an implication of the fact that God is essentially free. That property—but not any contingent property in particular—is a part of God's essence (though not, in any untoward sense, a part of God). So even if we agree that God in his perfection has necessary and contingent properties, it does not follow that God needed the actual or any creation in order to perfect himself.[35]

TEMPORAL PROCESS AND MODALITY

Another aspect of Hartshorne's thought, which again makes panentheism virtually inevitable, is his temporal understanding of modality. Significantly, he collapses the distinction between necessity and possibility and the distinction between abstract and particular into his all-encompassing doctrine of time.[36] This conflation serves his definition of creativity.[37] Without his doctrine of time, Hartshorne believes creativity would be an illusion.[38] So he insists that an actuality has no advance modal status. Actuality is not simply more than possibility for Hartshorne. Actuality is prior to possibility, not only epistemically, but also ontologically.[39] To say

---

[35]I will consider God's experiential dependence on things distinct from him in chapter eight, when we consider divine immutability. What Hartshorne has not established, apart from his understanding of experience as prehension, is that God is essentially dependent on the contingent objects of his knowledge.

[36]With respect to relation, time and not space is "the basic principle" (CSPM, p. 219). See also his "Real Possibility," The Journal of Philosophy 60, no. 21 (1963): 596-98; MVG, p. 271; and "The Meaning of 'Is Going to Be,' " Mind 74 (January 1965): 46-58, for evidence of his conflation of the modalities of time and necessity/possibility.

[37]So he claims: "Modal distinctions are ultimately coincident with temporal ones" (CSPM, p. 61). The universal is the possible; the abstract is the potential. The particular is the actual, the concrete. The past is the actual, whereas the present is the becoming actual (CSPM, pp. 118, 225). This treatment of modality shows that some of Hartshorne's thought is dated, especially when he says things like: "Modal logic (as Prior and others have been trying to show) is the logic of temporality. Eternity or the necessary is only an abstract aspect of temporality" (p. 84). This is hardly an uncontested truth in modal logic.

[38]RSP, p. 201; LP, p. 165. He is fond of Bergson's dictum: "Time is creation or nothing," quoted in "Logic of Panentheism," p. 509. One should note that Hartshorne's view of time goes well beyond simply endorsing what McTaggart famously called the A Series view of time. According to McTaggart's distinction, time has two separable features. The A Series refers to the notion that time has a past/present/future aspect, in a way that the present has a status as the present that in some significant way differs from both the past and the future. The B Series refers to the fact that time is made up of events that are related to each other through succession and simultaneity. "A theorists" endorse both these aspects of time. "B theorists" deny that the present has any substantial or unique ontological status in comparison to the past or future. This is a complicated but interesting debate. Clearly in these terms, Hartshorne would qualify as an A theorist, but his views on time go beyond the intuition that the present has some special quality. One can be an A theorist without conflating logical and temporal modality, as Hartshorne does.

[39]This leads Hartshorne to deny that future events have a determinate truth value prior to their actualization. Although he says that the principle of excluded middle does not apply to future events (e or ~e), what he likely means is that the principle of bivalence does not apply to future events. That is, where t is the present, then for an event e at t +1, e is not true or does not obtain at t. Even on Hartshorne's terms, however, one could still say that e or ~e is true at t.

otherwise, he believes, contradicts real creativity.[40]

From the brief analysis of necessity in chapter two, we can see why it is a mistake to confuse logical and temporal modality. If a contingent actuality has no modal status prior to its actuality, this means it is neither necessary, possible nor impossible prior to its becoming actual. But surely prior to my birth on July 12, 1967, it was possible that I could be born on that day. In fact, it seems clear that this would always have been possible, even if things had turned out differently. Hartshorne's confusion of logical with temporal modality makes nonsense of counterfactual discourse.

His understanding of modality seems to fit best in the system S4, which we discussed briefly in chapter two.[41] Recall that in S5, the modal status of all propositions is necessary. This means that if a proposition *p* is possible in some world, then it is possible in every world. Not so with S4. In S4, some propositions are possible in some worlds but not in others. This is an inadequate analysis of logical necessity, but it does seem to capture temporal modality. If we think of the past as one set of worlds and the future as another, it is plausible to suppose that the future is accessible to the present in a way that the past is not. Once an event is past, certain possibilities are forever shut off, even if those possibilities are not logically impossible. But this change in modal sta-

---

[40]*CSPM*, pp. 62-68. For Hartshorne, the only sense in which the possible precedes the actual is that the past determines what is possible in the present. However, since the present determines or restricts what is possible tomorrow, the actual precedes the possible (p. 102). This way of putting things betrays Hartshorne's conflation of temporality and modality. The only strictly eternal object is "the necessary or eternal aspect of deity" (ibid., p. 65). All other universals "emerge in the creative process involving both divine and non-divine purpose, concepts, anticipations, or other forms of the experience of what could be or (in less definite outlines) must be" (ibid., p. 68). To say God exists necessarily is just to say that his existence has characterized the future of every past event; see "Necessity," *Review of Metaphysics* 21 (1968): 294. This understanding of necessary existence requires that there has been an infinite past for each thing of which God's existence has characterized its future. Moreover, he can claim: "*Reality is protean, not for our ignorance merely, but in itself or for the most ideal form of knowledge you please*" (*CSPM*, p. 67, his italics). So becoming is inclusive of being, not vice versa.

[41]This judgment is shared by Norman M. Martin in "Taking Creativity Seriously: Logical Structure," *The Philosophy of Charles Hartshorne*, ed. Lewis Hahn (LaSalle, Ill.: Open Court, 1991), p. 345. Hartshorne apparently agrees in *A Reply to My Critics* in the same volume, p. 657. However, Hartshorne's unfamiliarity with the details of modal logic prevents him from defending one system as the most adequate interpretation of his modal intuitions. He does not quite get clear on the meaning of accessibility between possible worlds, as he admits (pp. 658, 664). He concedes that process philosophy has not yet reconciled its view with "the technical procedures of recent mathematical logic" (p. 659). In S4, accessibility between possible worlds is reflexive and transitive, but not symmetrical. See the discussion in chapter two, note 30.

tus between possible worlds does not accurately map logical modality. The modal characteristics of time are not identical to the modal characteristics of logical necessity. As previously noted, S4 may be an adequate interpretation of temporal modality, but S5 is more adequate for the modalities of logical necessity and possibility. Hartshorne's conflation of the two leads to some confusions in his treatment of necessity.[42]

He rarely if ever refers to past events as necessary; rather, they are "determinately true." How this differs from "true" is not clear. He claims that the past, since it "contains a series of previous futures, . . . involves possibilities."[43] As past, the possibilities that failed to obtain are no longer possible. So there are certain things that become impossible. Herein hides a problem in Hartshorne's argument. To avoid confusion, one must distinguish this type of impossibility from the impossibility of the logically impossible. For if something can become impossible, then certain things (namely, the negation of such impossibilities) can become necessarily true. This contradicts his claim that necessary truths are eternal, that they are always true. But if his definition of necessity—that which must always be true[44]—is adequate, then surely it is equivalent to that which may never be false.

While he does not intend it, on his view past events necessarily obtain. Consider some past event e. Since e is past, $\sim e$, then it's impossible that e be false (again, assuming S4 as an analysis of temporal modality). And if $\sim\diamond\sim e$ (*it is not possible that not e*) is equivalent to $\square e$ (*necessarily e*), why is e not now necessarily true on Hartshorne's view? In such cases, events now past would necessarily obtain, because they could not now be otherwise.[45]

---

[42]H. G. Hubbeling contends that Hartshorne's temporal modality implies S4 but that Hartshorne's ontological argument presupposes S5, which his temporal view seems to repudiate. Hubbeling thinks that Hartshorne's project would be stronger if he had made up his mind on one or another logical system. H. G. Hubbeling, "Hartshorne and the Ontological Argument," in *The Philosophy of Charles Hartshorne*, ed. Lewis Hahn (LaSalle, Ill.: Open Court, 1991), pp. 365-66.

[43]Hartshorne, "Necessity," p. 293.

[44]The necessary is "what is true no matter what" (*A Reply to My Critics*, p. 661). I am not sure how this reconciles with a temporal understanding of necessity. I suspect he presupposes a type of logical necessity that is not accommodated by temporal modality.

[45]This argument may uncover a formal difference between temporal and logical modality. In logical modality, $\sim\diamond\sim e = \square e$. With temporal modality, $\sim\diamond\sim e$ does not $= \square e$, where $\square$ is defined as in S5. It might be easier to speak of different senses of possibility, distinguishing that which emerges from the passing of time from logical possibility.

This problem surfaces because Hartshorne misses the difference between some event now being unchangeable and its being necessarily true. Indeed, by conflating temporal and logical modality, he cannot account for the difference. He sometimes recognizes the problem since he calls some things, such as God's existence, unconditionally necessary, in contrast to the particular past, which is conditionally necessary.[46] But conflating temporality and modality muddles this distinction,[47] for it is never clear what unconditional necessity means. He seems to slide back and forth between construing modality in more perspicuous logical terms, which I have argued is best interpreted by S5, and in temporal terms, which is something like that modeled by S4.[48]

I argued that essentialist distinctions closely approximate our intuitions about logical necessity and that logical necessity is best interpreted by the system S5, in which the modal status of propositions is the same across possible worlds, whether or not they are actual. We may conceive of God as acquiring some contingent or accidental properties at some time, that is, temporally. But essentialism does not require that God be temporal (whether or not, all things considered, we decide to include temporal relations among God's contingent properties). Defining modality wholly in temporal terms, however, prevents Hartshorne from understanding God's essence or nature other than temporally. For Hartshorne, God requires time for his essential properties as much as for his contingent ones. By conflating temporality and logical modality, he makes it still more difficult to understand God's choice to create as radically free, hence implying panentheism. For Hartshorne, time is not dependent on God, so much as God is dependent on time.

Again, if logical modality is just temporality, then it is impossible to distinguish between something being the case at every past time t and something being necessarily the case. If the series of past events is infinite, then to say that at every past time t there is a creation, is equivalent to saying that there is a creation in every possible world. So Hartshorne can hardly avoid making some or another creation necessary.

---

[46]*A Reply to My Critics,* p. 661.

[47]Martin does not see this as a problem; see "Taking Creativity Seriously," p. 348.

[48]Of course there are disputes among logicians over the adequacy of S4 as an analysis of temporal modality. My point is that even if S4 suffices for temporal modality, it does not suffice for the modalities of broadly logical necessity and possibility.

However, if temporal succession is part of creation itself, then at every time *t*, creation may be actual; nevertheless, creation itself could still be contingent, since, without creation, there may be no succession of discrete temporal states. So to avoid making creation necessary, we need an analysis of logical necessity different from Hartshorne's in this respect. And since his analysis fails to make some crucial distinctions concerning modality generally, we are free to reject it.

None of this is to deny that time has some sort of objective modality; it is simply that modalities of time and the modalities of logical necessity and possibility are different. They are no doubt related, but conflating them leads to confusion. Distinguishing them as we have here helps resolve these conceptual difficulties, all while avoiding panentheism.

INTERNAL AND EXTERNAL RELATIONS

Hartshorne, unlike earlier idealists, maintains the distinction between internal and external relations and defends the existence of asymmetrical relations. As in other areas, he seeks an understanding that mediates between unstable extremes. However, unlike the essentialist understanding of relations—which can also account for the reality of internal, external and asymmetrical relations—Hartshorne understands relations primarily as temporal and epistemic categories. Since his modality is temporal, however, all relations to the past are internal. Only "relation to contemporaries and the future" are external.[49] So the temporal relation is an important example of an asymmetrical relation.[50] Similarly with respect to knowledge: Internal and external relations are relations between a subject and object. The knowledge relation "is external to the known, internal to the knower."[51] He speaks of the knowing subject as the relatum that is "relative" to the object. The relation is epistemic, but Hartshorne construes it in terms of prehension, which requires that a knowing subject be acquainted with and "feel" the object.[52] To be a subject,

---

[49]As John B. Cobb Jr. puts it in "Hartshorne's Importance for Theology," *The Philosophy of Charles Hartshorne,* ed. Lewis Hahn (LaSalle, Ill.: Open Court, 1991), p. 174.

[50]*CSPM*, p. 210; Nancy Frankenberry, "Hartshorne's Method in Metaphysics," in *The Philosophy of Charles Hartshorne,* ed. Lewis Hahn (LaSalle, Ill.: Open Court, 1991), pp. 304-7; Devlin, "Hartshorne's Metaphysical Asymmetry," pp. 276-81.

[51]*DR*, p. 7.

[52]Ibid., p. 98.

then, is to be relative. So a mind or subject by definition cannot be "absolute," at least not in every respect. God's knowledge in particular, since it is infallible, will depend wholly on what is the case, and in this sense, it is the most relative and dependent.[53]

While Hartshorne employs the terminology of internal and external relations, he alters their traditional meaning. Where philosophers have traditionally placed the joint between these categories between essential and contingent,[54] Hartshorne puts the joint between past and future and between knower and known. Therefore the arguments that employ his idiosyncratic meaning of internal and external relations cannot be used to demonstrate that, say, past relations are essential to an entity (in the essentialist sense).[55]

Hartshorne's description of temporal relations again exhibits his confusion of temporal and logical modality. It is precisely that confusion that leads him to define relations to the past and to a known object in a theologically objectionable sense—that is, as essential to God. In contrast, with the clear distinctions that essentialism provides, we can avoid panentheism while affirming unambiguously that God is related to contingent realities.

Consider the case of finite beings. For example, *marrying Ginny on May 25, 1991* is one of my properties acquired in the past. If past events cannot be reversed, then this is a property I can no longer lack. But if we have any apprehension of logical modality, then clearly this is not one of my essential properties. I could easily have married on another day. Less easily but possibly I might not have married at all. So *having married Ginny on May 25, 1991,* while no doubt an important and (now) unchangeable property, is not one of my essential properties. As such, it is an external relational property. It is only by conflating logical and temporal modality that I would be tempted to say otherwise.[56]

---

[53]Ibid., pp. 11-12.

[54]Timothy Sprigge's definition of internal property is representative of the traditional one: "By an internal property of a thing, I mean a property of a thing such that the thing could not but have it." That is, an internal property is an essential property of an entity. An internal relation is an essential relation, a *sine qua non* of that entity. See "Internal and External Properties," *Mind* 71 (1962): 197.

[55]Concerning God's epistemic relation, his comments have some force as a critique of a certain type of divine immutability; I will take this up in chapter eight.

[56]Still, there does seem to be a sense in which the past is necessary. What seems clear is that this necessity is different from logical necessity. Some philosophers have referred to the necessity of the past as an accidental necessity or a necessity *per accidens*. See Edward R. Wierenga's discussion in *The Nature of God* (Ithaca, N.Y.: Cornell University Press, 1989), pp. 86-115.

We can make a similar distinction with respect to God. *Having created the actual world* and *knowing the actual world as actual* are two of God's properties. They are relational properties or entail relational properties. And they do seem to be properties God could not now freely lack. But if these properties resulted from God's free choice, why must they be his internal properties? They do not, as long as we distinguish temporal and logical modality.

Additionally, *God's having created the world* is surely as good an example as any of an asymmetrical relation. For while *creating the actual world* is one of God's external properties (or, as I prefer to say, contingent properties), surely *being created by God* is one of the world's internal—that is, necessary—properties. If the doctrine of creation is true, then every entity distinct from God is essentially a creature. So we can agree with Hartshorne that there are theologically relevant asymmetrical relations, but their existence does not entail panentheism. The actual world exists; God is related to it; neither it nor his relation to it is essential to him; the world's relation to God, on the other hand, is essential to it.[57]

So God's relations, responses, sympathy with this world and its constituents are all accidental properties—he could be fully God without them, that is, if he had not created anything distinct from himself. Nevertheless, since God chose this world, he now possesses these properties permanently, so to speak. Since God is, for example, Creator of Augustine, presumably God is no longer at liberty to lack that property.[58] His having that property in the first place is wholly the product of his free will. Still, that choice was *self-implicating*.

Notice, however, that since we can distinguish the permanence of the past from logical modality, it's possible to avoid seeing such past properties as essential or internal divine properties in any sense. At the same time, we can agree with Hartshorne that such properties are no longer properties God is free to have or not to have. They are permanently accidental properties. So the actual world

---

[57]Hartshorne allows that God in his abstract aspect is externally related to other entities. However, since the world makes a difference, so to speak, to God in his concrete aspect, as concrete he is internally related to the world (*MVG*, pp. 237ff.). Again, this seems to be a different claim than the essentialist use of internal and external relations. It also depends on his concept of divine dipolarity, which I discuss below.

[58]I have not established this. It just seems intuitively plausible.

and God's relations to it are indeed significant to God. Having chosen them, they are a permanent part of his life and actuality. They will never fail to be so. God will never be God without the actual world. That is, God will never be such that the actual world never existed. Nevertheless, *having created the actual universe and its constituents* is not now nor will it ever be an essential divine property.

DIVINE DIPOLARITY

The concept of divine dipolarity has an important metaphysical function. It allows Hartshorne to attribute certain dualities or contrasts, such as abstract-concrete, necessary-contingent, absolute-relative, to God without contradiction. Without Hartshorne's assumptions, however, we need no such a distinction in order to attribute necessary and contingent properties to God.

Hartshorne also needs this distinction because he consigns necessity to the merely abstract realm. Since only contingent actualities are real or particular, he equates the factual and the contingent. Similarly, he cannot conceive of any necessary states of affairs. States of affairs can only be contingent. For this reason, God's existence cannot be a state of affairs or a fact, since it is necessary.[59] But what justification is there for this banishment of necessity to the nonfactual?[60] What sense does it make to say that $5 + 5 = 10$ is necessarily true, but is not a fact? Or that *God necessarily exists* is true, but not factual?

Apparently the reason he withholds the moniker *fact* from necessary truths is because he accepts Karl Popper's falsifiability criterion for an empirical fact. For a state of affairs to be an empirical fact, for Popper, it must be possible that it be falsified. But why assume that? In any case, without this assumption, his definition of fact is hardly obligatory.[61]

---

[59] Charles Hartshorne, "Is God's Existence a State of Affairs?" in *Faith and the Philosophers,* ed. John Hick (New York: St. Martin's Press, 1964), p. 26.

[60] He seems to concede to Wittgenstein and positivism that metaphysical statements are not factual, but he insists that they are nevertheless necessary—that is, necessarily true or necessarily false. This requires that he remove necessary truths from the realm of the factual. For example: "Metaphysical truths are necessary, not factual. But when Wittgenstein says that necessary propositions 'say nothing' I want to add to 'nothing' the words 'factual or contingent' " (*CSPM,* p. 158). So metaphysics on his view is the study of "non-restrictive existential affirmations" (p. 162; see also *LP,* p. 295).

[61] He rejects certain forms of positivism (*CSPM,* p. 170). Hartshorne's loyalty to positivism is not of the verificationist variety. Rather, he joins Karl Popper in accepting falsificationist criteria for meaning. See, for example, *CSPM,* pp. 159, 171. He seems to assume that a statement (other than a necessary one) that could not be falsified does not "make sense" (p. 161).

Another problem with this dichotomy between necessity and fact is that it makes it hard to see how any actuality could ever have necessity as one of its components. Whatever is necessary must always dwell in the ghostly primordial realm of the abstract, which for Hartshorne is nonactual and nonconcrete. But why assume this? Apparently he believes this because of how he thinks we come to know necessary and contingent truths. We can know the latter only purely empirically, but the former we know in most cases by abstraction from concrete experience. So necessary truths cannot be falsified and are known by abstracting from concrete experience. Hence, for Hartshorne, they are nonfactual.

As it stands, then, his argument is quite tenuous, since it rests of assumptions that are easy to doubt. In fact, Hartshorne's dichotomy between the abstract and the concrete may not even be coherent. Consider the nature of properties. How is a necessary property any more abstract or concrete than a contingent one? They are both properties, and as properties, they are not concrete objects of sense perception. So for Hartshorne, they are abstract. It is not at all clear that having necessary properties is any more abstract than having contingent ones.

This applies to surrelativism, with its emphasis on the fundamental concreteness of actual events. For what do actual events—those paradigms of concreteness—have in common? They have a certain definiteness, a positivity, by which they rule out alternatives. But is not definiteness itself a property, and thus abstract?[62] How then can actualities be so estranged from the abstract, and why need the necessary be so estranged from the contingent? Why would only contingent states of affairs be facts? Why could God not have both types of properties? And why do we need a distinction between primordial and consequent natures to understand this?

Besides his Popperian definition of fact, another reason Hartshorne disallows God's concrete necessary existence is his emphasis on event-states.[63] According to Hartshorne, God's concrete actuality is always contingent. God's existence as necessary is never actual but always abstract. This picture provides

---

[62]Eugene Peters almost makes this point in *Hartshorne and Neoclassical Metaphysics* (Lincoln: University of Nebraska Press, 1970), p. 122.

[63]One could say that, for Hartshorne, God does not exist concretely (*CSPM,* pp. 283, 291).

a background contrast to the actuality of the contingent world.[64] He correctly notes that a conjunctive proposition with one contingent and one necessary conjunct is a contingent proposition.[65] For instance, the proposition *Five is prime, and it will rain tomorrow* is contingent, because one of its conjuncts is contingent. He infers from this that since God exists in concrete states, he is always actually contingent. (He also says obscurely that this means "the contingent can include the necessary."[66]) But if event-states are not fundamental, then God can necessarily exist in any given state while still having some contingent property, such as hearing[67] Augustine's prayer at some moment. For instance, *At time t, God exists necessarily and hears Augustine's prayer* may describe a contingent state of affairs. It takes contingently and necessarily true propositions to describe such a situation. It does not follow that God, his essence or existence is contingent in that state of affairs, or that his existence is less concrete than the state of affairs. We do not need the distinction between God's primordial and consequent natures to make this point.

These criticisms are suggestive, but rather than continue to list problems with Hartshorne's use of abstract and concrete, we should consider an essentialist alternative. God, we have said, has certain essential properties, which are just those properties he has in every possible world. Among them are the traditional perfections, such as perfection of power, knowledge, freedom and goodness. Because God is free to choose among alternatives, he also has contingent properties. All those properties that he has as a result of choosing this actual world are contingent external relational properties, which he now possesses of his own volition. They are his properties, but they are not essential. As such, they are not a part of his essence, nor are they equivalent to his essence. His freedom itself is essential, but not the specific properties that exist because of his exercise of that freedom. Clearly God's choice among alternatives means that he foregoes possibilities. If the creation is contingent, this seems to follow unequivocally. But does this not violate the classical claim that God is Pure Actuality? Perhaps on some in-

---

[64]Ibid., p. 284.

[65]For example, *CSPM*, p. 267.

[66]Ibid., p. 271.

[67]Obviously, speaking of God as hearing a prayer requires a certain metaphorical use of language, which we will not fret over here.

terpretations it does.[68] If it does, this seems to be a case where the PP or the SAC inspired an expression not fully consistent with the revealed truth that God freely chose to create. If there is a conflict between God as *Actus Purus* and the contingency of creation, then the traditional formula rather than the revealed truth is the element to modify. (But see chapter 9.)

While theological essentialism has certain problems (which I will try to resolve in the conclusion), it can accommodate two divine aspects, like Hartshorne's dipolar theism, without describing God as having two natures.

CONCLUSION

Hartshorne's proposal is useful in demonstrating the need to posit contingent divine properties and to rethink certain formulations of divine immutability and simplicity. Hartshorne also alerts us to important truths, such as the reality of necessary and contingent properties in God, of internal, external and asymmetrical relations, and of the importance and irreversibility of temporal actuality.

However, his metaphysic, especially his panentheistic understanding of the God-world relation, flatly contradicts the SAC. Since essentialism can incorporate his insights without running afoul of the SAC, it is more adequate for a Christian doctrine of God than is Hartshorne's surrelativist theology.

---

[68]However, some argue that Hartshorne's depiction of the classical doctrine of God as Pure Actuality is a caricature. See David Burrell, "Does Process Theology Rest on a Mistake?" *Theological Studies* 72 (1982): 127-30.

8

THE DIFFICULT DOCTRINE OF
DIVINE IMMUTABILITY

In the next two chapters we will consider the two classical divine attributes that, some may suspect, are most likely to conflict with essentialism—simplicity and immutability. With a bit of nuance, we can interpret these doctrines in a way that upholds their classical motivation as well as much of their traditional content. And since these are the most difficult classical attributes to accommodate, clearly a similar strategy could be pursued for the other classical attributes as well.

Of course, I can't reconcile every version of divine immutability and simplicity with essentialism. Fortunately, as we will see, there is little reason for the Christian to do so. Let us first focus on immutability, which is much easier to handle than simplicity.

THE DEFINITION OF AND MOTIVATION FOR THE DOCTRINE

The classical doctrine of divine immutability concerns God's capacity for change. To say God is immutable is to say that he cannot change. In a general sense, immutability is grounded in biblical texts such as Malachi 3:6: "For I the LORD do not change." Similarly, James tells us: "Every generous act of giving, every perfect gift, is from above, coming down from the Father of lights, with whom there is no variation or shadow due to change" (Jas 1:17). And a little more obliquely, Hebrews 13:8 says, "Jesus Christ is the same yesterday and today and forever."[1] The doctrine developed, however, not simply from biblical interpretation but from theological reflection on such truths as the dis-

---

[1]See also Jas 1:17; Num 23:19; Ps 33:11; Is 14:24; 46:8-11.

tinction between Creator and creature. So Thomas Aquinas, after quoting Malachi 3:6 and noting that God as pure act has no potentiality, concludes: "Hence it is evident that it is impossible for God to be in any way changeable."[2] While there are kinds of change that seem inappropriate to attribute to God, whether we need to be so unqualified as Thomas remains to be seen.

Immutability is a modalized version of a more general property, namely, being unchanging. But there are two ways to be unchanging: contingently or essentially. For instance, if God had never created the world and had existed in an unchanging eternity, perhaps it could have been that he never changes. But this might have been only a contingent fact, so that it was still possible that God change. Or it might be that God not only happens to be unchanging but also that he is essentially unchanging. Edward Wierenga defines immutability accordingly:

(I) x is immutable if and only if x is essentially unchanging.[3]

This is how classical theists have normally understood immutability, which is one of several incommunicable properties that distinguish God from the continually changing creation.[4] The classical theist usually arrives at the doctrine of divine immutability by applying the *via negativa*. To say God is immutable is to say that he does not change and decay like the world and the objects within it. And since the doctrine preserves the contrast between Creator and creation, it simultaneously expresses the doctrines of creation, divine aseity and sovereignty.[5]

It also seems to stem from a certain intuition about what it is to be perfect.[6]

---

[2]*Summa Theologica* 1.Q.9.A.1.

[3]Edward R. Wierenga, *The Nature of God* (Ithaca, N.Y.: Cornell University Press, 1989), p. 170.

[4]As is clear, for example, in Thomas's *Summa Theologica* 1.Q.9.A.1-2.

[5]Many theologians also argue that we can deduce immutability from the doctrine of creation. So H. P. Owen says, "We can deduce other divine properties from the concept of creation. If God is Creator he must be personal, omnipotent, omniscient, self-existent, necessary, eternal, immutable and good." See *Christian Theism* (Edinburgh: T & T Clark, 1984), p. 12. While I agree that these claims are related, I am less confident that all of these attributes are deducible from creation *simpliciter*. What is more likely is that the doctrines, given certain additional premises, presuppose each other and are mutually implicatory. In particular, I suspect that certain intuitions about aseity and perfection also play a part.

[6]Immutability as an expression of perfection is a common intuition in the literature. See, for example, Norman Kretzmann, "Omniscience and Immutability," *Journal of Philosophy* 63 (July 1966): 409-21; Eleanor Stump and Norman Kretzmann, "Eternity," in *The Concept of God,* ed. Thomas V. Morris (Oxford: Oxford University Press, 1987), p. 249; and William E. Mann, "Simplicity and Immutability in God," in *The Concept of God,* ed. Thomas V. Morris (Oxford: Oxford University Press, 1987), p. 261: "It is ultimately the 'logic of perfection' which gives us the DDS [doctrine of divine simplicity] and DDI [doctrine of divine immutability]."

The idea is that God's lacking the ability to change is not a deficiency, since changeability or mutability is not strictly a power that it is better to have than to lack; rather, it is a deficiency that besets finite things. Since God is perfect and radically distinct from the world, any change he might undergo could only be a change for the worse.[7] And it is presumably better to be essentially unchanging, rather than merely contingently so.

Now that we have the concept clearly in front of us, we can consider the possibilities that God is immutable in every respect, in some respects or in no respects. If we seek to preserve the traditional claim that God is immutable insofar as this is congruent with biblical revelation and other claims based on that revelation, then we can reject the third option at the outset.

God is immutable in every respect just in case no aspect of God is susceptible to change in any sense, that is, just in case there is no divine property (in our sense of property) that either changes or can possibly change. If we think

---

[7]Immutability is related to other classical divine attributes, such as God's eternality or atemporality and his impassibility. Therefore anything we say about immutability is likely to be relevant to God's impassibility and eternity. So Thomas claims: "The idea of eternity follows immutability, as the idea of time follows movement" (*Summa Theologica* 1.Q.10.A.2). For example, if God had temporal properties, then, since things change in time, God would change at least in his relations to them. And if God could be affected either by himself or something outside himself, then he would be passible and mutable in some sense. Nevertheless, immutability, impassibility and eternity have distinct aspects. Whereas immutability has to do with ability to change, impassibility has to do with ability to be affected, a species of which is the capacity for suffering.

God's capacity for suffering is a subject of frequent dispute in contemporary theology and Christian philosophy. Richard Creel's *Divine Impassibility* is probably the most extensive treatment. Creel defends impassibility in most senses, and Kelly James Clark gives it sympathetic treatment in "Hold Not Thy Peace at My Tears: Methodological Reflections of Divine Impassibility," in *Our Knowledge of God*, ed. K. J. Clark (The Netherlands: Kluwer Academic, 1992), pp. 167-93. The contemporary trend, however, is to reject divine impassibility and in particular to embrace the notion of divine suffering. See, for example, Nicholas Wolterstorff, "Suffering Love," in *Philosophy and the Christian Faith*, ed. Thomas V. Morris (Notre Dame, Ind.: University of Notre Dame Press, 1988, n.p.); Paul Fiddes, *The Creative Suffering of God* (New York: Oxford University Press, 1988); Jürgen Moltmann, *The Trinity and the Kingdom* (New York: Harper & Row, 1981). Eternity often has to do with God's lack of temporality, or at least his lack of the deficiencies that afflict finite beings.

Impassibility and immutability are not necessarily coextensive when abstractly considered. For instance, it is possible that x be impassible in some sense but still be mutable in the same sense. This would be true just in case x were not susceptible to change from an entity outside itself, and so be impassible, but still be capable of changing itself, and so be mutable. However, the converse does not hold. If x is passible, then x is certainly susceptible to change, that is, mutable, at least in the same sense in which x is passible. So even if one concluded, for instance, that God can be mutable in will (with respect to contingent matters compatible with his essence), it does not follow that he is passible in will. However, if one argued that God is passible in will, it would follow that he is mutable in will. In fact, I think God is mutable but still impassible in will. As such, he is the exemplar of freedom.

this is incorrect or too difficult to defend, then we will opt for the second option, for which there are many possibilities. In considering these, we must delineate and account for the various ways God might be mutable or immutable. Richard Creel's distinctions concerning divine impassibility are a helpful starting point. He argues that God could be impassible in four relevant ways: in his nature, will, knowledge and feelings. Maybe God is impassible, for example, in nature (or essence) and will and passible in knowledge and feeling. If we understand these options to be jointly exhaustive, then there are sixteen possibilities to ponder.[8]

If God enjoys moral perfection, then we will include immutability of God's moral consistency and resolve within the immutability of his essence. And in fact, some theologians and philosophers have argued that moral consistency alone satisfies the burden of the biblical texts traditionally cited in favor of immutability. The monograph *Divine Immutability* by I. A. Dorner probably deserves to be called the classical defense of this view. Dorner argues that despite historical and metaphysical accretions, the taproot for the claim that God is immutable is the conviction that God's perfection consists in his ethical actuality.[9] For similar reasons, many contemporary biblical scholars and theologians recommend that we say only that God's character is supremely steadfast and trustworthy. By refusing to say more, they argue, we can escape the troublesome questions raised by the broader concept of immutability.[10]

While this strategy has some appeal, it hardly seems adequate to say that God's character is merely contingently reliable and steadfast. If God is perfect, then surely God is essentially reliable and steadfast, since it is surely better to be reliable and steadfast in all possible worlds than in only some. So grounding God's reliability and unchangeableness in his essence makes sense. And while not explicitly articulated in the biblical texts, this strategy also seems to capture the general biblical teaching concerning God's nature.

---

[8]Richard Creel, *Divine Impassibility* (Cambridge: Cambridge University Press, 1986), p. 11.

[9]I. A. Dorner, *Divine Immutability: A Critical Reconsideration* (Minneapolis: Fortress, 1994), pp. 87, 166. Unfortunately Dorner interprets God's ethical actuality in such a way that entails God's creation, thus compromising divine freedom (p. 182). He seems to assume that if God's relation to creation is accidental, then his love for it is arbitrary and its existence is unimportant to him. This does not follow.

[10]Richard Swinburne takes immutability of character to be the central sense of the claim that God is immutable, and he judges other stronger senses to be unnecessary for the needs of Christian theism. See, for example, *The Coherence of Theism* (Oxford: Oxford University Press, 1977), p. 212.

Moreover, why restrict God's immutability only to his character, that is, to his moral qualities? After all, commitment to divine perfection and aseity seem to require immutability (i.e., essentiality) of God's other perfections as well. If God's essence could change (ignoring for the moment the fact that this would render his essence nonessential), then obviously enough, it would be possible that he lack some or all of his essential properties, including his perfections. But then God might lack a perfection *p,* which would obviously be worse than if he possessed perfection *p* essentially. So whatever perfections God does in fact possess, such as omnipotence, omniscience, perfect goodness, freedom and faithfulness, he must possess immutably. That is, if God is perfect with respect to his positive attributes, then he is immutable with respect to those attributes. God has certain essential properties by virtue of being perfect; so he cannot change in those respects. This much is not only compatible with but also entailed by an essentialism committed to central Christian themes.

Furthermore, for the essentialist God's essence is not only immutable; immutability is the very quality that distinguishes God's essential properties from his accidental ones: the essential properties are, by definition, unchanging, since they are the same in every possible world. The essentialist consigns change or the potential for change only to God's accidental properties.

In fact, this sense of immutability seems to capture most of the concerns of classical theists. For example, according to Reformed Scholastic Heinrich Heppe, Heidan makes three distinctions with respect to divine immutability:

> This unchangeability of God is: (1) 'an immutability of essence'; for it is not 'liable to any conversion into another essence, to an alteration, to any change of place; (2) an 'immutability of nature or essential attributes'; for the latter 'are and remain unchangeable to all eternity'; and (3) an 'immutability of God's decrees and promises': for 'whatever God has decreed from eternity or whatever He has promised is immutable.'[11]

Nothing in this definition of immutability contradicts essentialism per se. However, Heppe adds Heidegger's definition of immutability to Heidan's distinctions. Heidegger said that immutability is the attribute "by which He alone is *per se* and *a se,* in actuality and in potency, devoid of all succession, change or variation, remaining the same eternally without even the faintest

---

[11]Ibid.

shadow of transmutation."[12] So Heidegger seems to take immutability more broadly than Heidan.

Heppe assumes that if God is immutable in his essence, essential properties, decrees, and promises, then God is "devoid of all succession, change or variation." But this does not follow, for God could have accidental properties that in no way compromise the immutability of any of the above. Heppe probably made this inference because he denied that God has accidental properties. So we can accommodate the traditional commitment to God's immutability when we detach immutability from the claim that God has no accidental properties.[13]

THE ESSENTIALIST QUALIFICATION OF STRONG DIVINE IMMUTABILITY

Since the essentialist maintains that God has accidental or contingent properties, however, there still seems to be sense in which God can change. If so, then he is not immutable in every sense. Does this violate the Principle of Perfection (PP) or the Sovereignty-Aseity Conviction (SAC)? Some theologians seem to think so. For example, H. P. Owen has claimed, "If God could change in any of his attributes he could change in all of them. Also if he could change by the increase of an attribute he could also change by the decrease of one. We cannot set limits to contingency. But if God could decrease in some of his attributes he could decrease in all of them; and so, eventually, he could pass out of existence altogether."[14]

However, elsewhere Owen claims that God's knowledge of actuality in the world changes with the world. Therefore he may mean to say that none of God's essential attributes or properties could change, because, if one of God's essential properties could change, it is conceivable that any or all of them could change. This is indeed an unsavory proposition. But since Owen says that God's knowledge of actuality changes, his view entails that God has accidents.

To say that God has essential and accidental properties does not imply that because some of God's properties could change, any or all of them could. The distinction between essential and accidental is precisely the limit of contin-

---

[12]Heinrich Heppe, *Reformed Dogmatics,* ed. Ernst Bizer (London: George Allen & Unwin, 1950), p. 67.

[13]In the next chapter, I will make clear what an accidental property is and what it is not.

[14]Owen, *Christian Theism,* p. 13.

gency that Owen thinks eludes us. The fact that contingent or accidental properties do or at least could change entails nothing about the mutability of God's essence or essential properties.

But what about the claim that God could have accidental properties that are susceptible to change? Does this impugn divine perfection? There are certainly some types of change that entail movement for the worse, such as a change in perfection of knowledge. If God could change from the state of knowing every truth that it is logically possible that he know, what could this mean but that he fail to know some truths? Surely it is better to be immune from such ignorance than to be susceptible to it.

Other types of change, however, seem just as obviously not to have this sort of evaluative dimension. Think, for example, of some variations in knowledge. For instance, while it is better for God to know everything that he can know than to lack some knowledge relevant to his purview, is it better to know the truth that (1) *John Brown runs at t* than that (2) *John Brown does not run at t?* It is hard to see how. What is important is to know which of these propositions is true, rather than to believe one falsely. And if (1) is true in some possible worlds and (2) is true in others, it would hardly be a deficiency for God's knowledge to change depending on which state of affairs obtains. In fact, the truth is just the opposite. It is surely better to know what is the case than to be immune to change in knowledge. So every type of change does not violate the PP.[15] If divine freedom requires that God's contingent properties could change, there is no good reason to conclude that this contradicts divine perfection. (As we will see below, however, this contingency of the content of God's knowledge is subtly different from literal change in his knowledge.)

The fact that some of God's properties may vary seems to follow straightforwardly from the fact that God exercises libertarian freedom in choosing to create the world. If God had to create the world, then God's creative activity was not free. In contrast, recognizing that God could have done otherwise captures

---

[15]At this point I am not saying that God's knowledge actually changes in this way. I am only considering whether it is a deficiency that God's knowledge could change in this way. To affirm the former proposition, I would need the additional premise that God's knowledge relation to the world is temporal. This point is distinct from God's immutability, although eternality and immutability are often conflated.

the fact that God was free in creating, the graciousness of his choice to do so and the contingency of the world he has created.

To say God could have done otherwise does not exhaust what it means to say God's choice is or was free. No doubt divine freedom is in many ways qualitatively different from the mundane variety. Moreover, to say God created the world freely is quite compatible with our partial or total ignorance of God's reasons for doing so. At the same time, there is no good reason to assert that speaking of divine freedom here is illicitly anthropomorphic. Quite the contrary. The error would be to deny that choice was an element of God's creative freedom. For surely God is at least as free in creating the universe as I am in choosing between strawberry and vanilla ice cream. If saying that God is free has any real sense, then choice among alternatives—in the sense that God could have done otherwise—must be one of its necessary elements, even if it is not a sufficient one. This implies that God will have contingent or accidental properties, that is, properties that could change. Those contingent properties concerning God's relation to a contingent creation are the expression of his freedom, as are all his contingent properties; so they do not imply any significant ontological dependence of God on the world.

DOES DIVINE ETERNITY SAVE STRONG IMMUTABILITY?

To this point, then, the argument is that God's knowledge relation can and does change, for the simple reason that, in order for God to know what is the case, he will have to know what is the case at a time. And what is the case at time t will usually differ from what is the case at time $t + 1$. So, given God's omniscience, if John Brown is running at time t, and John Brown is not running at $t + 1$, then God will know *John Brown is now running* at t, but he will know *John Brown is not now running* at $t + 1$. So presumably, if God is omniscient, then his knowledge will change to account for changes in what is the case. To avoid this inference, it seems that one would have to deny God's omniscience, which is surely a deeper theistic conviction than is immutability of God's knowledge.[16]

Notice, however, that this argument presupposes that God or at least God's

---

[16]For an extensive treatment and defense of this argument, see Richard Gale, *On the Nature and Existence of God* (Cambridge: Cambridge University Press, 1991), pp. 57-97.

knowledge is temporal (at least subsequent to creating the world), but many in the tradition have denied this. Historically, many theologians and philosophers have claimed that God is eternal not only as everlasting but also as atemporal or time-transcendent. He is outside time. His life and existence are of a different order from the successive before and after that we experience as temporally circumscribed beings. The classical expression of divine eternity in this sense is Boethius's: "Eternity . . . is the complete possession all at once of illimitable life."[17] Thomas Aquinas defends this definition in his *Summa Theologica,* arguing that it applies to God as a consequence of God's immutability.[18] So divine eternity in this sense—call it eternalism—means that God not only has no beginning or end but also has no succession.[19] The eternalist must argue that the relations of before and after (or earlier and later) are in reality not tensed relations. Rather, they are static, unchanging relations.[20] For example, the Battle of Hastings is always before the Battle of Waterloo, whether they are past, present or future to us.[21]

Eternity in this sense may be interpreted as simple timeless,[22] or it may include the notion of simultaneity. If the latter, then one might describe God as existing in an eternal now, in which he observes and knows all things simultaneously, so to speak, which to us are past, present or future. So God does not foreknow the future but knows it as simultaneous with his eternal living presence.[23] A spatial analogy is helpful for explaining this concept of eternity: eter-

---

[17]Boethius, *The Consolation of Philosophy,* 5.6. The pedigree of this definition may be traced from Parmenides through Plato to Plotinus. See Stump and Kretzmann, "Eternity," p. 221, nn. 4, 6. Notice that Boethius's definition speaks of God's "illimitable life" rather than his state of knowledge or relations.

[18]*Summa Theologica* 1.Q.10.A.2.

[19]*Summa Theologica* 1.Q.10.A.1. This concept has become somewhat unpopular in contemporary theology and Christian philosophy, although it still has defenders, especially among Thomists.

[20]As Thomas Aquinas seems to do in *Summa Theologica* 1.Q.10.A.1.

[21]I must thank William Lane Craig for clarifying this point for me.

[22]A excellent recent defense of timeless eternity is Paul Helm's *Divine Eternity: A Study of God Without Time* (Oxford: Clarendon, 1988).

[23]In "Distinguishing God from the World," in *Language, Truth and Meaning,* David Burrell clearly misinterprets Thomas. He says, "Not even God can [know what will take place], concurs Aquinas, since 'the future' does not yet exist, and what does not exist is not there to be known." He cites *Summa Theologica,* Ia.14.13. However, in this article Thomas explicitly says the opposite: "God knows future contingent things." What Thomas denies is that such things are future to God. Rather, they are future to us but present, and so presumably actual, to God.

nity is to time as the center of a circle is to its circumference.[24]

Since simultaneity is a temporal notion, however, many have argued that this definition of eternity is incoherent. The problem is that it seems to make times that are not simultaneous to be simultaneous for God.[25] How can two events circumscribed by different times also be simultaneous with each other?

In a well-known article, "Eternity,"[26] Eleanore Stump and Norman Kretzmann argue that there could be a type of "static" simultaneity compatible with the temporal succession we experience in the created order. The crucial component of their argument is the notion of ET-simultaneity. Unlike mundane simultaneity, ET-simultaneity refers to the unique "simultaneity" that obtains between two distinct frames of reference or perspectives, namely, the eternal and temporal frames of reference. The theory of relativity provides the analogy for introducing such a type of simultaneity. As the theory "relativizes" time to the reference frame of a given observer, so eternity and time serve as distinct reference frames. Stump and Kretzmann offer the following formalized definition of ET-simultaneity:

(ET) For every x and for every y, x and y are ET-simultaneous if and only if

either x is eternal and y is temporal, or vice versa; and

for some observer, A, in the unique eternal reference frame, x and y are both present—i.e., either x is eternally present and y is observed as temporally present, or vice versa; and

for some observer, B, in one of the infinitely many temporal reference frames, x and y are both present—i.e., either x is observed as eternally present and y is temporally present, or vice versa.[27]

---

[24]Another helpful analogy is the psychological image of a specious present, in which we conceive of a temporally extended event in a single moment. If this is a coherent concept, it might be extended, *mutatis mutandis,* to the divine case. See William Alston's treatment in "Hartshorne and Aquinas: A Via Media," in *Divine Nature and Human Language* (Ithaca, N.Y.: Cornell University Press, 1989), pp. 136-38.

[25]For example, Swinburne, *Coherence of Theism,* p. 221.

[26]In *Concept of God,* pp. 219-52. The force of my argument below does not depend on the particulars of the Stump/Kretzmann account. It could be formulated in light of a number of the other recent defenses of divine timeless eternity.

[27]Ibid., p. 231.

While this definition does little to clarify the relation between time and eternity, it does provide an apparatus for blocking the inference that because two events occur at different times in the temporal reference frame, they need occur at different times in the divine reference frame. It also blocks the inference that because these same two events are simultaneous in the divine eternal reference frame, they must be simultaneous in the temporal reference frame. So ET-simultaneity is different from the run-o'-the-mill temporal simultaneity in just the ways necessary to prevent the offending inferences.[28]

Although I have quibbles with this analysis and doubt that God must be strictly timeless,[29] let us concede it for the sake of argument.[30] Accordingly, let

---

[28]Philosophical disputes abound here, especially the dispute between the A and B Series aspects of time. I do not engage this debate here because, so far as I can see, it does not offer a way out of my argument. The issue hinges on one's view of the status of the present in relation to the past and the future. If one accepts that the actual world (past, present and future) has a different status from all possible but nonactual worlds, then one will still need to modify the strongest form of the doctrine of divine immutability.

[29]See especially Helm, *Divine Eternity,* pp. 23-40.

[30]In truth, I have doubts about and attractions to this concept of eternity. On the one hand, on this view it seems that God could never know such indexed things as (1) *Jay is now writing a book.* The most God could know are such items as (2) *Jay writes his book in April 2002* or (3) *Jay writes his book after he graduates from high school.* By my lights, any argument that trivializes the difference between these two truths is thereby weakened. (Readers familiar with the debate on the status of time will recognize that I am endorsing what has been called the A Series dimension of time as well as the B Series.) It seems clear to me that (1) is different from (2) and (3), and that it is worse for God not to be able to know (1) than for his knowledge relation of contingent actual entities to be temporal or successive. Of course, this inability of God's might be only apparent, like his inability to scratch his arm, since he has no arm. So these arguments appear inconclusive. Still, it is more difficult to conceive of such an eternity subsequent to divine creation than *sans* creation. More importantly, it seems to make the incarnation very difficult to defend.

On the other hand, I think Boethian eternity is less troubling than the alternative idea (embraced by Hartshorne and others) that God has existed through an infinite series of past moments. And I certainly want to avoid depicting God as dependent on time as creatures are or as constituted by temporal parts. As Anselm says in *Proslogion* 18: "There are no parts in God or in the eternity which He is." For a detailed discussion and attempted resolution of these difficulties, see William Lane Craig, *God, Time and Eternity: The Coherence of Theism II* (Netherlands: Kluwer Academic, 2001).

In any event, I am not convinced that the Boethian concept of eternity is incoherent. It might even be true. Time is a strange thing. We should not flippantly trifle with it. Be that as it may, I do not think either PP or SAC requires the Christian theologian to uphold it. Boethian eternity is certainly not entailed by anything in Scripture, nor does the theologian necessarily flout Christian duty or conviction by questioning it. See Oscar Cullman, *Christ and Time* (London: SCM Press, 1962), p. xxvi. While Cullman argues that a timeless eternity is foreign to Scripture, James Barr argues that the biblical testimony is inconclusive. James Barr, *Biblical Words for Time* (London: SCM Press, 1962), p. 80. Christian philosopher Nicholas Wolterstorff argues that everlastingness is a preferable idea for expressing God's temporal status than is "eternity" in the Boethian sense. See his "God Everlasting," in *God and the Good,* ed. C. Orlebeke and Lewis Smedes (Grand Rapids, Mich.: Eerdmans, 1975).

us assume that we come to know things only successively, either when they come into actuality temporally or come into our awareness or perception. In contrast, God somehow knows, intuits and relates to all actualities, truths, relations, and such either in an eternal present, or perhaps timelessly. God does not know one thing at time t and something else at $t + 1$. In that sense, God's knowledge does not change from moment to moment. What is to us future but not yet actual is somehow actual to God, so that when it passes from future to actual for us, it does not so change relative to God's knowledge of it. Anything that ever was, is or will be actual, God knows as actual.

Even with such concessions, however, this argument still does not preserve the immutability of God's knowledge in every sense. For insofar as God did not have to make actual what he freely chooses to make actual, he knows these things as actual that he might not have known as actual. He might have known other things as actual, or he might have known nothing other than himself as actual, just in case he had chosen to create different things or to create nothing at all.

So, even if we construe divine knowledge of actual entities (past, present and future) in such a way that God's knowledge relation is eternally unchanging and nonsuccessive, God cannot be essentially immutable in knowledge, since a contingent creation entails—or perhaps presupposes—counterfactual possibilities. If God had created a different world w_d than the one he did create (w_a), there would be other actualities than there are. And God would then know w_d and its constituents as actual. So there are other possible worlds in which God knows something different from what he knows in the actual world. Thus even if God does know past, present and future actualities in an eternal now, he cannot know entities that could have been actual as actual but never will be actual, for the simple reason that they are not now and never will be actual. And he certainly would not believe falsely that they were actual.

To put it differently, even if in the actual world God's knowledge is un-

More relevant to the current discussion is that Boethian eternity seems to be fed from the same stream as strong immutability. (So Thomas begins his response in *Summa Theologica* I.10.1 on the eternity of God: "The idea of eternity follows immutability, as the idea of time follows movement. . . . Hence, as God is supremely immutable, it supremely belongs to Him to be eternal.") So if we find it appropriate to qualify divine immutability in some way, we would cease to have clear motivation for barring such qualification with respect to divine eternity.

changing, it does not follow that it is impossible that God's knowledge change. And impossibility of change is what we need in order to fully accommodate the classical understanding of divine immutability. So the thesis that God knows temporally successive actualities from a nonsuccessive eternity does not save the thesis that God's knowledge is essentially immutable. Insofar as the creation's existence or actuality is contingent, God's knowledge of its existence or actuality is contingent. It could have been otherwise.

Notice, however, that there is a slight equivocation in my argument. What it establishes is that God's knowledge could have been different even if it does not actually change. But does the fact that God's knowledge could be different mean that God's knowledge could change? If the eternalist is correct, then there does seem to be a difference between the two. For, given eternalism, it might be that while God could be different—just in case he had chosen to create a different world—nevertheless, since he is immutable, he could never change from one state to the other. The essentialist insists that God could have been different, since he has many properties that he might not have had and that he has by no force of necessity. The eternalist could agree but still maintain that God cannot change.

Does this solution fully satisfy the doctrine of divine immutability? I'm not sure. I would be pleased to say that essentialism is compatible with a quite strong doctrine of immutability, if only because it is impressive to reconcile two ideas that seem incompatible. But perhaps it satisfies the letter of the traditional understanding but not the spirit. Or perhaps not. The possibility of God being different looks like a qualification of the doctrine of divine immutability, even if it is not literally a type of temporal change from one state to the other. This is probably why most defenders of strong divine immutability will not be satisfied with this result, as we will see below.

Moreover, if one is willing to admit that God, while still perfect and sovereign, could have been different, then why insist that he could still never change? If counterfactual difference of contingent properties does not violate God's perfection, why would contingent change do so?

In any case, essentialism combined with eternalism comes quite close to meeting even the strongest version of divine immutability. Strictly speaking the only mutability that essentialism requires is a counterfactual type, which allows God to have contingent properties. God could have been different in his knowledge and his choices. To say that God knows some contingent truth *x* contingently in no way entails the contingency of the perfection of his knowledge, which would still be one of God's essential properties. It is just to say that what God knows perfectly could be different from what he actually does know, because God in his freedom could have created different actual entities than he has created. So mutability of knowledge in this sense follows not from any untoward dependence of God on the world, but rather from the freedom of his will.

CONTINGENT VERSUS CAMBRIDGE PROPERTIES

One committed to strong divine immutability could insist on a distinction between the content of God's knowledge, that is, what God knows, and God's knowledge or omniscience as such. A number of defenders of the classical doctrine have pursued this strategy, including William E. Mann.[31] Mann concedes that the content of God's knowledge could have been different in some other possible world but maintains that this implies nothing about the mutability of God. This sounds like Thomas and Anselm's admission of merely relational change among God's external relations, although we have to account for different philosophical contexts. Now I also affirm the immutability of God's omniscience, since it is one of his essential properties. So this is not the point of conflict between Mann's suggestion and essentialism. The conflict is over the propriety of attributing accidents to God.

This becomes clear in a later article by Mann responding to criticisms by Thomas V. Morris similar to those here.[32] In this essay Mann construes such items as *knows that Augustine prays* as merely extrinsic or so-called Cambridge properties of God, which are not really divine properties.[33] This seems to be a required strategy for the partisan of what we might call "strong immutability" (and "strong simplicity")[34]: designate any divine "property" that is susceptible

---

[31]William E. Mann, "Simplicity and Immutability in God," in *The Concept of God,* ed. Thomas V. Morris (Oxford: Oxford University Press, 1987), p. 263.

[32]Thomas V. Morris, "On God and Mann: A View of Divine Simplicity," *Anselmian Explorations* (Notre Dame, Ind.: University of Notre Dame Press, 1987), pp. 98-123.

[33]William E. Mann, "Simplicity and Properties," *Religious Studies* 22 (1986): 348-51.

[34]Barry Miller disagrees, although I am not sure why, in *A Most Unlikely God* (Notre Dame, Ind.: University of Notre Dame Press, 1996), p. 99, n. 3.

to change (or that could be different) as a mere Cambridge property.[35] Clearly essentialism as I have defended it implies more change in God than "Cambridge change"[36] or merely relational change.

It is difficult to offer a precise analytical distinction between a real but contingent change and a merely relational change or property, such as Cambridge change. (To avoid implying that the issue is about temporal change, I will speak of contingent and Cambridge properties in what follows.) A mere Cambridge property captures some trivial or irrelevant relation between two things. Admittedly, this is inadequate as a definition; but even if we cannot get a tight analytic definition of the distinction between a contingent and Cambridge property, examples are easy enough to come by. For instance, it might be true (unbeknownst to me) that at 1:35 p.m. there is a squirrel running a few feet outside my house, and at 1:36 p.m. that the squirrel has departed. So at 1:35 I am such that there is a squirrel running outside my house, and at 1:36 I am such that there is not a squirrel running outside my house. There is some picayune sense in which I have changed, since my relation to this squirrel has changed from 1:35 to 1:36; nevertheless, clearly on this count there is no real change in me. The change has to do wholly with the squirrel. I am implicated only trivially, for the change in the squirrel's position from 1:35 to 1:36 provides no substantive information about me. Similarly, gerrymandered disjunctive properties, such as the "property" *either I am human or six is prime,* seem to be good examples of Cambridge properties (even if one of the disjuncts, as in this case, is an essential property).

We can imagine all sorts of Cambridge properties for God as well, such as *being such that Augustine prays* and *being such that Augustine does not pray.* Such items have not traditionally been thought to compromise God's immutability.[37] There are some properties in God, however, that, because of divine acts such as creation and incarnation, are accidental or contingent but not trivial. That

---

[35]And it is the course taken by contemporary defenders of these two doctrines. Miller designates all divine relational properties as Cambridge properties, which are compatible with strong divine simplicity; ibid., pp. 6, 9, 18, 22-27, 43, 37, 55, 93, 106-12, 145, 151.

[36]Perhaps the seminal essay arguing that God's relations to the world are Cambridge changes is Peter Geach, "God's Relation to the World," in *Logic Matters* (Berkeley: University of California Press, 1972), pp. 318-27.

[37]Or simplicity. See Eleanore Stump and Norman Kretzmann, "Absolute Simplicity," *Faith and Philosophy* 2, no. 4 (1985): 372.

is, they are real divine properties and not merely properties of the world. Even the state of Augustine's prayer life seems to qualify, since God is omniscient. Thus, unlike me in my state of squirrel-location ignorance, God would know which of Augustine's states obtains.

This suggests a clear example of a contingent divine relation that is not a mere Cambridge property, namely, God's knowledge of contingent truths and entities.[38] Such a relation is rightly called an accidental or contingent property. *Being such that Augustine prays* might plausibly be counted as a Cambridge property. But *knowing that Augustine prays* is surely not.

Another more specifically Christian difficulty with this argument is the incarnation. If all of God's apparently contingent properties were mere Cambridge properties, then this would include the relation of the Word to the human nature in Jesus. This would make it very difficult to defend the personal union of Christ's person, since one would have to say that the relation between Christ's two natures is trivial and irrelevant. (Recall that an irrelevant relation is the criterion by which we distinguish a mere Cambridge property from a contingent but real property.) Surely this is unacceptable for the Christian. Without allowing the Word to have real contingent relations to Jesus' human nature,[39] the only other option is to make the human nature essential and thus eternal to God the Son, which obviously introduces another host of difficulties.[40]

This debate seems to reveal conflicting convictions about what is most important to uphold in a Christian doctrine of God and what constitutes a real versus a Cambridge property. Because of Mann's commitment to strong divine

---

[38]There are other such relations, although the types of relations that God has with the world are limited by the fact that the world is constituted by its relation to God, while God is not so constituted by his relation to the world. Knowledge and love in particular seem to be appropriate relations of God to world, as Burrell notes: "The only way open for the One to relate to everything else existing in virtue of it, is through knowing and loving" (*Knowing the Unknowable God,* p. 72).

[39]One should note, however, that the relation between the two natures in the one person Jesus is an asymmetrical relation. That is, the relation of the human to the divine nature is essential to the human nature. The distinct human nature of Jesus as an individual does not and did not exist apart from the hypostatic union. To say otherwise is to commit the Nestorian heresy. The relation of the divine to human nature in Jesus' person, however, is real but contingent. That is, the Word can and did exist apart from his union with a human nature in the incarnation, but chose to become not only related to but also united with human nature in Jesus Christ.

[40]The more I reflect on this issue, the more I think it is a devastating problem for the Christian who seeks to claim that all divine contingent relations and properties are Cambridge properties. Because it would take us too far afield from the main argument of this chapter, however, I will leave this issue as little more than a suggestion for now.

simplicity and immutability, he cannot admit the distinction between essential and accidental divine properties. I find it implausible to count God's knowledge of Augustine's prayer as a Cambridge property. It looks to me like a fine example of a contingent property. More substantially, Christian theology seems to require that the Christian scholar not treat the relation of the divine and human natures in Christ as a mere Cambridge relation. This is much more apparent to me than is the fear that attributing such accidents to God is problematic.

DEPENDENCY OF THE OBJECTS OF DIVINE KNOWLEDGE

Another strategy to deflect the claim that God's knowledge of actuality is mutable would be to maintain a type of idealism with respect to God's knowledge of contingent entities. That is, one could deny that God is affected by or passive before the things that he knows. Rather, God produces or creates the objects of his knowledge in the act of knowing them. In this way, God's relation to objects of knowledge is reversed from the typical realist construal of knowledge for human beings. For human beings—assuming epistemic realism—the knower depends on the object of knowledge, in the sense that at least something in the object known affects the knowledge of the knower. One might argue that this is not the case for God. The objects of God's knowledge are dependent upon his knowing them for their very existence. This is Thomas Aquinas's conception of divine knowledge. Since God's knowledge is the cause of things, he is not passive before the objects of his knowledge. God knows, for example, things which are future to us, but it is "not that the futurity of things is the cause why God knows them." (In addition, for Thomas God just knows them; he does not foreknow them.) So with respect to God, Thomas denies Aristotle's thesis: "The thing known is prior to knowledge, and is its measure."[41]

There is a somewhat trivial sense in which known objects are dependent on God's knowledge for their reality. For nothing other than God could be actual unless it is possible and actualized by God. And God's knowledge of possibility is presumably exhaustive.[42] But even if God's knowledge determined all its

---

[41]*Summa Theologica* I.14.8. See also William Mann, "Epistemology Supernaturalized," *Faith and Philosophy* 11 (1985): 436-56.

[42]See Creel, *Divine Impassibility*, pp. 175-79.

objects in some stronger sense, the most that this argument would establish is that God's knowledge is impassible. It cannot establish that God's knowledge is immutable with respect to contingent entities. That is, even if God's knowledge is not affected by or passive before contingent actual objects, insofar as things are actual in some states of affairs or possible worlds and not in others, God's knowledge of such facts could be accordingly different, whether or not such difference in his knowledge is caused by the different objects themselves.[43] Even if from eternity God knows what he chooses to create, if God's choice to create is free in the libertarian sense, then he could have chosen differently. In that case, what God would have known from eternity as actually created would be different from what he actually has created.[44] Therefore we should conclude that God is immutable in those respects relevant to his essential perfection and aseity but "mutable"[45] with respect to certain contingent properties because of his freedom.

---

[43]I do not consider other contingent relations that make unqualified divine immutability difficult to defend, such as divine action in and response to a contingent world. For instance, in *Coherence of Theism*, p. 214, Swinburne argues that denying responsiveness in God may make him appear "lifeless." I tend to agree. The arguments offered here with respect to God's knowledge could be extended to other cases such as these.

[44]The Thomist W. Norris Clarke has offered what he deems a creative appropriation of Thomas by arguing that God has the immutability befitting a personal being. By means of the notion of intentionality, he argues that while God is essentially immutable, he is "truly related to creatures by an intentional relation of personal consciousness." See "A New Look at the Immutability of God," in *Explorations in Metaphysics* (Notre Dame, Ind.: University of Notre Dame Press, 1994), pp. 194-97. I am not sure this argument is a faithful interpretation of Thomas, but clearly Clarke accepts a certain type of nonessential mutability in God.

[45]In the sense that such properties could be different, even if in fact there is no time t at which they actually change.

9

THE DIFFICULT DOCTRINE
OF DIVINE SIMPLICITY

The claim that God is simple is as obscure to most modern Christians as it is prominent in classical theism. Most sweepingly stated, to say that God is simple is to say, as philosopher Barry Miller puts it, "In God there is no composition of any kind whatever."[1] As noted earlier, simplicity is not really a divine attribute or perfection but rather a "formal feature" of divinity.[2] Catholic philosopher David Burrell says simplicity "defines the manner in which such properties might be attributed to God."[3]

THE DEFINITION OF AND MOTIVATION FOR THE DOCTRINE

While the doctrine of divine simplicity is a common theme in the Christian tradition,[4] Thomas Aquinas is the first to treat it with systematic rigor. Indeed, in his *Summa Theologica,* he treats the doctrine before all the divine attributes

---

[1]Barry Miller, *A Most Unlikely God: A Philosophical Inquiry* (Notre Dame, Ind.: University of Notre Dame Press, 1996), p. 11.

[2]As is eternity according to David Burrell, in "Distinguishing God from the World," in *Language, Meaning and God,* ed. Brian Davies (London: Geoffrey Chapman, 1987), p. 75; and *Aquinas: God and Action* (Notre Dame, Ind.: University of Notre Dame Press, 1979), pp. 14-17. Burrell even goes so far as to say that "God's simpleness and God's eternity are part of what assures us we are talking about divinity" ("Distinguishing God from the World," p. 77).

[3]David Burrell, *Knowing the Unknowable God* (Notre Dame, Ind.: University of Notre Dame Press, 1986), p. 46.

[4]For philosophical and theological antecedents of the concept of divine simplicity, see Christopher Stead, *Divine Substance* (Oxford: Clarendon, 1977), pp. 180-89.

or perfections,[5] since he believes it should qualify how we should attribute all other things to God. Moreover, it appears to be the main reason he insists that we cannot predicate properties to God and creatures univocally but only analogically.[6] So he begins with the simplicity of God's being and, in its light, develops his understanding of the divine attributes rather than beginning with God's properties or perfections and then considering how one might predicate them of God.[7] In speaking of simplicity, then, we are not merely reflecting on one of several divine attributes but are considering how the classical theist understands God's essence and of the propriety of attributing things to God in general. Perhaps we should think of the doctrine, then, as a regulative principle that states something like this: However we attribute properties and an essence to God, we should do so in a way that doesn't require or imply that he is composed of them.

In the last century, many theologians have criticized the doctrine of divine simplicity as a piece of unjustifiable philosophical speculation, derived not from Scripture or salvation history but from the concept of God as the Absolute or the One of the ancient philosopher Parmenides.[8] There may be some

---

[5]In fact, the value Thomas saw in the doctrine of simplicity seems to have increased throughout his career, since it is closer to the beginning, as well as systematically more determinative in the *Summa Theologica* than in his earlier *Summa Contra Gentiles*.

[6]See, for example, his argument in *Summa Theologica* 1.Q.15.A.5 and *Compendium Theologiae* 27. See discussion of the role of simplicity in Thomas's doctrine of analogical predication in Christopher Hughes, *On a Complex Theory of a Simple God: An Investigation in Aquinas' Philosophical Theology* (Ithaca, N.Y.: Cornell University Press, 1989), pp. 57-59.

[7]Hughes, *On a Complex Theory*, p. 58.

[8]So Emil Brunner contends: "Anyone who knows the history of the development of the doctrine of God in 'Christian' theology, and especially the doctrine of the attributes of God, will never cease to marvel at the unthinking way in which theologians adopted the postulates of philosophical speculation on the Absolute, and at the amount of harm this has caused in the sphere of the 'Christian' doctrine of God" (see his *Dogmatics*, 3 vols. [London: Lutterworth, 1949], 1:242. See this quote and other anti-simplicity comments from kerygmatic theologians in Frederik Gerrit Immink, *Divine Simplicity* (Uitgeversmaatschappij: J. H. Kok-Kampen, 1987), pp. 15-20.

Such criticism is not limited to the twentieth century. Charles Hodge leveled a similar charge against the doctrine over a century ago: "To say, as the schoolmen, and so many even of Protestant theologians, ancient and modern, were accustomed to say, that the divine attributes differ only in name, or in our conceptions, or in their effects, is to destroy all true knowledge of God. . . . We must, therefore, either give up the attempt to determine the divine attributes from our speculative idea of an infinite essence, or renounce all knowledge of God, and all faith in the revelation of Himself, which He has made in the constitution of our nature, in the external world, and in his Word. Knowledge is no more identical with power in God than it is in us." See his *Systematic Theology*, 3 vols. (reprint ed.; Grand Rapids, Mich.: Eerdmans, 1995), 1:371-72.

truth in their charge; but it is an overstatement since, as we will see, central aspects of the doctrine follow from commitment to God's perfection and aseity. For that reason, we should try to oblige as much of the doctrine as possible, insofar as it is compatible with other basic Christian commitments.

So what are the traditional motivations for defending divine simplicity? Many see it as arising from the idea that God's existence is self-explanatory, that he is an absolutely perfect being of pure actuality.[9] Similarly, Alvin Plantinga attributes it to a "sovereignty-aseity intuition" held by most traditional theists.[10] This intuition inspires theologians to preserve in theological formulations God's "uncreatedness, self-sufficiency and independence of everything else" as well as "his control over all things and the dependence of all else on his creative and sustaining activity."[11] Burrell asserts that divine simplicity or "simpleness," along with eternity, "assures God's distinction from 'all things'" and provides "the ground for asserting the gratuity of creation."[12] Unlike immutability, there is no proof text for this doctrine in Scripture, although Scripture does say that God is love (1 Jn 4:8). While the claim that God is love does not entail simplicity, the claim is entailed by certain versions of divine simplicity. Despite a lack of direct biblical affirmations, however, we might see divine simplicity as a philosophical extension of the biblical concept of God's holiness, by which the biblical authors distinguish God from his creation.[13]

When Thomas Aquinas takes up the topic early in his *Summa Theologica* as part of his natural theology, he first treats it as a conclusion of the *via negativa*. Immediately following his discussion of the existence of God, he says:

> When the existence of a thing has been ascertained there remains the further question of the manner of its existence, in order that we may know its essence. Now, because we cannot know what God is, but rather what He is not, we have no means for considering how God is, but rather how He is not. . . . Now it can

---

[9]Eleanore Stump and Norman Kretzmann, "Absolute Simplicity," *Faith and Philosophy* 2, no. 4 (1985): 353.

[10]Alvin Plantinga, *Does God Have a Nature?* (Milwaukee: Marquette University Press, 1980), p. 28.

[11]Ibid., pp. 1-2.

[12]Burrell, "Distinguishing God from the World," p. 78. Burrell also claims more strongly that this distinction is "the central issue" with respect to divine simpleness.

[13]See N. H. Snaith, *The Distinctive Ideas of the Old Testament* (London: Epworth, 1956), p. 30; Otto Proksch, "Simplicity" in *Theological Dictionary of the New Testament*, 10 vols., edited by Gerhard Kittel and Gerhard Friedrich (Grand Rapids, Mich.: Eerdmans, 1968), 1:93; and Immink, *Divine Simplicity*, 1:163-64.

be shown how God is not, by denying of Him whatever is opposed to the idea of Him—viz., composition, motion, and the like.[14]

So for Thomas, in this passage at least, simplicity is a product of negative theology.[15]

But this fact does not give us Thomas's motivation for affirming divine simplicity. For we can still ask, Why does Thomas feel the need to engage in such denials as required by the *via negativa?* Similarly, one might ask, Why should the theologian distinguish God from the world, as Burrell advises? Presumably, among other reasons, we should do so because of the radical and asymmetrical dependency relation between God and the world. The world is utterly dependent on God for its continued existence and essence, while God has no analogous ontological need for the world. God has no cause outside himself, whereas the creation's essential cause is found in God. Preserving this asymmetry in our theological formulations suggests some elements of the doctrine of divine simplicity, even if it does not require or justify every version of the doctrine. I have sought to capture this motivation by speaking of the Sovereignty-Aseity Conviction (SAC).

There are other manifestations of the doctrine of simplicity besides the claim that God is not made of parts. For instance, some have claimed, in the name of simplicity, that God is identical with his essence and that all of God's properties are really identical with his essence and with each other. So the question is whether commitment to the SAC requires one to affirm these things. To answer, we need to tease out the various senses of the doctrine of divine simplicity.

THE SENSES OF SIMPLICITY
As with immutability, so with simplicity we may consider whether God is sim-

---

[14]*Summa Theologica* 1.Q.3.

[15]Some Thomists see its apophatic function as the essence of simplicity doctrine in general, although others disagree. For example, Brian Davies agrees with others in saying that "from first to last the doctrine of divine simplicity is a piece of negative or apophatic theology and not a purported description of God." See "The Doctrine of Divine Simplicity," in *Language, Meaning and God,* ed. Brian Davies (London: Geoffrey Chapman, 1987), p. 59. He also sees Thomas's motivation to be commitment to God as existing *a se* as the uncaused cause (p. 63). Similarly, David Burrell contends that saying God is simple is "a way of remarking that no articulated form of expression can succeed in stating anything about God." See his *Aquinas: God and Action* (London: Routledge & Kegan Paul, 1979), p. 18. In *A Most Unlikely God,* Miller disagrees, arguing that the doctrine allows us the concept of God as a limit case and as pure actuality (pp. 158-68).

ple in all respects, in some respects or in no respects. Any purported defense of simplicity will conclude that God is simple in at least some respects, so we will ignore the last option. Now obviously God is not simple in just any sense. One meaning of "simple," after all, is "unintelligent." So we should specify in what sense we mean that God is simple. It should then become clear that there are several crucial senses in which we should say that God is simple and a few senses in which we should deny it.

Among the senses of simplicity that appear in Christian theology are the following:

(1) All divine properties are possessed by the same self-identical God.

(2) God is not composite, in the sense that he is made up of elements or properties more fundamental than he is. He has no external cause(s), such as Platonic Forms.

(3) God's essence is "identical with" his act of existing. (Or perhaps: God's existence is not extrinsic to his essence.)

(4) All God's essential properties are coextensive.

(5) All God's perfections are identical.

(6) All God's properties are coextensive.

(7) God's essential properties and essence are (strictly) identical with God himself.

(8) All God's properties are (strictly) identical with God himself.

Of these, (1) is the easiest to accommodate; (8) is the most difficult. In fact, of these eight possibilities, we can defend plausible renderings of (1), (2), (3), (4) and perhaps (5). But it should become clear that the Christian must deny senses (6), (7) and (8), at least on certain contemporary interpretations; but see the conclusion for an important qualification. Interestingly, there seems to be an asymmetrical entailment relation between these theses going from (8) to (1). So, for instance, (8) entails (7), but (7) does not entail (8), and so on. If this is correct, then (8) is clearly the strongest form of simplicity and (1) is the weakest. We should not mistake the strongest version of the doctrine, however, with the most traditional. It may be that the strongest versions of the doctrine have resulted from misinterpreting certain traditional claims.

In fact, I suspect that sense (2) is the primary burden of the traditional doctrine, rightly interpreted.

The most perplexing features in this list are implicit in (7) and (8). Strictly speaking, if either were true, it would be incorrect to say that God has properties or even that he has an essence. Rather, these would be identical with God and, a fortiori, identical with each other, unless, obscurely, one denies classical identity. So to say God is simple in senses (7) and (8) may be to deny that God has properties or an essence.[16]

Some affirm God's simplicity because of the conviction stated in (1), that the divine attributes or perfections all refer to one and the same God.[17] In this form, simplicity is more or less synonymous with God's unity[18] and expresses the monotheistic conviction common to Judaism, Christianity and Islam.[19] So obviously any monotheist would affirm sense (1). Philosopher Richard Swinburne claims that so long as a theological proposal preserves divine unity, it need not be shackled with the more difficult aspects of the doctrine.[20] Commitment to God's unity, however, is not the only traditional motivation for defending divine simplicity.

Sense (2) is closely linked to the notion of divine aseity, transcendence and sovereignty, for if God were dependent on universals like being or goodness or knowledge as platonic Forms or causal powers, so that he were somehow composed of these things, then God would not be self-existent. Presumably he would depend on those things of which he was composed. Moreover, if God were composed of (metaphysical) parts, one could construe those parts as God's formal causes for his being what he is,[21] an idea that surely contradicts the claim that God exists *a se*. Further, anything made of parts could seemingly

---

[16]As Davies notes in "Doctrine of Divine Simplicity," pp. 58-59.

[17]See *CSPM*, p. 257. "That divine essence, divine existence, and divine individuality are the same is traditional, and is correct." But divine actuality is distinct and much richer according to Hartshorne. Paul Helm also understands the doctrine in this way in *Eternal God: A Study of God Without Time* (Oxford: Clarendon, 1988), p. 25.

[18]So Barth, after harshly criticizing the classical form of divine simplicity, defends it for among other reasons because it means "that in all that He is and does, He is wholly and undividedly Himself" (*CD* 2/1, p. 445). For Barth, simplicity rightly understood also expresses God's freedom.

[19]Burrell, *Knowing the Unknowable God*, p. 50.

[20]Richard Swinburne, *The Christian God* (Oxford: Clarendon, 1994), pp. 160-63.

[21]Ibid., p. 40. See *Summa Theologica* 1.Q.3.A.7.

come apart. So in the sense of "noncomposite,"[22] simplicity seems well founded. This sense may come closest to preserving the basic motivation behind various classical defenses of the divine simplicity. For that reason, let us postpone treating (2) until we have analyzed senses (3) through (8). (Incidentally, if I am correct, then it would have been better for Christian theology if the doctrine had been called divine noncomposition rather than divine simplicity. But it is too late now.)

The central questions for evaluating senses (3) through (8) are, To what degree does the claim that God is noncomposite require the various identity theses (3) through (8)? Can we reject or qualify some or all of (3) through (8) while maintaining that God is noncomposite in the relevant sense?

Sense (3) is particularly tricky because its meaning shifts from the medieval to the modern philosophical context. If we are not careful, we could perceive disagreements where none really exist. In his *Summa Theologica* Thomas says both that God is the "same as" his essence and that essence and existence are the "same in" God.[23] This sounds baffling to a modern essentialist, who might respond, "How could God, who is the actual living God on whom all things depend, be identical with a set of facts or truths such as an essence, which is just a set of essential properties?"[24] This is a reasonable question, assuming the modern, essentialist definition of properties and essences. However, this is not Thomas's conception. One should not assume he means what I would mean with these words. As Nicholas Wolterstorff notes, we, or at least those of us who engage in essentialist discourse, now speak of an entity as having an essence, as essentially exemplifying it. Wolterstorff calls this view "relation ontology," in which an essence as such is an abstraction or, more precisely, a way of describing the set of fundamental facts or truths about an entity's existence in the world. One who understands "essence" in this way would not be inclined to identify God with his essence. God is not simply a set of facts or truths.

But Thomas and other medievals thought of an essence of a thing as a "*what-it-is-as-such*." That is, for them, an "entity does not *have* a certain [essence] in the way that it has a certain property. It *is* a certain [essence]." When

---

[22]Or perhaps "essentially noncomposite."

[23]*Summa Theologica* 1.Q.3.A.3-4.

[24]This is akin to Plantinga's objection in *Does God have a Nature?* (p. 57).

they speak of an entity as "having" a nature or essence, they meant it as "having as one of its constituents" rather than as exemplifying it.[25]

In addition, Thomas denies that God has an essence, in the sense that God is one instance of some more general essence of divinity.[26] For Thomas and Aristotle, individuals such as Socrates and Plato have the same—human—essence. That is, one of their constituents is the essence "human." How then are they individuated? They are individuated by the matter that uniquely constitutes them as individuals, as well as by their various accidents, not by their abstract individual essences or haecceities as a modern essentialist conceives them. This is not the case for an immaterial entity, since such an entity is not composed of matter. Moreover, it cannot be the case for God, since that would require that he be a composite of matter and form, which Thomas wisely denies.[27] It would also imply that God merely instantiates a generic kind essence of divinity. So for God as for other immaterial entities, it would be natural for Thomas to say that God "is identical with" his own essence.[28] When he speaks in this way he is not really asserting an identity relation between God and his essence in the Leibnizian sense of the indiscernibility of identicals, even if his words sometime suggest this. So Thomas's claim is understandable, given his philosophical context, although modern essentialists will want to state things a little differently, to avoid the impression that we are identifying God with an abstraction.

But what about the claim that essence and existence are the same in God? Is this an identity claim, meaning that there is simply nothing to God other than that he exists? Could we translate this assertion into the formula God's essence = God's existence? Is God "just a lump or bit of existence"?[29] If a mod-

---

[25]Nicholas Wolterstorff, "Divine Simplicity," in *Our Knowledge of God*, ed. Kelly James Clark (Netherlands: Kluwer Academic, 1992), pp. 140-41.

[26]It is in this sense that Thomas says God cannot be defined. So Diogenes Allen describes Thomas's program following Aristotle: "The divine essence is not that God is this or that sort of being, but God is an act of independent existence. So we have no categories by which to define God." See his *Philosophy for Understanding Theology* (Atlanta: John Knox Press, 1985), p. 142.

[27]*Summa Theologica* 1.Q.3.A.2.

[28]In interpreting Thomas on this point, Hughes notes with respect to immaterial entities like angels and God: "Given the premiss that an immaterial substance is a form that subsists *per se*, and the premiss that the (substantial) form of an immaterial thing is its essence, we can move from its immateriality to its identity with its own essence or nature" (*On a Complex Theory*, p. 93).

[29]Wolterstorff, "Divine Simplicity," p. 144.

ern essentialist were to say that God's essence and existence are the same, this would be a reasonable inference to make. For instance, if I were to say that God's essence equals God's existence, I would mean

For any property *P* of God's essence, *God's essence* has *P* if and only if *God's existence* has *P*.

From this I could infer that since God's essence is exemplified in all possible worlds, God is exemplified in all possible worlds. And that certainly sounds strange. What I would want to say is not that God is exemplified in all possible worlds but that he exists in all possible worlds. But, once again, we may be led astray by Thomas's way of speaking. Perhaps we should join Nicholas Wolterstorff in preferring Thomas's formulation in chapter 22 of the *Summa Contra Gentiles:* God's "essence or quiddity is not something other than his being." That is, "God's existence is not something distinct from God's [essence]."[30] Better, God's existence is not extrinsic to or separable from his essence. Thomas's point seems to be that unlike finite creatures, God necessarily exists. Unlike the rest of us, the "whatness" of God includes his existing, even if we cannot deduce this to produce a self-evidently valid ontological argument for God's existence. Such a claim is of course unproblematic for the essentialist.

On this interpretation, it is clear why some contemporary Thomists regard the fundamental burden of the doctrine of simplicity to be the identity of God's essence with his act of existing.[31] This interpretation has two senses, both translatable into essentialist terms. The first sense, as Burrell puts it, is that the existence of anything presupposes the notion of its essence as *that which is,* and so the existence of a substance or essence cannot be accidental to the entity.[32] A fortiori, existence cannot be accidental to God. So in defending the claim that essence and existence are the same in God, Thomas quotes Hilary, who says, "*In God existence is not an accidental quality, but subsisting truth.* Therefore what subsists in God is His existence."[33] As Wolterstorff explains it, for

---

[30]Ibid.

[31]For example, Burrell, under the subtitle "The Case for Divine Simpleness," says that "the positive reason underlying every negation is the identity of God's essence with God's very existing" ("Distinguishing God from the World," p. 84). See also his *Knowing the Unknowable God,* pp. 19-50.

[32]*Knowing the Unknowable God,* pp. 19-50.

[33]*Summa Theologica* 1.Q.3.A.4.

Thomas, only potentiality for existing belongs to every nondivine essence; existing itself belongs to the divine. Again, rather than a real disagreement, we have a translation problem.

This sense of (3) alone is so modest, however, that according to it every substance or essence, and not just God, is simple when translated into the contemporary essentialist idiom. For this reason, it probably does not fully capture the doctrine of simplicity. For as noted in chapter two, in essentialist terms, everything that exists, exists essentially, because nothing can exist in any possible world in which it does not exist. Existence is for every entity either an essential property, or, if Kant is correct, a necessary condition for having any essential properties.

In essentialist jargon, what distinguishes God absolutely from created things in this regard is that he exists necessarily. So here we have a second sense in which God's existence is identical with his essence, to put it in Thomas's terms: since God necessarily exists, it is one of his essential properties that he necessarily exist. In contrast, in the case of any finite creature such as Socrates, his essence as human can be distinguished from his contingent existence. Socrates' existence is essential *to* him, but his existence as such is contingent. Moreover, there could have been humans, that is, human nature or essence could have been instantiated, even if Socrates had never existed. In God's case, there is no such distinction. There is no possible world in which God's essence could be instantiated but God not exist, since there is no world in which God does not exist. His essence is necessarily instantiated or exemplified. His essence and existence are coextensive. We cannot get the daylight between God's essence and existence as we can with finite creatures. This fact, which marks a profound "distinction" between God and the created world,[34] is not just compatible with Christian essentialism; it is entailed by it. So I concur with Thomas that existence is not an accidental quality in God.

The claim that all God's essential properties are coextensive, (4), is another sense of simplicity we can endorse. This is one of two theses in William E. Mann's defense of simplicity, and it seems to account for much in the views of

---

[34]As Burrell puts it in *Knowing the Unknowable God*, pp. 2ff.; also Robert Sokolowski, *The God of Faith and Reason* (Washington, D.C.: University Press of America, 1982, 1995).

Thomas and other classical theists.[35] Mann maintains that one can preserve simplicity by defending the following theses:

(A) **All the divine attributes are necessarily coextensive. According to this thesis, it would be impossible for any being to instantiate the attribute being omniscient, say, without also instantiating the attribute being omnipotent, and vice versa.**

(B) **Necessarily coextensive attributes are necessarily identical.[36]**

Now, (A) is clearly unproblematic, so long as "attributes" refers only to God's essential properties. For according to the essentialist, God has all his essential properties in all possible worlds. There is no world in which he has one but not the others. Therefore they are necessarily coextensive. This does not establish that, abstractly considered, the properties *being omnipotent* or *being perfectly good* are coextensive. What we can maintain is that God's omniscience and perfect goodness, for example, are coextensive. But this is no deficiency for essentialism, since God exists necessarily. So God exemplifies all his essential properties in every possible world.[37] Moreover, there is no omniscience other than God's omniscience.[38] This formulation also corroborates a commitment to divine unity, since it is impossible that God's essential properties could "come apart" or cease to be divine properties.[39]

Mann's inference from (A) to (B), however, requires a doubtful premise,

---

[35]William E. Mann, "Simplicity and Immutability in God," in *The Concept of God,* ed. Thomas V. Morris (Oxford: Oxford University Press, 1987), p. 256, and "Divine Simplicity," *Religious Studies* 18 (1982): 451-71. This is also how Hartshorne takes simplicity; so he can argue that God is simple in essence but not in actuality.

[36]Mann, "Simplicity and Immutability," p. 256.

[37]This may also accommodate the traditional claim that God's perfections can be derived from each other (as Allen describes in *Philosophy for Understanding Theology,* p. 144), although establishing this would require more argument than I provide here.

[38]This is not merely an anthropomorphic maximalizing of positive human characteristics, as some critics charge of Perfect Being theology. See, e.g., Miller, *A Most Unlikely God,* pp. 3, 85, 159-60. While there may be some semantic overlap between ascribing, say, power to God and to human beings—without any overlap such ascription would be senseless—the modal chasm between God's power and human power is as wide as the gap between contingency and necessity. And this is to say nothing of the unique and incomprehensible aspects of divine power. It would be difficult to conceive a more secure or preeminent mode of existence. For more on this, see William P. Alston, "Irreducible Metaphors in Theology" and "Referring to God," in *Divine Nature and Human Language* (Ithaca, N.Y.: Cornell University Press, 1989).

[39]Thomas V. Morris sees this virtue but does not understand the view as a sense of simplicity, as I do here. See his *Anselmian Explorations* (Notre Dame, Ind.: University of Notre Dame Press, 1987), p. 122.

namely, that properties—at least in the case under consideration—are nothing more than a function from possible worlds to individuals. They are certainly not abstract entities, and not even meanings or facts. But this view of properties seems a bit coarse-grained, since it does not capture what most people mean when they refer to properties or attribute them to various entities. I discuss the relationship between identity and coextensiveness of properties below, so I will not rehearse criticisms of this view of properties here. But whatever can be said on its behalf, it is a contemporary way of understanding properties and is surely not equivalent to the traditional way of viewing properties either in broadly Aristotelian or Neo-Platonic terms. Although securing coextensiveness of essential divine properties is necessary for capturing the identity of divine perfections—a goal of Mann's simplicity doctrine—it is not sufficient.

Let us skip (5) for a moment and consider (6), the claim that all God's properties are coextensive. (6) is a "sense of simplicity" incompatible with Christian essentialism, since the distinction between essential and accidental properties entails that such properties are not modally coextensive. An entity has its essential properties in every world in which it exists. Since God exists necessarily, he exemplifies his essential properties in every possible world. Accidental properties, however, are properties an entity has in some worlds in which it exists but lacks in others. In saying God has essential and accidental properties, we are saying that God's properties are *not* all coextensive. So we must deny that God is simple in sense (6) and, a fortiori, in senses (7) and (8).[40]

Most traditional defenders of divine simplicity do not unambiguously affirm senses (6), (7) and (8). Denying that God has accidents is common among traditional advocates of divine simplicity, including Thomas

---

[40]Some traditional claims of divine simplicity seem to imply (6), (7) and (8). See, for example, Augustine *De Trinitate* 5.5.6 and Anselm's *Monologion*. However, as I have suggested, this may be a misreading, carried into the present by contemporary defenders of simplicity who mistakenly take the traditional identity claims of, say, Thomas, to mean strict identity. If this is the case, then I have done all that is needed to accommodate the various traditional affirmations of divine simplicity. In any case, deciding this question would require detailed exegesis of Thomas and others on divine simplicity, which I will not attempt here. In what follows, therefore, I will be considering various contemporary defenses of divine simplicity, some of which do affirm (6), (7) and (8). I will call (6), (7) and (8) the strong senses of simplicity, to distinguish them from (1) through (5). But this does not imply that the stronger a sense is, the more faithful it is to the tradition. See also footnote 91 below.

Aquinas,[41] Anselm[42] and Augustine.[43] Superficially, one might suppose that essentialism directly contradicts their claim. On closer inspection, however, we discover another translation problem, since they are not denying what the modern essentialist is affirming. Thomas at least does not include among accidents all the things we do, so he would not bother distinguishing between senses (4) and (5). Whereas the essentialist includes contingent relations as divine accidents, Thomas would define such relations as either extrinsic "operative" relations or actions of God *ad extra* rather than "entitative" properties of God *in se*.[44] As such, he would not count them among God's properties. So the conflict between Thomas and essentialism on this point is somewhat indirect. The conflict becomes explicit with certain contemporary defenders of Thomas who argue that God's external relations are for Thomas and other medievals mere Cambridge properties. But Thomas did not have the distinction between real and Cambridge properties, so it may be somewhat anachronistic to attribute it to him.[45]

Another fact that narrows the distance between the classical and essentialist perspectives is the traditional motivation for denying that God has accidents. Thomas, Anselm, and other classical theists who deny that God has accidents do so to forestall the suggestion that such things as goodness, justice and wisdom are merely divine qualities. To say this would be to imply that God merely participates in his perfections, in the way finite creatures do. For example, when we say that an individual subject such as Plato is wise, we are speaking of a quality Plato happens to have, namely, being wise. At the same time, it is possible that Plato might not have been wise. There is nothing about Plato as such that entails that he be wise. Wisdom is one of Plato's qualities in the actual world, but he might have been dropped as a baby and rendered quite dull. In essentialist lingo, Plato has wisdom contingently or accidentally.

---

[41]*Summa Theologica* 1.Q.3.A.6, and *Summa Contra Gentiles* 1.23.

[42]*Proslogion, Monologion.*

[43]*City of God* 11.10.

[44]Allen, *Philosophy for Understanding Theology*, p. 141.

[45]For this interpretation, see Miller, *A Most Unlikely God*, pp. 106-12; Stump and Kretzmann, "Absolute Simplicity," p. 372. To be precise, Thomas considers Creator as a name of God rather than a mere external relation.

Clearly this is an inadequate way of describing God's relation to wisdom.[46] Such notions as wisdom are for God perfections. God does not merely have justice as I might have it by habitually acting in a just manner. God is essentially just; he exemplifies justice and his other perfections necessarily.[47] As Thomas puts it, God's perfections are to be attributed to him per se rather than merely *de subjecto.*[48] So the traditional denial that God has accidents is at least in part an insistence that God's perfections are not accidents as they are in creatures. And of course the essentialist happily concurs with this. For the essentialist, God has many accidents, but the divine perfections are not among them.

So our treatment of simplicity reduces to two questions: Are all God's essential properties identical? and, Does God have accidents in another sense, namely, as the result of his free choices? This leads to sense (7), the claim that God's essential properties and essence are identical with God himself. This is the less strict version of the thesis that (all) God's properties are identical with his essence, with God himself and with each other. Since essentialism distinguishes God's essence and accidents, some might surmise that the essentialist could still defend simplicity of essence in sense (6). That is, presumably one could argue that although God has accidents other than the ones classically denied and that while God's contingent properties are certainly not equivalent to God's essential ones, nevertheless all his essential properties are equivalent to each other. Since God's essence includes only his essential properties, one could still argue that God is simple in essence, even if in actuality he has sundry contingent properties, since there are many facts about God that would not be facts in every possible world. So God would still be simple in sense (6).

Some of Thomas's arguments, as well as other traditional defenses of the

---

[46]So Thomas says in considering whether any name can be applied to God in its literal sense: "Our knowledge of God is derived from the perfections which flow from Him to creatures, which perfections are in God in a more eminent way than in creatures" (*Summa Theologica* 1.Q.13.A.4). Also, in *Summa Theologica* 1.Q.3.A.6, in his reply to objection 1, he argues, "Virtue and wisdom are not predicated of God and of us univocally. Hence it does not follow that there are accidents in God as there are in us"; and *Summa Theologica* 1.Q.6.A.3: "Whatever belongs to others accidentally belongs to Him essentially; as, to be powerful, wise, and the like." See also Anselm, *Monologion* 16.

[47]Immink, *Divine Simplicity,* pp. 92-93.

[48]*Summa Theologica* 1.Q.3.A.6. See also Immink, *Divine Simplicity,* p. 176.

doctrine, seem to suggest that God is simple in the sense that all of God's properties are identical to his essence—and to each other, if we assume that any two things identical to a third are equivalent to each other. Interpreting Thomas and other medievals is very difficult on this point, however, since they do not explicitly defend identity in Leibnizian terms, such as with the indiscernibility of identicals.[49] So we should avoid attributing this view to them without qualification. Of course, when strong identity *is* explicitly joined with the denial that God has accidents—as in some contemporary defenses of simplicity—we get (7). Let us set aside the claim that God has accidents and consider first the claim that God's perfections (a subset of his essential properties) are identical. Can we uphold this more modest claim?

I am initially inclined against the notion that, say, perfect or infinite goodness, knowledge and power are just the same properties, even in God, whether we understand them as maxima or some kind of infinite limit case. While the perfections are coextensive in God, coextensiveness is clearly not synonymous with identity. For instance, trilaterality and triangularity are coextensive properties of triangles, but they are surely different properties. Similarly, all necessary truths are coextensive; that is, they are true in the same set of possible worlds, namely, all of them. So, the propositions *All red things are colored* and *All bachelors are unmarried* are both true in all possible worlds and so they are coextensive. Nevertheless, these propositions are not identical.

Still, there are arguments that go some way toward making the equivalence of the divine perfections plausible. The best effort is probably William Mann's. Mann concedes that while, say, *being knowledgeable* and *being powerful* are not the same properties, since they have different connotations, nevertheless, in God, who possesses the maxima of these properties (according to Mann), they

---

[49]Thomas's concept of identity is terribly complicated, especially when he attempts to square simplicity with the Trinity. Hughes treats the matter with care and thoroughness in *On a Complex Theory*, pp. 218-38. Thomas speaks of *identitas secundem rem* and *identitas secundem rationem* as well as *identitas secundem rem et rationem*. He uses *identitas secundem rem* interchangeably with *idem realiter* (really the same), thus suggesting that *identitas secundem rem* just is identity. However, at times he seems to make *identitas secundem rem et rationem* classical identity (which entails substitutivity and indiscernibility), while suggesting that *identitas secundem rem* is some weaker relation. At times, he may be interpreted as denying a principle of substitutivity rather than indiscernibility per se. Thus armed, he aspires to reconcile his doctrine of simplicity with the doctrine of the Trinity. I do not intend to treat such complicated exegetical matters here. I intend to show *only* that strong simplicity, with classical or Leibnizian identity, contradicts the Christian concept of the free and triune God.

converge or coalesce.[50] The idea is something like this. When we speak of different perfections, like omniscience or omnipotence, we connote different things, so the assertions have different meanings. Nevertheless, perhaps all of these different meanings have the same denotation, that is, perhaps they refer to some single capacity in God. That does not seem implausible. After all, the perfections do seem to relate to each other, and in fact, maybe being omnipotent entails being omniscient, maybe being perfectly loving entails being perfectly just, and so forth. If Mann is correct, then sense (5) is another sense of simplicity that we can accept. In any case, it does not contradict anything intrinsic to my argument.

In another recent argument Miller defines the divine perfections not as maxima but as limit cases, which—owing to their infinity—are identical in God, who is pure subsistent existence.[51] Since the concept of limit case is such as to prevent much comprehension, I do not know how to evaluate Miller's argument. But even if correct, Mann's and Miller's arguments can apply only to God's perfections. For God has other essential properties for which their arguments are ineffectual, namely, the specifically trinitarian attributes, which are a sine qua non for any Christian doctrine of God.

THE INCOMPATIBILITY OF TRINITARIAN DOCTRINE WITH THE STRICT IDENTITY OF ALL ESSENTIAL DIVINE PROPERTIES

Christian theologians have traditionally recognized that some divine attributes concern God's essence generally, while others concern the three divine persons

---

[50]William E. Mann, "Simplicity," *Religious Studies* 18 (1982): 461. So he claims that the friend of simplicity does not argue that God is identical with, say, omniscience *simpliciter* but with *God's* omniscience, which is his property instance. God is identical with his "rich property," "a conjunctive property whose conjuncts are all and only the essential and accidental properties of a person." See Mann, "Simplicity and Properties," p. 344. Morris, in "On God and Mann," notes that this leaves the distasteful impression that God is a mere instance of certain properties that are ontologically anterior to him, like platonic Forms. In response to Morris's article, Mann repairs his view by arguing that God's omniscience is "extensionally equivalent" to omniscience itself, and so, equivalent to it. As such, we should not imagine generic or abstract properties as ontologically prior to God. See Mann, "Simplicity and Properties," p. 353. I have not considered Mann's unnuanced original position separately, because I doubt any defender of simplicity would claim that God is a mere property-instance of some more fundamental platonic Form.

[51]Miller, *A Most Unlikely God*, pp. 7-14. If God's perfections are limit cases rather than intrinsic maxima, then Anselm's claim—that God is that than which none greater can be conceived—is a necessary thing to attribute to God, but it is not sufficient.

individually. In some sense, then, trinitarianism requires that we gingerly distinguish between two classes of attributes.[52] If trinitarianism is true, then all these attributes are coextensive. Nevertheless, even if we claimed more strongly that the attributes shared by the three persons were equivalent in God, the trinitarian claim requires that at least some of the attributes or properties in the second class, namely, those that distinguish the divine persons, *not* be identical. Therefore, the Christian (assuming all Christians are trinitarians) should not affirm simplicity in the sense of equivalence or identity of all essential divine properties. It should not be surprising, incidentally, that recent defenses of strong divine simplicity lack any consideration of the problems the doctrine of the Trinity raises for the notion.[53]

The most basic trinitarian claims[54] are impossible to square with simplicity[55] in senses (7) and (8). Consider for example the "person-constituting" relations of paternity, filiation and spiration.[56] Paternity is the relation the Father has from eternity with the Son and the Spirit. More precisely, paternity is the property that expresses that relation. Filiation is the Son's eternal relation to the Father, and

---

[52]For example, Augustine *De Trinitate* 5.9-15. See also Gillian R. Evans, *Anselm and Talking About God* (Oxford: Clarendon, 1978), pp. 59-60. This is often combined with a methodological or epistemic claim about God's attributes. So Thomas, in *Summa Theologica,* argues for God's perfections as a part of natural theology and for God's trinitarian attributes later, as a part of revealed theology.

[53]Two important recent defenses of simplicity are Miller, *A Most Unlikely God,* and Immink, *Divine Simplicity.* While both are Christians, neither considers the unique problems that the doctrine of the Trinity presents for their defense of simplicity. Hughes, in *On a Complex Theory,* does examine simplicity in light of the Trinity. Not surprisingly, he concludes that strong simplicity is not compatible with either the doctrines of Trinity or incarnation. Hughes's argument, pp. 215-40, 269-71, bears some resemblance to mine, although my argument was developed independently of his. One difference is that he attributes strong simplicity to Thomas and so concludes that Thomas's natural theology conflicts with his revealed theology. I demur on this charge, because I am unsure whether Thomas affirms strong simplicity as I have defined it. And I give some reason to suspect that he does not, at least not consistently.

[54]Clearly simplicity in senses (7) and (8) are also incompatible with some of the more controversial claims of contemporary social trinitarianism, such as the argument that the divine persons have a distinct subjectivity or self-consciousness. See, for example, Cornelius Plantinga Jr., "Social Trinity and Tritheism," and David Brown, "Trinitarian Personhood and Individuality," in *Trinity, Incarnation and Atonement* (Notre Dame, Ind.: University of Notre Dame Press, 1989); and Jürgen Moltmann, *The Trinity and the Kingdom* (San Francisco: HarperSanFrancisco, 1991).

[55]Dorner recognized the problem over a century ago but did not develop it in detail. See *Divine Immutability,* pp. 136-37.

[56]For discussion, see Catherine Mowry LaCugna, *God for Us: The Trinity and the Christian Life* (San Francisco: HarperSanFrancisco, 1991), pp. 179-80, n. 133. It does not follow that we know much about how these properties differ. What is required is at least that we maintain that they do differ somehow.

spiration is the Spirit's eternal relation to the Father and perhaps the Son. Insofar as these constitute the divine persons uniquely (although they do not exhaust them—the divine persons are not merely relations without remainder) and distinguish them from each other, clearly we cannot identify or equate them or claim they are the same as God's essence.[57] For example, if paternity is equivalent to filiation, then it is true to say of the Father that he exemplifies filiation, and of the Son that he exemplifies paternity. But if we say that, we have obliterated the very claim by which we secure the distinction between Father and Son.

One could say that there is only one relation between Father and Son. Nevertheless, that relation is asymmetrical. The Father and the Son could not change places. There is some fact about the Father that makes him the Father and not the Son, and some fact about the Son that makes him the Son and not the Father, even if we can refer to these separate facts by means of a single asymmetrical relation. Moreover, the relation of the Father to the Son is not the same as the relation of the Father to the Spirit. Therefore, if one wishes to retain the trinitarian distinctions, one must deny that every essential divine property or relation is strongly equivalent.[58]

The problem here is not with trinitarianism per se but with trinitarianism shackled with strong simplicity. Given the centrality of the trinitarian claim to the Christian doctrine of God, if there is such a conflict between it and strong simplicity, then surely the latter should give way.[59] Let us take Barth's advice on this point: Grant marginal control to the Trinity, and trump any form of simplicity that compromises it.

---

[57]Incidentally, Thomas argues that these are real relations in God (*Summa Theologica* 1.Q.28.A.1) and that they are really distinguished from each other (*Summa Theologica* 1.Q.28.A.4); but he also says in the same question that relation in God is the same as his essence (*Summa Theologica* 1.Q.28.A.3). This way of speaking certainly contributes to the problem.

[58]There is a way to block this argument, but it exacts a high price. One could say that paternity and filiation are the same as God's essence but distinct from each other. To say this, one would have to say that two things could be equivalent or identical to a third but not identical to each other. This is as close to a bare repudiation of logic as we are likely to get, since the identity relation is the most basic and probably the most intuitively unimpeachable component of logic. The theologian who denies the identity relation would presumably forfeit the right to charge an alternative theological conception with incoherence or contradiction. At the very least, one should avoid such a strategy in theology if possible. And any doctrine that tempts us to affirm it should be subject to severe scrutiny. If trinitarianism can be saved only by denying this aspect of identity, it is in serious trouble.

[59]Note that Thomas's operative/entitative distinction cannot apply in this instance, since no trinitarian argues that the trinitarian distinctions only apply to God *ad extra*—as Thomas makes clear.

If simplicity in sense (7) is incompatible with trinitarianism, then it is hardly a deficiency of essentialism that it is incompatible with simplicity in either sense (7) or sense (8). If not even God's essential properties are equivalent to each other, then the fact that God's contingent properties are not equivalent to his essence, essential properties or each other is no argument against the claim that God has contingent properties or accidents.[60]

DOES ESSENTIALISM IMPLY THAT GOD IS COMPOSITE?

So the strongest senses of simplicity—(6), (7) and (8)—are not compatible with a thoroughly Christian doctrine of God in general and so are not binding for essentialism in particular. However, simplicity in sense (2), that God is not composite, is surely binding on anyone who seeks to affirm God's aseity and sovereignty.[61] In fact, this seems to be the main burden of the doctrine of divine simplicity, despite the complicated ways in which it is often expressed. Plainly if God were composed of his properties, then he would be constituted by them. They would be metaphysical parts. At best, God would somehow supervene on his properties and essence, making him dependent on them.

In question three of part one of the *Summa Theologica*, Thomas Aquinas

---

[60]There may be another strategy available here to the partisan of simplicity in sense (7). Perhaps she could retreat from the stronger claim that all God's essential properties are equivalent to each other and assert instead only that all those properties shared by the three divine persons are equivalent to God himself, his essence and each other. This would include the divine perfections as well as more obscure properties such as *being one of the three members of the Godhead* and *being eternally related to two divine persons*. However, I see no virtue in this view. For if one agrees that speaking of one God is compatible with maintaining certain essential trinitarian distinctions, then what motivation could there be for continuing to maintain the equivalence of the essential properties common to the Godhead? Why would that sort of equivalence be necessary to preserve divine unity or aseity? How would the need to distinguish God as Creator from creation require or entail it (as Miller asserts without benefit of argument in *A Most Unlikely God*, p. 94, n. 11)?

Such a strategy seems implicitly to concede the charge that trinitarianism really is not compatible with monotheism, divine aseity, transcendence or unity. Such a concession seems unwise for a Christian theologian to make. If deep reflection on the biblical witness leads us to affirm trinitarianism, then the more prudent course of action is to deny that divine aseity, unity, perfection or whatever require that all of God's essential properties—person-constituting or otherwise—must be strictly equivalent to God himself, his essence or each other. Nevertheless, God's perfections could still all denote a single power or capacity in God, as suggested in sense (5).

[61]Even Hodge, no friend of the doctrine of simplicity in some of its manifestations, sees this aspect of the doctrine as worthy of protection. So he argues, "We must not represent God as a composite being, composed of different elements," in *Systematic Theology*, 1:369.

mentions eight ways God is not composite. He is not composite by being composed of (i) body and soul, (ii) matter and form, (iii) quiddity, essence or nature and subject, (iv) essence and existence, (v) genus and difference, (vi) subject and accident, (vii) potentiality and actuality or (viii) things outside of him versus things inside of him.

But since essentialists do claim that God has several properties that are in some sense distinct and even distinguish between two fundamental types of properties, essential and accidental properties, do they imply that God is composite and thereby violate this requirement of simplicity? There are several reasons to suppose this is not the case.

What we want to preserve is the conviction that God is not dependent on properties or on his essence in a way that compromises his aseity. As Plantinga says, "There is a difference between thinking of God as *having* properties and thinking of his properties as *constituents* of him."[62] Recall that properties, as I have defined them, are simply facts or truths about an entity.

Nothing about essentialism implies that God is composite in senses (i) through (v) and (viii).[63] So our concern is with (vi) and (vii), thus reducing the

---

[62]Plantinga, *Does God Have a Nature?* p. 55.

[63]I concur with Thomas that God is not composite as bodies are composite, either by way of physical or temporal parts that constitute God. (A concern to deny divine parts seems to underlie Anselm's less explicit endorsement of simplicity. He runs together denial of parts with identity of divine properties in *Proslogion* 18: "Thus life and wisdom and the rest are not parts of thee, but all are one, and each of them is the whole that thou art, and what all the rest are.")

A fortiori, God is not composed of matter and form (*Summa Theologica* 1.Q.3.A.2). More precisely, for the Christian essentialist, God is not essentially a composite of form and matter. This does not preclude the possibility that, say, the Son could assume a human nature, including a human body. While such a divine assumption would be essential to the human nature that is assumed (i.e., the human nature could not exist or be instantiated apart from union with the eternal Logos), it would be contingent or accidental to God as the eternal Logos or Son. That is, God could have existed eternally as a Trinity even if he had not created a material world in which to become incarnate. As it actually is, however, God has eternally but freely chosen to be the one who became incarnate as Jesus Christ. So the fact that human nature is accidental to the Logos says nothing about the significance or stability of the hypostatic union, even for the life of God. Also, since essentialism allows us to articulate the conviction that God exists necessarily and that he has his perfections not only essentially but necessarily, we can accommodate some of Thomas's claims that God is the same as his essence and that existence and essence are the same in God—so long as we do not take these as Leibnizian identity statements. The essentialist can also deny that God is a composite with the things he has created, so that it is inappropriate to view God and world as a single entity.

Perhaps more relevantly, God is not composite in the sense of participation. God does not participate in the properties that he exemplifies, in the way particular finite entities participate in their constituent and accidental properties. See, for example, *Summa Contra Gentiles* 38. Also, in *Summa Theologica* 1.Q.3.A.7, Thomas says, "every composite is posterior to its component parts, and is dependent

issue at stake to a single question: Is it appropriate to attribute to God any real multiplicity or diversity with respect to actuality and potentiality and essence and accidents? Does Thomas's claim that God is "altogether simple" or "absolutely simple"[64] entail that all of God's properties are strictly identical with each other, with God's essence and with God himself? We have already seen that Christians must deny this strongest form of the doctrine of divine simplicity because they are committed to at least one type of essential, internal, eternal distinction in God, namely, the person-constituting differences of the three eternal divine persons. Speaking of multiplicity or distinction of some sort, however, need not be equivalent to speaking of composition *simpliciter.* Here we must insist on the difference between ontological diversity or multiplicity and composition per se. To say that God exists eternally as three persons, for instance, is not to say that God is composed of the three persons like cogs on a wheel or fingers on a hand. Nothing in trinitarianism or essentialism implies that the divine persons are a divine triumvirate that made a pact to exist eternally together.

If we allow essential distinctions of the divine persons with respect to their

---

on them; but God is the first being." Nor does God participate in being itself. He is rather the primary source of all these things, and so the source of his own being. Similarly, Anselm expresses God's simplicity: "But certainly, whatever thou art, thou art through thyself, and not through another. Thus thou art the very life by which thou livest, and the wisdom by which thou art wise, and the very goodness by which thou art good to the good and to the wicked—and so with all thine attributes" (*Proslogion* 12). Whereas creatures exist *per participationem,* God exists *per essentiam* (Immink, *Divine Simplicity,* p. 14). God exemplifies his properties necessarily. We may instantiate some of our properties essentially, but we never necessarily exemplify them, since our existence is contingent.

Modern essentialism such as I have endorsed is a type of realism, if by realism we mean that properties are not mere constructions of human beings or their linguistic or conceptual activities. So essentialism gives rise to questions similar to Platonism concerning the status of universals. While the essentialist admits properties, necessary truths and the like into her ontology, she need not confer on them the status of Plato's Forms. They are not active or personal in any sense; their reality is abstract, and so they do not imply a denigration of concrete realities. (See Immink, *Divine Simplicity,* pp. 51-56.) If anything, abstract entities are of a somewhat lower grade ontologically than concrete individuals, even if they have an independence stronger than Aristotle would countenance. They most certainly are not formal causes of concrete individuals. At least on my account, God holds exclusive rights to that privilege. See the conclusion for more on this.

The essentialist also can agree that God is not a species or a genus differentiated or derived by species-specific properties, since we cannot separate God's existence from his essence as we can with any member of a natural genus. Since we say God exists necessarily, we can accommodate Thomas's claim that "if God were in any genus, He would be the genus 'being,' because, since genus is predicated as an essential it refers to the essence of a thing" (*Summa Theologica* 1.Q.3.A.5).

[64]*Summa Theologica* 1.Q.3.A.7.

person-constituting properties, we have already admitted that simplicity in its strongest senses, which are (7) and (8) above, contradicts basic requirements for any Christian concept of God. So it cannot be reinstated to deflect the distinctions between essence and accident and potential and actual. (For the essentialist, the potential/actual distinction is virtually impossible to separate from the essential/accidental one.) There may be some other reason to reject these distinctions in a doctrine of God, but for the trinitarian, strong simplicity cannot be the weapon of choice.[65]

We need to make these distinctions, not because of requirements extrinsic to the doctrine of God or from penchant for novelty in theology, but simply because Christians speak of the gratuity and freedom of God's creating, and a fortiori of the contingency of creation itself. For instance, if God is free in creating the actual world (w_a), then he could have refrained from doing so or could have created a world different from the one he has created. But in such a case, God exists with countless potentialities, that is, unactualized possibilities, which are just those things he could choose to do but does not, and those things precluded because of the choices he does take. So if God could have created a world w_d different from and incompossible with the world he actually created (w_a), then he has a potentiality to create w_d which can never be realized, since it is precluded by his actually creating w_a.

On this point, Thomas's denial, again, does not quite contradict essentialism in its contemporary manifestation; for one of his motivations for denying "potency" in God was his belief, following Aristotle, that the movement from potency to act and from essence to accident is how individuals who share a common essence are individuated.[66] To have accidents in this sense would be to be one contingent individual who instantiates a generic common or "kind" essence. Given his broadly Aristotelian intellectual frame-

---

[65]There are inappropriate types of potential and accidental attribution. The essentialist could and should deny that God could exist in potentiality with respect to any of his essential properties, including all the divine perfections, as well as the person-constituting properties of the three persons. None of these properties could be mere qualities or divine accidents. To say otherwise compromises divine perfection, aseity and sovereignty.

[66]So Thomas, in arguing that God does not have accidents, says, "A subject is in some sense made actual by its accidents" (*Summa Theologica* 1.Q.3.A.6).

work, then, Thomas would have been remiss to ascribe accidental properties to God. The modern essentialist can also deny that God has accidents or "potencies" in this Aristotelian sense.

So our disagreement is less with Thomas than with those contemporary scholars, such as James Ross, Barry Miller and perhaps David Burrell, who take Thomas's claim as denying potentiality or possibility in the modern sense and seek to defend it accordingly. Their interpretations augment Thomas's view in various ways. As mentioned above, their first strategy is to construe all relational properties of God *ad extra* as Cambridge properties, like *being such that Augustine prays* or *being such that 2 is the only even prime*. However, this argument is clearly unsuccessful for certain relational properties, such as God creating the actual world and the Word uniting with human nature in Christ.[67] On the face of it, such examples look like paradigms of real but contingent properties. In fact, among contemporary defenders of strong simplicity, the very reason for construing such properties as Cambridge properties is a prior commitment to strong simplicity.[68] But God's choosing to create the world itself, or God the Son actually uniting with human nature in Jesus, are clearly not extrinsic in the mere Cambridge sense.

To take the first example, how can God's willing to create be contingent, if God's willing is identical with every other one of his properties? Again, Miller and others who pursue this strategy must argue that while the creation is contingent and God is free in creating it, nevertheless God has no choice or alternative in the matter. So Miller contends, "Although choice may entail freedom, freedom entails neither choice nor the possibility of a change of mind." To say otherwise is to attribute a potentiality or ability to God that he might not exercise, which is not possible since God is Pure Actuality.[69] "*Choice* is alien to God because it entails potentiality, but *willing* is not."[70] He argues that there is no "moment" either temporally or logically in which God could survey a range

---

[67]As with immutability, simplicity is difficult to reconcile with the doctrine of the incarnation, especially the relation between Christ's human and divine natures.

[68]Miller, for instance, frequently deduces the lack of potentiality and accidents in God from the proposition that God is utterly simple (*A Most Unlikely God,* p. 95).

[69]Ibid., p. 166.

[70]Ibid., p. 105.

of options and choose one. Nevertheless, he is free in creating the universe, which is therefore contingent.

Miller goes beyond other advocates of this view—who offer little explanation—by distinguishing between internal and external uses of the modal operator, superficially akin to the distinction mentioned in chapter two (n. 35) between a necessity of the consequent and necessity of the consequence. (*If a, then necessarily b* is a necessity of the consequent. *Necessarily, if a, then b* is a necessity of the consequence.) For example, he argues that since God is absolutely simple, it is incorrect to say,

Even if God had not created the Universe, he could nevertheless have done so.

To preserve divine simplicity, one must say

Even if God had not created the Universe, it was possible that (God create the universe).

Presumably, the latter imputes no potentiality to God.[71] Similarly, instead of saying that God contingently creates the universe, we should say

God's creation of the Universe is an object of the divine will in less than every possible world. (Because it holds in less than every possible world, this proposition is a contingent one.)[72]

And instead of saying that

God can either create the Universe or not create it

we should say (according to Miller)

It can be that (God create the Universe), or it can be that (God not create the Universe).[73]

I find this argument not only unpersuasive but utterly perplexing. How could it be that God not create the universe if he had no alternative in so doing? If I were to say that it could be so, part of what I would *mean* would be that God had some alternative, that he could have done otherwise. Miller's distinction here bears little analogy to the clear analytical cut between the neces-

---

[71]Ibid., p. 165.

[72]Ibid., p. 167.

[73]Ibid., p. 102. Miller capitalizes "Universe" in these quotes.

sity of the consequence and necessity of the consequent. The first ascribes necessity to the conditional as a whole—*Necessarily (if a, then b)*. The second ascribes necessity to the consequent within the conditional—*If a, then necessarily b*. In contrast, Miller's claim fails to capture any such nuance. It seems to make God's creative freedom far more obscure than it need be and depends on an ineffable distinction without a difference. Moreover, it fails to accommodate the truth that God could have created a universe different from the one he actually created, which is entailed by the claim that the constituents of the universe are contingent.

Perhaps most importantly, the primary reason for marshalling such recondite distinctions is to preserve strong divine simplicity at all costs. Such esoterica surely outstrip the meaning of Christian theological discourse. Admittedly, Miller has an additional, unique motivation: He seeks to defend the cogency of God as Uncaused Cause and pure, *simple,* subsistent existence or Pure Actuality, because he believes he has proven the existence of such a Being in a previous work.[74] This is an understandable and even noble motive. Nevertheless, it is incompatible with any robust doctrine of divine triunity. It is telling that while he defends his view as the proper Christian conception of God philosophically and theologically, he makes no reference to the complexities the Trinity and incarnation pose for his theory.[75] His commitment to strong divine simplicity determines his options, and he sticks to them consistently.

Baldly asserting freedom without choice is no solution. Thomas, incidentally, does not take this course but rather claims there are different ways the world may have been. Contrary to Miller, he says flatly, "We must simply say that God can do other things than those He has done."[76] This may not comport well with Thomas's additional claim that there is no potentiality in God; but his conviction that freedom includes choice—at least with respect to divine creation—apparently forces him into an inconsistency at this point. I suspect that the problem is that Thomas's Aristotelian understanding of potentiality did not provide him with a conceptual tool adequate to make the distinction

---

[74]Barry Miller, *From Existence to God* (London: Routledge, 1992).

[75]Miller, *A Most Unlikely God,* p. 168.

[76]*Summa Theologica* 1.Q.25.A.5-6. See also Hughes, *On a Complex Theory,* p. 109.

he needed to make. Miller resolves the inconsistency by opting for strong simplicity over divine choice.

Miller is not the only one to take this route. For instance, in treating divine
simplicity Burrell says that God's "freedom need not (and I contend, ought
not) primarily to be considered as freedom of choice." He admits this "defies
our articulation" but notes,

> "The sense in which creation is at once gratuitous yet utterly fitting, according
> to the axiom that 'good diffuses itself,' reminds us that divine freedom may be
> better understood on the model of Zen 'resonance' than on that of a western
> penchant for *decisions*."[77]

God as good, then, invariably if not necessarily diffuses himself by creating.

Perhaps there is some narrow sense of freedom that applies in such a
scenario. At best, however, such a freedom would be the compatibilist sort
that God has with respect to his essence. This type of freedom allows us to
say that there is never a time at which God does not affirm his essence, that
he never feels constrained by it. God never finds himself shackled with,
say, necessary omniscience. Similarly on Burrell's proposal, God never fails
to affirm the existence of creation, which is determined by his self-diffus-
ing nature. While there is no sufficient external cause for God's creating,
there is also no alternative. At best, this is a diminutive sense of freedom,
and not the robust type appropriate to divine freedom in creation. It is
much more restrictive than Leibniz's view, in which God is under a moral
but not logical necessity to create the best world (if he creates at all). Such
necessitarianism, when combined with language of diffusion and reso-
nance, is also reminiscent of Neo-Platonist immanationism and even pantheism,[78] which for the Christian theist should suggest that Burrell has
made a mistake somewhere.

---

[77]Burrell, "Distinguishing God from the World," p. 86.

[78]The Dionysian principle that goodness is essentially self-diffusive was common in medieval thought,
so Burrell is not alone in appealing to it. However, it is not compatible with the claim that God enjoys
libertarian freedom in creating the world, as Burrell seems to recognize. For more on this medieval
principle, see Norman Kretzmann, "Goodness, Knowledge and Indeterminacy in the Philosophy of
Thomas Aquinas," *Journal of Philosophy* 80 (1983): 631-49. This principle seems more helpful in the
exposition of divine love, which essentially expresses itself in the Father's begetting of the Son and
the Spirit's procession in eternal triune communion.

So what exactly is the problem with God exercising choices and making decisions? Quite clearly, the problem is that they are inconsistent with a type of simplicity that denies the distinctions of essence and accident and actual and potential in God. So the person enamored by strong simplicity must settle for a truncated definition of divine freedom.

By my lights, neither Miller's nor Burrell's suggestion preserves what most mean when they say that creation is contingent and that God's creating is free. Certainly God's freedom exceeds our own in incomparable ways, not least because he need not work on a preexistent substratum as all finite creatures must. Nevertheless, if choice and alternatives must be positively barred from our understanding of God's creation of the world, one should conclude that God is not even as free as we are in many situations.[79] This denial of choice does not imply a supereminent but rather an anemic freedom in God. Claiming that creation is contingent while denying that God had any choice in creating it empties the word *contingent* of all determinate logical and theological sense.

If, as I have argued, the strongest form of simplicity is incompatible with the Christian doctrine of God for trinitarian reasons, then why should the Christian accept it in this instance? The better course seems to be to retain the claim that God is free, at least with respect to some things, in the libertarian sense. God could have created a world different from the one he actually did create, or he could have created none at all. And the presence of the actual world, or of any world for that matter, neither increases his perfection nor assails his aseity. In choosing to create this actual world, God closes off all alternatives not compatible with that choice. This is because of his free choice and not from any necessity intrinsic or extrinsic to him. He chooses eternally to create the actual world and by implication to be the Creator, Sustainer and Redeemer of this world. We attribute a type of potentiality to God, not because we conceive of him as built up from fundamental parts of potency and act but because he is free. His essential freedom is the source of his potentiality and

---

[79]Burrell is perhaps correct to note that "it would seem jejune to presume, without further analysis, that God's freedom in creating would be given adequate expression by a mere freedom of choice" (*Knowing the Unknowable God,* p. 104). Mere freedom of choice may not be sufficient to express divine freedom, but certainly it is necessary. Surely God is at least as free as we are when we exercise freedom (assuming, as I do, that we sometimes exercise libertarian freedom).

contingency.[80] Therefore we should affirm that God is simple in just those senses—and only those senses—appropriate to, and compatible with, his perfect, free, sovereign and trinitarian reality.

---

[80]We can express this with the modalities of S5 modal logic, which, as noted in chapter two, are different from the temporal modalities more characteristic of S4. In this way we can maintain divine choice without necessarily implying divine deliberation or succession of thought in the act of creation. So, for instance, we can say straightforwardly that *God contingently creates the actual world* without any implication that there was some time t at which God chose this world, instead of another world or no world. Contingency is here a logical not a temporal distinction. There is of course a type of necessity that attaches to the world and God's free choice as actual, but it is innocuous. It is a conditional necessity, according to which

(1) Necessarily, if God creates w_a, then w_a exists (a necessity of the consequence).

But (1) does not entail

(2) If God creates w_a, then w_a necessarily exists (a necessity of the consequent)

anymore than

(3) Necessarily, if Ginny knows Jay is typing, then Jay is typing

entails

(4) Ginny knows Jay is typing, then Jay is necessarily typing.

The only difference between these examples is that, if temporal succession is only part of the created universe (whether or not God can or does freely enter the temporal realm is another matter), then there is no time t at which (1) is not true. But this is quite compatible with the contingency of creation itself, and the robust freedom of God's creating it. By grounding essentialism in S5 modal logic, we can differentiate potency-act and contingency-necessity from temporality in a way that Thomas and Aristotle could not. On Thomas's identification of potentiality with temporality, see Hughes, *On a Complex Theory*, pp. 41-50.

CONCLUSION

O ur solution to the conceptual dilemmas lurking in the classical Christian doctrine of God may be intellectually coherent and even satisfying; but some may still be uneasy. To put words on an intuition, they might ask, Since we are left with myriad divine properties, of which God has some necessarily and some contingently, are we not implying that God participates in or depends on entities more fundamental than he is?[1] When we talk about properties, universals, states of affairs, modal truths and individual essences, these can sound like necessarily existing abstract entities. As such, do they not compromise God's sovereignty, since it is not up to God, so to speak, whether they exist or not? Do we not end up with a swarming pantheon of necessary existents sharing eternity with God?

We may sense the Sovereignty-Aseity Conviction (SAC) prompting us to say that God simply creates such things, that it is up to God whether they exist. In the sense in which *Socrates exists* is up to God, so too it is up to God that *it is possible that Socrates exist*. Just as God creates human beings by his free choice, so too does he make it true that *it is possible that human beings exist*. And just as God made there be seven hills in Rome, so too he could have made $2 + 1 = 7$.

It is tempting to say these things, but they do not stand up to scrutiny. To

---

[1] I have already argued that God not be thought of as participating in properties anterior to him, but rather in some sense as preeminently and essentially exemplifying them. However, he does not exemplify properties as contingent entities do so, namely, by instantiating a transcendent universal. We may note in passing that some of the inclination against speaking of divine properties in the plural may stem from insufficient care in avoiding the connotation that properties are physical parts. Additionally, in chapter five we considered the costs of claiming that God chooses his essence or essential properties (from among alternatives) in any strong sense. So I will not retrace those reasons.

see this, recall the discussion from chapter two. If S5 comes close to capturing the modal intuitions relevant to broadly logical necessity and possibility (even if it does not explain them), and if those intuitions approximate the truth of the matter, then such claims could not be more than bald and senseless assertions. For if anything is possible, we said, then it is necessarily possible. That is, it is possible in every possible world. If this is the case, then there is no possible world in which God makes *t* either necessarily true or necessarily false (that is, impossible). And this does seem a bit troubling, since it seems to limit God's power. So, in defense of divine sovereignty, we may be tempted to conclude, so much the worse for S5 modal logic.

More modestly, we might want to say that God somehow causes these things, that they are creatures that God necessarily creates. The problem is that if God has an essence and properties, then there would seem to be a sense in which God causes himself or at least his essence.

ESSENTIALISM AND THE DOCTRINE OF DIVINE IDEAS

But we have another option: the doctrine of divine ideas or exemplars. This doctrine saved theologians with Neo-Platonic sympathies, such as Augustine, Anselm and Thomas Aquinas, from the appearance that they were populating heaven with unwelcome guests. So too may the contemporary essentialist appeal to it to interpret properties, universals, necessary truths and the like. Originating with Philo, the doctrine of divine ideas offers a way to reconcile the best elements of realism (about abstract "objects") with a thoroughgoing theism.

The doctrine provided Augustine with a way to domesticate the Platonic Forms in a universe ultimately dependent on the God of the Christian faith. Essentialists will understand the doctrine a little differently, since essentialism does not construe universals, properties, and the like as Platonic Forms or abstract entities per se, insofar as this suggests that they are discrete, independent members of reality. According to the doctrine of divine ideas, abstract entities are best interpreted as eternal objects of divine thought. They are objects in the sense that our language about properties, essences, logical and mathematical truths, and the like, have real referents and are not merely fictional artifacts or reifications of human language. But they are not entities or universals independent in their own right, standing over against God; rather, they are something like the content of God's intellectual activity.

Thomas endorsed the doctrine of divine ideas and even admitted that they were many, as truths are. Nevertheless, because of his commitment to divine simplicity, he maintained paradoxically that they were the same as God's essence.[2] At the very least we too can affirm that God, his essence, essential properties and knowledge of all necessary truths and abstracta are coextensive through all possible worlds. On this view, the domain of possible worlds and the abstract entities they contain are not an independent *plenum* of passive possibilities, like a modal version of the Forms in Plato's *Timaeus,* from which God creates the universe.[3] Rather, they are God's knowledge of the consistency, plenitude and expanse of his own being and of the extent and implications of his own power and freedom.

We refer to these as abstract objects precisely because we abstract them from concrete entities, the objects of our sense perception, into universals, using reason, modal intuitions and the like. And in that sense, universals transcend their instantiation in contingent objects as well as our perception of them. According to the doctrine of divine ideas, however, God thinks them preeminently and primarily.[4] And he thinks first of goodness, knowledge, power, love and so on neither as abstractions from contingent objects nor by consulting Platonic Forms but by reflecting on his own being. To us, they are abstractions we cannot help but refer to, somewhat obscurely, as objects. To God, they are immediately evident thoughts in whatever preeminent way God can be said to have thoughts.[5]

---

[2]*Summa Theologica* 1.Q.15.A.2.

[3]On this point I depart from Richard Creel's proposal in *Divine Impassibility* (Cambridge: Cambridge University Press, 1986), pp. 64-79. He appeals to just such a plenum to circumvent what he takes to be insuperable difficulties with the doctrine of *creatio ex nihilo.* Although Creel does well in deflecting the criticism that his model compromises divine sovereignty as well as monotheism, I do not find his arguments against creation *ex nihilo* nearly impressive enough to resort to such drastic measures.

[4]See Frederk Gerrit Immink, *Divine Simplicity* (Uitgeversmaatschappij: J. H. Kok-Kampen, 1987), p. 103.

[5]There is a great deal more to be said than my brief endorsement of the doctrine of divine ideas; but that is the subject for another book. Strictly speaking, this doctrine transforms realism into a type of theistic conceptualism. Such a conceptualism, however, is not beset with the difficulties of a conceptualism or antirealism located at the individual or societal level. Since God exists in every possible world, he thinks his ideas in every possible world. So modal truths, states of affairs, properties and the like exist as divine thoughts in every possible world. They are independent of human thought but not of divine thought. This solution promises to accommodate well-founded intuitions of realism and conceptualism or antirealism. It accommodates the realist intuition that truths are not things we make up, nor are they mere artifacts of language or conceptual schemes. They are not epistemic, for in-

Admittedly, this solution does not fully satisfy the intuitions nurtured by the SAC, for God, with respect to necessary truths, still could not do otherwise than to think them. God thinks them in every possible world. As previously argued, however, the Christian should not give the SAC free reign in the doctrine of God. It has a prima facie but defeasible authority. We have no obligation to extend it beyond its proper domain, especially since we know that, thus overextended, it generates contradictions. Whereas the contingent creation is the product of God's free choice to create, these divine ideas are objects of God's thought but not of his free choice or will.

Still, we would like to express the knowing relation between God and his ideas or exemplars as an asymmetrical, dependent relation, so that the ideas somehow depend on God's eternal noetic activity. We could say that, because God exists necessarily,

For any necessary truth p, if God thinks p, then p is true.

So God's thinking p is a sufficient condition for p. This solution is superficial, however, since, if p is a necessary truth and God is omniscient, then the conditional holds the other way around, so that

For any truth p, if p is necessary, then God thinks p.

This makes it seem that God's noetic relation is dependent on certain necessary truths, which is not much help.[6] Rather, we want to say that, for any necessary truth p, p is true if and only if God thinks p. Or perhaps more strongly, we want to say that the cause of p's truth is that God thinks p. Then God's noetic activity, albeit eternal, is the necessary and sufficient condition for all the necessary truths, and by extension, we could include essences, properties, states of affairs and the whole horde of abstract entities.

---

stance, in such a way that the truth that dinosaurs once roamed the earth is dependent on whether some human community knows or can verify it. It also accommodates the antirealist skepticism that truths, propositions and the like could not be utterly independent of mind *simpliciter*. They seem to have intrinsically intellectual characteristics. For more on the convergence of realism and antirealism via "divine creative anti-realism," see Alvin Plantinga, "How to Be an Anti-Realist," *Proceedings and Addresses of the American Philosophical Association* (April 1982): 47-70.

[6]Thomas V. Morris has a similar but independent argument in which he considers the propositions (1) If there were no God, there would be no abstract objects, versus (2) If there were no abstract objects, there would be no God. This generates the same dilemma. See his "Absolute Creation," in *Anselmian Explorations* (Notre Dame, Ind.: University of Notre Dame Press, 1987), p. 164. He notes that one strategy, which I will not pursue, would be to refuse assent to subjunctive conditionals having necessarily false antecedents.

In "Absolute Creation," Thomas Morris and Christopher Menzel suggest a way to describe God's ideas as dependent on God's causal powers. They note that while there is a symmetrical logical dependence from such propositions as (G) and (P), we can still insist that there is an asymmetrical causal or onto-logical dependence from (G) to (P). This is plausible, since abstract entities are causally inert and conceptual, whereas God is the preeminently active causal agent. The difference between divine causation of abstract entities and of con-tingent creation is that the former type of causation is purely intellective and does not involve the sort of libertarian freedom that God exercises in creating the actual world. They are freely caused in the diminished sense that God's in-tentionality produced them rather than any force or cause external to God. Can we understand God's relation to his own essence in the same way, without resurrecting the problems of strong actualism? While we cannot have the type of absolute control implied by choice that an unrestrained SAC might encour-age, can we affirm that all abstract truths are still caused by God's eternal in-tellective activity?[7]

It seems not. There is certainly an important distinction between God as the preeminent active causal agent and the eternal objects of his thought, which do not call anything into existence. And we clearly want to maintain that God's ideas are not outside of him, that they illicitly dictate what he is and what he can do or that they are independent of God's thinking them. Still, the boot-strapping problem rears its ugly head again, since Morris and Menzel's pro-posal implies that God has, necessarily and eternally, caused his essence and essential properties to exist, not by an exercise of free will—as in strong actu-alism—but by his eternal thought.[8] But this would entail, for example, that God is all-powerful just because, from eternity, God has reflected on the fact that he is all-powerful. But clearly, for this to be possible, God would have had to have the property P_{O1} of being able to think his omnipotence into existence. But perhaps, one might retort, God also thought *that* property into existence from eternity. Well, then he would have had to have another property P_{O2}, and off, once again, goes an infinite regress.

---

[7] I have paraphrased their suggestions from "Absolute Creation" reprinted in *Anselmian Explorations*, pp. 165-72. The article was originally published by Thomas V. Morris and Christopher Menzel in *American Philosophical Quarterly* 23 (1986): 352-62.

[8] I must thank Greg Welty for helping me see this point clearly.

There are other complexities here, many worth discussing. But none, so far as I know,[9] offer an alternative to perhaps the only way to avoid the contradictory idea of divine self-creation: Stop the regress of explanation, not with God's causal powers, whether grounded in his will or his intellect, but with God's eternal essence and actuality, which include his eternal thoughts and his free will. God's ideas, like his triune nature, perfect goodness, love and knowledge, are not independent entities and objects. They are aspects of who God necessarily *is*.

But what about those baffling claims of divine simplicity that recur as sub-themes in the Christian tradition, that God is not simply loving, all knowing and all-powerful; he *is* Love, Knowledge and Power? I should very much like to give an account of this practice, but I have left it to the very end, because I think this should be one of the last things the Christian says about God, not one of the first. These claims are confusing, very difficult to interpret, and suggest that we are reaching the limits of our capacity to speak of God. But perhaps we can shed a little light on them nonetheless. What seems to lie behind these obscure claims is a worry: If we ground everything about God in his essence and essential properties, then it seems that what truly exists *a se,* from itself, is not God but his eternal essence. God, in turn, depends on his essence by standing in the eternal relation of essentially exemplifying it, or at least essentialist language can seem to imply. But that is a problem only if God's essence is separate or distinct from God himself. Hence, the motivation to say that God just is his essence and essential properties.

I have maintained that we are well within our rights in using essentialist language and in applying it to God with the appropriate modifications, without deciding on the metaphysical nature of properties, essences, universals and the like. Moreover, by defining these things minimally as facts or truths about individual entities in the actual world, I think I have circumvented most of the problems that a more strongly Platonic view of abstract entities poses for God's sovereignty and aseity. Nevertheless, the status of such abstracta takes on a theological urgency here. To avoid these unsavory implications, what we should say is that God's perfect wisdom, goodness, and so forth, is ontologically prior to these abstractions in the order of ultimate explanation.

---

[9]I am not discounting the possibility that someone may resolve this problem. But I cannot think how it would be done.

God's being precedes the discrete universal properties, though universals eternally exist and are relevantly distinct, in the sense that God eternally abstracts them by reflecting on his own being. When we say that Socrates is wise, the claim is meaningful and true because of this prior act of God abstracting the concept of Wisdom by reflecting on the concrete actuality of his own being, one aspect of which is perfect wisdom. God's eternal thought also allows us to speak much more easily about God, using the language of properties and essences. It is God's intellectual activity that makes our intellectual and linguistic activity possible, not only in everyday contexts but also in theology.

A great deal more remains to be said, but I do think we are now in the neighborhood of preserving the essential core of the doctrine of divine simplicity.

DIVINE IDEAS AND UNINSTANTIATED INDIVIDUAL ESSENCES
Everyone may not be satisfied with this solution. James Ross, for instance, says:

> God's power is more awesome. Its domain is realized with its exercise. What is possible *ad extra* is a result of what God does. God has no exemplar objects. . . . All content *ad extra* is caused by God. In sum, God creates the possibility, impossibility, and counterfactuality that has content (real situations) involving being other than God.[10]

This objection is not directly targeted at my argument, since Ross aims his crosshairs at the view that there is a realm of possibility outside God (*ad extra*). But this is no implication of either essentialism or the doctrine of divine ideas. Still, Ross apparently wants to say that God's creative activity logically or ontologically precedes possibility and impossibility in the same or similar way that it precedes the existence and actuality of contingent entities. So, for instance, for Ross, if the universe did not exist, it would be neither possible nor impossible for it to exist. It would have no modal status whatsoever.

Since there are no merely possible individuals, he argues, there can be no modalized truth conditions about them. Possibility of *x* presupposes the actu-

---

[10]James Ross, "God, Creator of Kinds and Possibilities," in *Rationality, Religious Belief and Moral Commitment,* ed. Robert Audi and William Wainwright (Ithaca, N.Y.: Cornell University Press, 1986), pp. 318-39.

ality of *x*. He seems to be assuming that there must be concrete individuals in order for there to be things like kinds and essences. So there is no eternal truth concerning the modal status of contingent things.

However, Ross insists in a much earlier work that choice among alternatives is a requisite part of God's creative freedom.[11] Thus one could read him as saying that it is straightforwardly up to God to make such things as necessary truths true, such that he could have made them false or at least possibly true. Similarly, Alvin Plantinga says that the "sovereignty-aseity intuition" may suggest (if not checked) that every truth is up to God or within his control, such that for any proposition *P*, whether or not *P* is true, is up to God, and God could have made it false.[12] This idea is "repugnant to the intellect" and if allowed, would introduce incoherence into the doctrine of God in ways akin to the problems of strong actualism. Letting the abstract notion of free choice run rampant in this way quickly leads to grief. It entails among other things that God could have made it true that he never exist, that there be beings in no way dependent on him, that God love and save his creatures but never exist, and other such monstrosities. I seriously doubt Ross would allow such an outcome.[13]

But perhaps Ross's argument has a narrower range of application. Although God cannot create his own essence and essential properties, perhaps God is the Creator of all modalities and "abstract objects" relevant to contingent entities. This argument seems to hinge on his claim that there can be no merely possible individuals. From this, he concludes, "If there cannot be merely possible individuals, there cannot be ideas for them either."[14] Thus he denies that any modality applies to an individual *x* prior to *x* being actual.

In chapter two I also disavowed merely possible but nonactual individuals in the name of actualism. At the same time, I argued that there could have been individuals distinct from any individuals there actually are. To reconcile these two claims I introduced the notion of uninstantiated individual es-

---

[11]James Ross, *Philosophical Theology* (Indianapolis: Hackett, 1980), p. 289.

[12]Alvin Plantinga, *Does God Have a Nature?* (Milwaukee: Marquette University Press, 1980), pp. 77-84, 111.

[13]So he qualifies his claim by noting that there is an internal "perimeter" to God's power that includes internal consistency and compatibility with divine being. Ross, "God, Creator of Kinds and Possibility," pp. 318-19.

[14]Ibid., p. 329.

sences. So, to redirect Ross's critique to its intended object, we should consider this notion specifically.

Probably the most difficult aspect of essentialism to swallow is the notion of uninstantiated individual essences or haecceities.[15] And not surprisingly, it is precisely on this point that critics of views such as the one I have defended usually direct their attack.[16] With the doctrine of divine ideas, however, individual essences are much less obscure. To illustrate: If I am contingent, then I might not have existed. So there is some possible world $w_{~j}$ in which I do not exist. Nevertheless, in $w_{~j}$ it would have been possible that I exist, since God could have created me.[17] Similarly, if the only individuals possible are those who exist in the actual world, then God's freedom would be less extensive than if he could have created individuals distinct from every individual who actually exists. So, if God is perfect, he should have a freedom as extensive as is compatible with his other attributes (such as his perfect goodness, his trinitarian relations and the fact that God the Son became incarnate). Thus there could be individuals distinct from those God has chosen to create. No more than this is needed to give rise to the notion of an uninstantiated individual essence. Uninstantiated individual essences are God's knowledge of all the individuals he could have created but has chosen not to create for reasons hidden in his will. Even if Ross is right concerning our knowledge of actual individuals and general essences, God need not have such actualities before him in order to know them in some sense. How God knows such things is difficult

---

[15]Strictly speaking, these are not identical. For instance, one might endorse the existence of qualitative individual essences, which contain non-trivial essential properties had by one individual uniquely. A haecceity need not be purely qualitative but might simply be something like *being-Socrates* or *Socrateity,* which can be referred to directly via proper names but cannot really be described qualitatively. So far as I can tell, whether or not there are haecceities in this narrower sense—that is, non-qualitative—is not crucial to essentialism as defined here. That is, it is compatible with the existence and the nonexistence of such things. For discussion and defense of individual qualitative essences, see Linda Zagzebski, "Individual Essence and the Creation," in *Divine and Human Action,* ed. Thomas V. Morris (Ithaca, N.Y.: Cornell University Press, 1988), pp. 119-44.

[16]For example, Barry Miller, *From Existence to God* (London: Routledge, 1992), pp. 40-63; James F. Ross, "The Crash of Modal Metaphysics," *Review of Metaphysics* 43 (December 1989): 251-79, and "God, Creator of Kinds and Possibilities," pp. 315-34; David Burrell, "Distinguishing God from the World," in *Language, Meaning and God,* ed. Brian Davies (London: Geoffrey Chapman, 1987), p. 83. Miller argues against possible but nonactual individuals from inability of reference.

[17]Again, as noted in chapter two, this says nothing about whether or not the truth that *it is possible that I (or Jay) exist* could be asserted or expressed in $w_{~j}$.

to conceive,[18] but surely that alone does not impeach the proposal since most of us do not even know how we know the things we know. The idea is surely coherent; moreover, it gives some substance to the claim that the creation is contingent and God is free in creating it.

This is not to say that there are possible but nonactual individuals but only that there are uninstantiated essences of individuals God could have created. Strictly speaking, God knows these rather than non-actual individuals as actual. To say otherwise—that God knows individuals as actual that are not actual—would be nonsense.[19]

Finally, this strategy upholds the Aristotelian conviction of the priority of the actual but redirects it to the prior actuality of God. What it denies is that individuals God could create need be actual in order for him to know what sorts of individuals he could create, whether or not he does so. Uninstantiated individual essences are God's knowledge of uniquely qualitative properties— as well as relevant accidental properties—instantiated in possible worlds where individuals exist distinct from any that exist in the actual world.[20] God has the power to instantiate, that is, to make actual, these uninstantiated individual essences, but in creating the actual world, he has foregone doing so. Admittedly, such esoterica rarely enter the minds of pious believers. Still, it is surely a small triumph that the Achilles' heel of essentialism finds its best defense in a theistic context; and essentialism, so far from contradicting theism, finds its proper home there. It is an unexpected bonus that the doctrine of divine ideas helps essentialism overcome an otherwise serious objection. Appropriately, it is in theism that essentialism—fortified with contemporary modal logic—finds a secure conceptual dwelling place.

---

[18]This problem is related to the grounding objection leveled against the view that God has knowledge of counterfactuals of creaturely freedom, which are those things that free creatures would have done in states of affairs different from states of affairs that actually obtain. For more on the grounding objection and for an excellent defense of God's knowledge of such things, see Thomas Flint, *Divine Providence: The Molinist Account* (Ithaca, N.Y.: Cornell University Press, 1998).

[19]Some who doubt the existence of uninstantiated individual essences confuse the defense of such entities with a defense of the existence of merely possible individuals. For instance, Ross, "God, Creator of Kinds and Possibilities," p. 323.

[20]And perhaps also haecceities, if we distinguish these from individual qualitative essences. However, if haecceities are just the unique actualities of individuals, then God obviously would not know the haecceities of nonactual individuals.

BIBLIOGRAPHY

Adams, Robert Merrihew. "Must God Create the Best?" In *The Concept of God,* edited by Thomas V. Morris. Oxford: Oxford University Press, 1987.

———. Review of *The Nature of Necessity. Nous* 11 (1977): 175-90.

Allen, Diogenes. *Philosophy for Understanding Theology.* Atlanta: John Knox Press, 1985.

Alston, William P. *Divine Nature and Human Language.* Ithaca, N.Y.: Cornell University Press, 1989.

Anselm. *Monologion.*

———. *Proslogion: A Scholastic Miscellany.* Edited by Eugene R. Fairweather. Philadelphia: Westminster Press, 1956.

Aquinas, Thomas. *Compendium Theologiae.*

———. *Summa Contra Gentiles.* London: Burns, Oates & Washbourne, 1924.

———. *Summa Theologica.* New York: Benziger Brothers, 1947.

Arapura, John G. "Hartshorne's Response to Vedanta." In *The Philosophy of Charles Hartshorne,* edited by Lewis Hahn. LaSalle, Ill.: Open Court, 1991.

Aristotle. *Categoriae. The Basic Works of Aristotle.* Edited by Richard McKeon. New York: Random House, 1941.

———. *Prior Analytics. The Basic Works of Aristotle.* Edited by Richard McKeon. New York: Random House, 1941.

Audi, Robert, ed. *The Cambridge Dictionary of Philosophy.* Cambridge: Cambridge University Press, 1995.

Augustine. *The City of God.*

———. *De Trinitate.*

Balthasar, Hans Urs von. *Karl Barth: Darstellung und Deutung Seiner Theologie.* Köln: Verlag Jakob Hegner, 1951. Translated into English as *The Theology of Karl Barth.* San Francisco: Ignatius Press, Communio Books, 1992.

Barr, James. *Biblical Words for Time.* London: SCM Press, 1962.

Barth, Karl. *Anselm: Fides Quaerens Intellectum.* London: SCM Press, 1960.

—————. *Church Dogmatics,* 1/1. 2nd ed. Translated by Geoffrey W. Bromiley and T. F. Torrance. Edinburgh: T & T Clark, 1975.

—————. *Church Dogmatics,* 1/2. Translated by Geoffrey W. Bromiley and T. F. Torrance. Edinburgh: T & T Clark, 1956.

—————. *Church Dogmatics,* 2/1. Translated by Geoffrey W. Bromiley and T. F. Torrance. Edinburgh: T & T Clark, 1957.

—————. *Church Dogmatics,* 3/1. Translated by Geoffrey W. Bromiley and T. F. Torrance. Edinburgh: T & T Clark, 1958.

—————. *Church Dogmatics,* 4/1. Translated by Geoffrey W. Bromiley and T. F. Torrance. Edinburgh: T & T Clark, 1958.

—————. *Credo: A Presentation of the Chief Problems of Dogmatics with Reference to the Apostles' Creed.* London: Hodder, 1936.

—————. "Fate and Idea in Theology." In *The Way of Theology in Karl Barth,* edited by H. Martin Rumscheidt. Allison Park, Penn.: Pickwick, 1986.

—————. *Protestant Thought: From Rousseau to Ritschl.* New York: Harper & Row, 1959.

—————. *The Theology of Schleiermacher.* Edited by Dietrich Ritschl. Grand Rapids, Mich.: Eerdmans, 1982.

Berkouwer, G. C. *The Triumph of Grace in the Theology of Karl Barth.* Grand Rapids, Mich.: Eerdmans, 1956.

Boethius. *The Consolation of Philosophy.*

Brody, Baruch. *Identity and Essence.* Princeton, N.J.: Princeton University Press, 1980.

Brown, David. "Trinitarian Personhood and Individuality." In *Trinity, Incarnation and Atonement.* Notre Dame, Ind.: University of Notre Dame Press, 1989.

Brown, James. *Subject and Object in Theology.* New York: Macmillan, 1955.

Brunner, Emil. *Dogmatics.* Vol. 1. London: Lutterworth, 1949.

Burrell, David. *Aquinas: God and Action.* Notre Dame, Ind.: University of Notre Dame Press, 1979.

—————. "Distinguishing God from the World." In *Language, Meaning and God,* edited by Brian Davies. London: Geoffrey Chapman, 1987.

—————. "Does Process Theology Rest on a Mistake?" *Theological Studies* 72 (1982): 125-35.

—————. *Knowing the Unknowable God.* Notre Dame, Ind.: University of Notre Dame Press, 1986.

Busch, Eberhard. *Karl Barth.* London: SCM, 1976.

Cartwright, Richard. "Propositions." In *Analytical Philosophy,* edited by R. J. Butler. Oxford: Basil Blackwell, 1962.

Chavannes, Henry. *L'Analogie entre Dieu et le Monde Selon Saint Thomas d'Aquin et Selon Karl Barth*. Paris: Les Editions du Cerf, 1969.

Chisholm, Roderick M. "Identity Through Possible Worlds." In *The Actual and the Possible*, edited by Michael Loux. Ithaca, N.Y.: Cornell University Press, 1979.

————. "Problems of Identity." In *Identity and Individuation*, edited by Milton K. Munitz. New York: New York University Press, 1971.

Clark, Kelly James. "Hold Not Thy Peace at My Tears." In *Our Knowledge of God*, edited by K. J. Clark. The Netherlands: Kluwer Academic, 1992.

Clarke, W. Norris. "Charles Hartshorne's Philosophy of God." In *Charles Hartshorne's Concept of God*, edited by Lewis Hahn. Dordrecht: Kluwer Academic, 1990.

————. *Explorations in Metaphysics*. Notre Dame, Ind.: University of Notre Dame Press, 1994.

Cloots, Andres, and Jan Van der Veken. "Can the God of Process Thought Be 'Redeemed'?" In *Charles Hartshorne's Concept of God*, edited by Lewis Hahn. Dordrecht: Kluwer Academic, 1990.

Cobb, John B., Jr. "Hartshorne's Importance for Theology." In *The Philosophy of Charles Hartshorne*, edited by Lewis Hahn. LaSalle, Ill.: Open Court, 1991.

Colwell, John. *Actuality and Provisionality: Eternity and Election in the Theology of Karl Barth*. Edinburgh: Rutherford House Books, 1989.

Copan, Paul. "Is *Creatio ex Nihilo* a Postbiblical Invention? An Examination of Gerhard May's Proposal." *Trinity Journal* 17 n.s. (1996): 77-93.

Craig, William Lane. "Divine Foreknowledge and Future Contingency." In *Process Theology*, edited by Ronald Nash. Grand Rapids, Mich.: Baker, 1987.

Creel, Richard. *Divine Impassibility*. Cambridge: Cambridge University Press, 1986.

Cresswell, M. J. "The World is Everything That Is the Case." In *The Possible and the Actual*, edited by Michael J. Loux. Ithaca, N.Y.: Cornell University Press, 1979.

Cullman, Oscar. *Christ and Time*. London: SCM Press, 1962.

Cunningham, Mary Kathleen. *What Is Theological Exegesis? Interpretation and Use of Scripture in Barth's Doctrine of Election*. Valley Forge, Penn.: Trinity Press International, 1995.

Davaney, Sheila Greeve. *Divine Power: A Study of Karl Barth and Charles Hartshorne*. Philadelphia: Fortress, 1986.

Davies, Brian. "The Doctrine of Divine Simplicity," In *Language, Meaning and God*, edited by Brian Davies. London: Geoffrey Chapman, 1987.

Dembski, William, and Jay Richards, eds. *Unapologetic Apologetics: Meeting the Challenges of Theological Studies*. Downers Grove, Ill.: InterVarsity Press, 2001.

Dembski, William. *Intelligent Design: The Bridge Between Science and Theology*. Downers Grove, Ill.: InterVarsity Press, 1999.

Devlin, James P. "Hartshorne's Metaphysical Asymmetry." In *The Philosophy of Charles Hartshorne,* edited by Lewis Hahn. LaSalle, Ill.: Open Court, 1991.

Dombrowski, Daniel A. *Analytic Theism, Hartshorne and the Concept of God.* Albany, N.Y.: SUNY Press, 1996.

Dorner, I. A. *Divine Immutability: A Critical Reconsideration.* Minneapolis: Fortress, 1994.

Fiddes, Paul. *The Creative Suffering of God.* New York: Oxford University Press, 1988.

Flint, Thomas. *Divine Providence: The Molinist Account.* Ithaca, N.Y.: Cornell University Press, 1998.

Flint, Thomas P., and Alfred J. Freddoso. "Maximal Power." In *The Concept of God,* edited by Thomas V. Morris. Oxford: Oxford University Press, 1987.

Foley, Grover. "The Catholic Critics of Karl Barth: In Outline and Analysis." *Scottish Journal of Theology* 14 (1961): 136-55.

Forbes, Graeme. *The Metaphysics of Modality.* Oxford: Clarendon, 1985.

———. *Languages of Possibility.* Oxford: Basil Blackwell, 1989.

Frankenberry, Nancy. "Hartshorne's Method in Metaphysics." In *The Philosophy of Charles Hartshorne,* edited by Lewis Hahn. LaSalle, Ill.: Open Court, 1991.

Frankfurt, Harry. "Descartes on the Creation of the Eternal Truths." *Philosophical Review* 86 (1977): 36-57.

Frei, Hans. *The Eclipse of Biblical Narrative.* New Haven, Conn.: Yale University Press, 1984.

Gale, Richard. *On the Nature and Existence of God.* Cambridge: Cambridge University Press, 1991.

Geach, Peter. "God's Relation to the World." In *Logic Matters.* Berkeley: University of California Press, 1972.

———. "Omnipotence." In *Providence and Evil.* Cambridge: Cambridge University Press, 1977.

Gragg, Alan. *Charles Hartshorne.* Waco, Tex.: Word, 1973.

Griffin, David Ray. "Hartshorne's Postmodern Philosophy." In *Hartshorne, Process Philosophy and Theology,* edited by Robert Kane and Stephen H. Phillips. Albany, N.Y.: SUNY Press, 1989.

Gunton, Colin. *Becoming and Being: The Doctrine of God in Charles Hartshorne and Karl Barth.* Oxford: Oxford University Press, 1976.

———. "Karl Barth's Doctrine of Election as Part of His Doctrine of God." *Journal of Theological Studies* 31 (1980): 381-92.

Hardy, Edward R., ed. *Christology of the Later Fathers.* Philadelphia: Westminster Press, 1954.

Hartshorne, Charles. "The Aesthetic Dimensions of Religious Experience." In *Logic, God and Metaphysics,* edited by James F. Harris. Dordrecht: Kluwer Academic, 1992.

———. *Anselm's Discovery: A Re-examination of the Ontological Argument.* LaSalle, Ill.: Open Court, 1965.

———. *Aquinas to Whitehead: Seven Centuries of Metaphysics of Religion.* Milwaukee: Marquette University Press, 1976.

———. *Beyond Humanism: Essays in the New Philosophy of Nature.* Chicago: Willet, Clark, 1937.

———. "Clarke's Thomistic Critique." In *Charles Hartshorne's Concept of God,* edited by Lewis Hahn. Dordrecht: Kluwer Academic, 1990.

———. "Cloots and Van der Veken on Panentheism." In *Charles Hartshorne's Concept of God,* edited by Lewis Hahn. Dordrecht: Kluwer Academic, 1990.

———. *Creative Synthesis and Philosophical Method.* LaSalle, Ill.: Open Court, 1970.

———. *The Divine Relativity: A Social Conception of God.* New Haven, Conn.: Yale University Press, 1948.

———. "Is God's Existence a State of Affairs?" In *Faith and the Philosophers,* edited by John Hick. New York: St. Martin's Press, 1964.

———. "The Logic of Panentheism." In *Philosophers Speak of God,* edited by Charles Hartshorne and William L. Reese. Chicago: University of Chicago Press, 1953.

———. *The Logic of Perfection and Other Essays in Neo-Classical Metaphysics.* LaSalle, Ill.: Open Court, 1962.

———. *Man's Vision of God.* LaSalle, Ill.: Open Court, 1941.

———. "The Meaning of 'Is Going to Be.'" *Mind* 74 (January 1965): 46-58.

———. *A Natural Theology for Our Time.* LaSalle, Ill.: Open Court, 1967.

———. "Necessity." *Review of Metaphysics* 21 (1968): 290-96.

———. *Omnipotence and Other Theological Mistakes.* Albany, N.Y.: SUNY Press, 1984.

———. *Reality as Social Process.* Boston: Beacon, 1953.

———. "Real Possibility." *The Journal of Philosophy* 60, no. 21 (1963): 593-605.

———. *A Reply to My Critics.* In *The Philosophy of Charles Hartshorne,* edited by Lewis Hahn. LaSalle, Ill.: Open Court, 1991.

———. "Response to Peters." In *Existence and Actuality,* edited by John B. Cobb Jr. and Franklin Gamwell. Chicago: University of Chicago Press, 1984.

———. "A Revision of Peirce's Categories." *Monist* 63, no. 3 (July 1980): 285-86.

———. "Toward a Buddhist-Christian Religion." In *Buddhism and American Thinkers,* edited by Kenneth K. Inada and Molan P. Jacobson. Albany, N.Y.: SUNY Press, 1984.

———. "Whitehead's Idea of God." In *The Philosophy of Alfred North Whitehead,* edited by Paul Arthur Schilpp. Evanston, Ill.: Northwestern University Press, 1941.

————. *Wisdom as Moderation: A Philosophy of the Middle Way.* Albany, N.Y.: SUNY Press, 1987.

Hartwell, Herbert. *The Theology of Karl Barth: An Introduction.* Philadelphia: Westminster Press, 1964.

Helm, Paul. *Divine Eternity: A Study of God Without Time.* Oxford: Clarendon, 1988.

Hendry, George. "The Freedom of God in the Theology of Karl Barth." *Scottish Journal of Theology* 31 (1978): 229-44.

Heppe, Heinrich. *Reformed Dogmatics* (1861). Revised and edited by Ernst Bizer. London: George Allen & Unwin, 1950.

Hick, John. "Jesus and the World Religions." In *The Myth of God Incarnate,* edited by John Hick. London: SCM Press, 1977.

Hintikka, Jaako. "Individuals, Possible Worlds and Epistemic Logic." *Nous* 1 (1967): 33-63.

————. *Models for Modalities.* Dordrecht: R. Reidel, 1969.

Hodge, Charles. *Systematic Theology.* Vol. 1. Reprint ed. Grand Rapids, Mich.: Eerdmans, 1995.

Hubbeling, H. G. "Hartshorne and the Ontological Argument." In *The Philosophy of Charles Hartshorne,* edited by Lewis Hahn. LaSalle, Ill.: Open Court, 1991.

Hughes, Christopher. *On a Complex Theory of a Simple God: An Investigation in Aquinas' Philosophical Theology.* Ithaca, N.Y.: Cornell University Press, 1989.

Hughes, G. E., and M. J. Cresswell. *A Companion to Modal Logic.* London: Methuen, 1984.

————. *An Introduction to Modal Logic.* London: Methuen, 1968.

Hunsinger, George. *How to Read Karl Barth: The Shape of His Theology.* New York: Oxford University Press, 1991.

Immink, Frederik Gerrit. *Divine Simplicity.* Uitgeversmaatschappij: J. H. Kok-Kampen, 1987.

Irenaeus. *Adversus Haereses.*

Jager, Thomas. "An Actualistic Semantics for Quantified Modal Logic." *Notre Dame Journal of Formal Logic* 23 (1982): 335-49.

Jenson, Robert. *God After God: The God of the Past and the Future as Seen in the Work of Karl Barth.* Indianapolis: Bobbs-Merrill, 1969.

Jüngel, Eberhard. *Gottes Sein Ist im Werden.* Tübingen: J. C. B. Mohr, 1966. Translated into English as *The Doctrine of the Trinity: God's Being Is in Becoming.* Edinburgh: Scottish Academic Press, 1976.

Kaplan, David. "How to Russell a Frege-Church." In *The Possible and the Actual,* edited by Michael J. Loux. Ithaca, N.Y.: Cornell University Press, 1979.

————. "Transworld Heir Lines." In *The Possible and the Actual,* edited by Michael J.

Loux. Ithaca, N.Y.: Cornell University Press, 1979.

Kelsey, David. *The Uses of Scripture in Recent Theology*. Philadelphia: Fortress, 1975.

Kenny, Anthony. "The Definition of Omnipotence." In *The Concept of God*, edited by Thomas V. Morris. Oxford: Oxford University Press, 1987.

———. *The God of the Philosophers*. Oxford: Clarendon, 1979.

King, Sallie B. "Buddhism and Hartshorne." In *The Philosophy of Charles Hartshorne*, edited by Lewis Hahn. LaSalle, Ill.: Open Court, 1991.

Konyndyk, Kenneth. *Introductory Modal Logic*. Notre Dame, Ind.: University of Notre Dame Press, 1986.

Kreck, Walter. "Analogia Fidei oder Analogia Entis?" In *Antwort*, edited by Ernst Wolf, Ch. von Kirschbaum and Rudolf Frey. Zollikon-Zürich: Evangelischer Verlag, 1956.

Kretzmann, Norman. "Goodness, Knowledge and Indeterminacy in the Philosophy of Thomas Aquinas." *Journal of Philosophy* 80 (1983): 631-49.

———. "Omniscience and Immutability." *Journal of Philosophy* 63 (July 1966): 409-21.

Kripke, Saul. "A Completeness Theorem in Modal Logic." *The Journal of Symbolic Logic* 24, no. 1 (March 1959): 1-14.

———. "Identity and Necessity." In *Identity and Individuation*, edited by Milton K. Munitz. New York: New York University Press, 1971.

———. *Naming and Necessity*. Cambridge, Mass.: Harvard University Press, 1972.

———. "Some Semantical Considerations on Modal Logic." In *Reference and Modality*, edited by Leonard Linsky. Oxford: Oxford University Press, 1963.

LaCugna, Catherine Mowry. *God for Us: The Trinity and the Christian Life*. San Francisco: HarperSanFrancisco, 1991.

Leibniz, Gottfried. *Philosophical Writings*. Edited by G. H. R. Parkinson. London: Everyman's Library, n.d.

Lewis, David. "Anselm and Actuality." *Nous* 4 (1970): 186-87.

———. *Counterfactuals*. Cambridge, Mass.: Harvard University Press, 1973.

———. "Counterpart Theory and Quantified Modal Logic." In *The Possible and the Actual*, edited by Michael J. Loux. Ithaca, N.Y.: Cornell University Press, 1979.

Lewy, Casimir. *Meaning and Modality*. Cambridge: Cambridge University Press, 1976.

Loux, Michael. "Introduction." In *The Possible and the Actual*, edited by Michael J. Loux. Ithaca, N.Y.: Cornell University Press, 1979.

Lycan, William. "The Trouble with Possible Worlds." In *The Possible and the Actual*, edited by Michael J. Loux. Ithaca, N.Y.: Cornell University Press, 1979.

Mackie, J. L. "Evil and Omnipotence." *Mind* 64 (1955): 200-212.

Macintosh, H. R. *Types of Modern Theology: Schleiermacher to Barth*. Digswell Place, U.K.: James Nisbet, 1937; reprint, 1962.

Mann, William E. "Divine Simplicity." *Religious Studies* 18 (1982): 451-71.

———. "Epistemology Supernaturalized." *Faith and Philosophy* 11 (1985): 436-56.

———. "Simplicity and Immutability in God." In *The Concept of God,* edited by Thomas V. Morris. Oxford: Oxford University Press, 1987.

———. "Simplicity and Properties." *Religious Studies* 22 (1986): 343-53.

Marcus, Ruth Barcan. *Modalities: Philosophical Essays.* New York: Oxford University Press, 1993.

Martin, Norman M. "Taking Creativity Seriously: Logical Structure." In *The Philosophy of Charles Hartshorne,* edited by Lewis Hahn. LaSalle, Ill.: Open Court, 1991.

McCormack, Bruce L. *Karl Barth's Critically Realistic Dialectical Theology: Its Genesis and Development 1909-1936.* Oxford: Clarendon, 1995.

McIntyre, John. "Analogy." *Scottish Journal of Theology* 12 (1959): 1-20.

Meinong. "The Theory of Objects." In *Realism and the Background of Phenomenology,* edited by Roderick M. Chisholm. Glencoe, Ill: The Free Press, 1960.

Miller, Barry. *From Existence to God.* London: Routledge, 1992.

———. *A Most Unlikely God.* Notre Dame, Ind.: University of Notre Dame Press, 1996.

Moltmann, Jürgen. *The Crucified God.* London: SCM Press, 1974.

———. *The Trinity and the Kingdom.* San Francisco: HarperSanFrancisco, 1981.

Mondin, Battista. *The Principle of Analogy in Protestant and Catholic Theology.* The Hague: Martinus Nijhoff, 1963.

Moore, G. E. "External and Internal Relations." In *Philosophical Studies.* London: Routledge & Kegan Paul, 1922.

Morris, Thomas V. *Anselmian Explorations.* Notre Dame, Ind.: University of Notre Dame Press, 1987.

———. "The Metaphysical Doctrine of Creation." *The Asbury Theological Journal* 46, no. 1 (spring 1991): 95-112.

Morshauser, Scott N. "Created in the Image of God: The Ancient Near Eastern Background of the *Imago Dei.*" *Theology Matters* 3, no. 6 (November/December 1997).

Muller, Richard A. *Dictionary of Latin and Greek Theological Terms.* Grand Rapids, Mich: Baker, 1985.

Murphy, Nancey. *Reasoning and Rhetoric in Theology.* Valley Forge, Penn.: Trinity Press International, 1994.

Oderberg, David S. *The Metaphysics of Identity over Time.* New York: St. Martin's Press, 1993.

Owen, H. P. *Christian Theism.* Edinburgh: T & T Clark, 1984.

Pailin, David A. "Rigor, Reason and Moderation: Hartshorne's Contribution to the Philosophy of Religion and Philosophical Theology." In *Charles Hartshorne's Concept of*

God, edited by Lewis Hahn. Dordrecht: Kluwer Academic, 1990.

Pannenberg, Wolfhart. *Systematic Theology.* Vol. 1. Grand Rapids, Mich: Eerdmans, 1991.

Pearl, Leon. "The Misuse of Anselm's Formula for God's Perfection." *Religious Studies* 22 (1986): 355-65.

Peters, Eugene. *Hartshorne and Neoclassical Metaphysics.* Lincoln: University of Nebraska Press, 1970.

————. "Methodology in the Metaphysics of Charles Hartshorne." In *Existence and Actuality,* edited by John B. Cobb Jr. and Franklin Gamwell. Chicago: University of Chicago Press, 1984.

Pinnock, Clark et al., eds. *The Openness of God.* Downers Grove, Ill.: InterVarsity Press, 1994.

Plantinga, Alvin. "Actualism and Possible Worlds." In *The Possible and the Actual,* edited by Michael J. Loux. Ithaca, N.Y.: Cornell University Press, 1979.

————. "De Re et De Dicto." *Nous* 3 (1969): 235-58.

————. *Does God Have a Nature?* Milwaukee: Marquette University Press, 1980.

————. *God and Other Minds.* Ithaca, N.Y.: Cornell University Press, 1967.

————. "How to Be an Anti-Realist." *Proceedings and Addresses of the American Philosophical Association* (April 1982): 47-70.

————. *The Nature of Necessity.* Oxford: Clarendon, 1974.

————. "On Existentialism." *Philosophical Studies* 44 (1983): 1-20.

————. "On Ockham's Way Out." In *The Concept of God,* edited by Thomas V. Morris. Oxford: Oxford University Press, 1987.

————. "Replies." In *Alvin Plantinga,* edited by James E. Tomberlin and Peter Van Inwagen. Dordrecht: D. Reidel, 1985.

————. "Self-Profile." In *Alvin Plantinga,* edited by James E. Tomberlin and Peter Van Inwagen. Dordrecht: D. Reidel, 1985.

————. "Transworld Identity or World Bound Individuals?" In *The Possible and the Actual,* edited by Michael J. Loux. Ithaca, N.Y.: Cornell University Press, 1979.

————. "World and Essence." *Philosophical Review* 79 (1970): 461-92.

Plantinga, Cornelius, Jr. "Social Trinity and Tritheism." In *Trinity, Incarnation and Atonement.* Notre Dame, Ind.: University of Notre Dame Press, 1989.

Pöhlmann, Horst Georg. *Analogia Entis Oder Analogia Fidei?* Göttingen: Vandenhoeck & Ruprecht, 1965.

Pollock, John. "Plantinga and Possible Worlds." In *Alvin Plantinga,* edited by James E. Tomberlin and Peter Van Inwagen. Dordrecht: D. Reidel, 1985.

Prior, Arthur N. *Papers on Tense and Time.* Oxford: Oxford University Press, 1968.

————. *Past, Present and Future.* Oxford: Oxford University Press, 1967.

————. *Time and Modality.* Westport, Conn.: Greenwood, 1957.

Proksch, Otto. "Simplicity." In *Theological Dictionary of the New Testament.* Vol. 1. Edited by Gerhard Kittel and Gerhard Friedrich. 10 vols. Grand Rapids, Mich.: Eerdmans, 1968.

Przywara, Erich. *Analogia Entis.* Munich: Kosel & Pustet, 1932; reprint, Einsiedeln: Johannes Verlag, 1962.

Quine, W. V. O. "Reference and Modality." In *From a Logical Point of View.* New York: Harper & Row, 1961.

———. *The Ways of Paradox and Other Essays.* New York: Random House, 1966.

———. *Word and Object.* Cambridge, Mass.: MIT Press, 1960.

Rad, Gerhard von. *Old Testament Theology.* Vol. 1. New York: Harper & Row, 1962.

Richards, Jay W. "Barth on the Divine 'Conscription' of Language." *The Heythrop Journal* 38, no. 3 (July 1997): 251-52.

———. "Is the Doctrine of the Incarnation Incoherent?" *The Princeton Theological Review* 2, no. 3 (October 1995): 10-12.

Ross, James. "The Crash of Modal Metaphysics." *Review of Metaphysics* 43 (December 1989): 251-79.

———. "God, Creator of Kinds and Possibilities." In *Rationality, Religious Belief and Moral Commitment,* edited by Robert Audi and William Wainwright. Ithaca, N.Y.: Cornell University Press, 1986.

———. *Philosophical Theology.* Indianapolis: Hackett, 1980.

Schleiermacher, Friedrich. *The Christian Faith.* Edited by H. R. MacKintosh and J. S. Stewart. Edinburgh: T & T Clark, 1989.

Snaith, N. H. *The Distinctive Ideas of the Old Testament.* London: Epworth Press, 1956.

Söhngen, Gottlieb. "Analogia Entis in Analogia Fidei." In *Antwort,* edited by Ernst Wolf, Ch. von Kirschbaum and Rudolf Frey. Zollikon-Zürich: Evangelischer Verlag, 1956.

Sokolowski, Robert. *The God of Faith and Reason.* Washington, D.C.: The Catholic University Press of America, 1982.

Sprigge, Timothy. "Internal and External Properties." *Mind* 71 (1962): 197-212.

Stalnaker, Robert. "The Interaction of Modality with Quantification and Identity." In *Modality, Morality and Belief,* edited by W. Sinnott-Armstrong, D. Raffman and N. Asher. Cambridge: Cambridge University Press, 1995.

———. "Possible Worlds." In *The Possible and the Actual,* edited by Michael J. Loux. Ithaca, N.Y.: Cornell University Press, 1979.

Stead, Christopher. *Divine Substance.* Oxford: Clarendon, 1977.

Stump, Eleanore, and Norman Kretzmann. "Absolute Simplicity." *Faith and Philosophy* 2, no. 4 (October 1985): 353-82.

————. "Eternity." In *The Concept of God,* edited by Thomas V. Morris. Oxford: Oxford University Press, 1987.

Swinburne, Richard. *The Christian God.* Oxford: Clarendon, 1994.

————. *The Coherence of Theism.* Oxford: Clarendon, 1977.

Torrance, Thomas. *Karl Barth: An Introduction to His Early Theology, 1910-1931.* London: SCM Press, 1962.

Tracy, David. *The Analogical Imagination.* New York: Crossroad, 1981.

Van der Veken, J. "From Modal Language to Model Language: Charles Hartshorne and Linguistic Analysis." In *Hartshorne, Process Philosophy and Theology,* edited by Robert Kane and Stephen H. Phillips. Albany, N.Y.: SUNY Press, 1989.

Van Inwagen, Peter. "Plantinga on Trans-World Identity." In *Alvin Plantinga,* edited by James E. Tomberlin and Peter Van Inwagen. Dordrecht: D. Reidel, 1985.

Viney, Donald Wayne. "God Only Knows? Hartshorne and the Mechanics of Omniscience." In *Hartshorne, Process Philosophy and Theology,* edited by Robert Kane and Stephen H. Phillips. Albany, N.Y.: SUNY Press, 1989.

White, Alan R. *Modal Thinking.* Oxford: Basil Blackwell, 1975.

White, Roger. "Notes on Analogical Predication and Speaking About God." In *The Philosophical Frontiers of Christian Theology,* edited by B. Hebblethwaite and S. Sutherland. Cambridge: Cambridge University Press, 1982.

Wiehl, Reiner. "Hartshorne's Panpsychism." In *The Philosophy of Charles Hartshorne,* edited by Lewis Hahn. LaSalle, Ill.: Open Court, 1991.

Wierenga, Edward R. *The Nature of God.* Ithaca, N.Y.: Cornell University Press, 1989.

Wiles, Maurice. "Some Reflections on the Origins of the Doctrine of the Trinity." *Journal of Theological Studies* 8 (1957): 92-106.

Wolterstorff, Nicholas. "Divine Simplicity." In *Our Knowledge of God,* edited by K. J. Clark. The Netherlands: Kluwer Academic, 1992.

————. "God Everlasting." In *God and the Good,* edited by C. Orlebeke and Lewis Smedes. Grand Rapids, Mich.: Eerdmans, 1975.

————. "Suffering Love." In *Philosophy and the Christian Faith,* edited by Thomas V. Morris. Notre Dame, Ind.: University of Notre Dame Press, 1988.

Wright, G. H. von. *An Essay in Modal Logic.* Amsterdam: North Holland, 1951.

Wyschogrod, Michael. *The Body of Faith: God and the People of Israel.* Northvale, N.J.: Jason Aronson, 1996.

Zagzebski, Linda. "Individual Essence and the Creation." In *Divine and Human Action,* edited by Thomas V. Morris. Ithaca, N.Y.: Cornell University Press, 1988.

Author Index

Subject Index

Lightning Source UK Ltd.
Milton Keynes UK
UKHW040926241022
410996UK00001B/15